GLOBAL HEALT

SOCIOLOGY FOR GLOBALIZING SOCIETIES

Series Editor: David Inglis, Professor of Sociology, University of Exeter, UK

Responding directly to the globalization of society, this series combines survey, critique and original contribution, demonstrating what sociologists can bring to our global understanding of various areas of study. Individual volumes focus on the complex conditions of globalization in a particular sphere of human life, considering the philosophical, conceptual and methodological issues arising from globalization. Written by leading and emerging authors in their fields, each title simultaneously depicts the main contours of the area under investigation, while offering a unique perspective on the matters at hand. In this way, readers are challenged to really think about – rather than passively accept – the issues under discussion.

Also published

SOCIAL MOVEMENTS AND GLOBALIZATION
Cristina Flesher Fominaya

Forthcoming

GLOBALIZATION AND HUMAN RIGHTS
Darren O'Byrne

FAMILY, INTIMACY AND GLOBALIZATION
Raelene Wilding

GLOBAL HEALTH INEQUITIES

A SOCIOLOGICAL PERSPECTIVE

FERNANDO DE MAIO

palgrave
macmillan

First published 2014 by
PALGRAVE MACMILLAN

Palgrave Macmillan in the UK is an imprint of Macmillan Publishers Limited, registered in England, company number 785998, of Houndmills, Basingstoke, Hampshire RG21 6XS.

Palgrave Macmillan in the US is a division of St Martin's Press LLC, 175 Fifth Avenue, New York, NY 10010.

Palgrave Macmillan is the global academic imprint of the above companies and has companies and representatives throughout the world.

Palgrave® and Macmillan® are registered trademarks in the United States, the United Kingdom, Europe and other countries

ISBN 978-0-230-30437-6 hardback
ISBN 978-0-230-30438-3 paperback

This book is printed on paper suitable for recycling and made from fully managed and sustained forest sources. Logging, pulping and manufacturing processes are expected to conform to the environmental regulations of the country of origin.

A catalogue record for this book is available from the British Library.

A catalog record for this book is available from the Library of Congress.

Typeset by Cambrian Typesetters, Camberley, Surrey

Printed in China

In memory of María Rosa De Maio,
who taught me (and many others) how to write

Short Contents

Long Contents

List of Tables and Figures

Tables

Figures

List of Abbreviations

AIDS   Acquired Immune Deficiency Syndrome
ADI   Average/Deprivation/Inequality Framework
CSDH   Commission on the Social Determinants of Health
COPD   Chronic Obstructive Pulmonary Disease
CI   Confidence Interval
DALY   Disability-Adjusted Life Year
DNDi   Drugs for Neglected Diseases Initiate
GPELF   Global Programme to Eliminate Lymphatic Filariasis
GDP   Gross Domestic Product
HIV   Human Immunodeficiency Virus
IMF   International Monetary Fund
MDA   Mass Drug Administration
MSF   *Médecins sans Frontières*
MDGs   Millennium Development Goals
NDTs   Neglected Tropical Diseases
OR   Odds Ratio
OECD   Organisation for Economic Co-operation and Development
PIH   Partners in Health
SARS   Severe Acute Respiratory Syndrome
TRIPS   Trade-Related Aspects of Intellectual Property Rights
UNDP   United Nations Development Program
WASH   World Action on Salt and Health
WHO   World Health Organization
WTO   World Trade Organization

Acknowledgements

There are many people who deserve my gratitude for supporting my work on this book. Colleagues at Simon Fraser University (SFU), where I taught from 2005–10, were fundamental in shaping my thinking on global health. Steve Corber, in particular, offered mentorship and insight into chronic non-communicable diseases. Michel Joffres and Craig Janes offered advice at key stages. Eagan Kemp and Jeanette Somlak Pedersen – two of the many outstanding students I had the privilege of working with at SFU – read the manuscript and offered detailed comments, helping me to clarify key points and deepen central arguments. At DePaul University, where I have worked since 2011, I have benefited from the support of the Department of Sociology and the Master of Public Health Program. Grace Budrys and John Mazzeo offered constructive comments on a preliminary draft and, in general, have welcomed me to my new academic home. DePaul students also played a key role in helping me to develop the ideas in this book through lively class discussions.

I am also grateful to David Pevalin, at the University of Essex, whose comments on the typescript were very helpful. Vic Neufeld and the Canadian Coalition for Global Health Research (CCGHR) have been critical in strengthening my work. Graciela Dinardi and Ignacio Llovet – who I met thanks to the CCGHR's Summer Institute – have taught me about Chagas, and have proven to be remarkable collaborators. Eric Hershberg has been a wonderful mentor, and kindly invited me to American University to present my work on income inequality and health.

My work on the social patterning of chronic non-communicable diseases has benefited most from the collaboration of Bruno Linetzky, Daniel Ferrante, Jonatan Konfino, Carlos Boissonnet, Ana King, Sebastian Laspiur and Mario Virgolini at Argentina's Ministry of Health. My work in Argentina would not have been possible without the help of Branka Legetic and James Hospedales at the Pan American Health Organization.

Generous funding for this project was provided by the Social Sciences and Humanities Research Council of Canada, Simon Fraser University, and DePaul University. Giselle Liberman and Kathryn Berry were excellent research assistants, tracking down a wide range of sources.

Anna Marie Reeve, Beverley Tarquini, Lloyd Langman and the staff at Palgrave Macmillan helped steer the project from the beginning. David Inglis welcomed this book to the *Globalizing Societies* series, urging me to highlight my opposition to much of the 'north-centric' literature on globalization. I also benefited from the comments offered by the anonymous reviewers of the prospectus and the typescript.

The most important source of support for this project was my family. My wife, Christy Allen, deserves more thanks than I can convey in these pages. She offered the most detailed and insightful of comments on rough drafts, and never wavered in her confidence about the importance of the work. She has helped me in immeasurable ways. Lucy, our four-year-old daughter, ensured that drafts were suitably marked with crayons of all colours. Inspiration and support were always in good supply from my parents, Susana and Domingo, from my brother, Pablo, and from my *suegros*, Sharyn and Phil.

I hope that the book conveys a sense of urgency – that much can be done to reduce global health inequities. The staggering differences that we see *between* as well as *within* countries are not the outcomes of 'natural' forces; they are produced and maintained by political and economic policies that harm populations. I believe that the social sciences can be – and should be – key actors in the fight for social justice. Recognizing that globalization will not necessarily improve the health of the world's poor is an important aspect of that struggle.

The author and publishers would like to thank the copyright holders for permission to reproduce material from the following sources:

Figure 2.1: WHO (2005) 'Preventing Chronic Diseases: A Vital Investment' (Geneva: World Health Organization).
Figure 3.1: Mckeown, T. (1979) *The Role of Medicine: Dream, Mirage, or Nemesis?* (2nd edn) (Princeton, NJ: Princeton University Press).
Figure 3.2: McCracken, K. and Phillips, D. R. (2005) 'International Demographic Transitions', in G. J. Andrews and D. R. Phillips (eds) *Ageing and Place*, 36–40 (London: Routledge).
Figure 3.4: Omran, A. R. (1983) 'The epidemiologic transition theory. A preliminary update', *Journal of Tropical Pediatrics*, 29(6): 305–16 (Oxford: Oxford University Press).
Table 3.1: Vio, F. and Albala, C. (2000) 'Nutrition policy in the Chilean transition', *Public Health Nutrition*, 3(1): 49–55 (Cambridge: Cambridge University Press).
Table 3.3: Heuveline, P., Guillot, M. and Gwatkin, D. R. (2002) 'The uneven tides of the health transition', *Social Science & Medicine*, 55(2): 313-22 (Oxford: Elsevier).
Table 3.4: Martínez, C. S. and Leal, F. G. (2003) 'Epidemiological transition: Model or illusion? A look at the problem of health in Mexico', *Social Science & Medicine*, 57(3): 539-50 (Oxford: Elsevier).
Table 4.1: WHO (2008) *The global burden of disease: 2004 update* (Geneva: World Health Organization).

Table 4.2: Abegunde, D. O. *et al.* (2007) 'The burden and costs of chronic diseases in low-income and middle-income countries', *Lancet*, 370(9603): 1929–38 (Oxford: Elsevier).

Table 4.3: UNDP (2000) *Human Development Report* (New York: Oxford University Press).

Table 5.1: WHO (2010) *Working to Overcome the Global Impact of Neglected Tropical Diseases: First WHO Report on Neglected Tropical Diseases* (Geneva: World Health Organization).

Table 5.2: Conteh, L., Engels, T. and Molyneux, D. H. (2010) 'Socioeconomic aspects of neglected tropical diseases', *Lancet*, 375(9710): 240 (Oxford: Elsevier).

Figure 5.1: WHO (2010) *Working to Overcome the Global Impact of Neglected Tropical Diseases: First WHO Report on Neglected Tropical Diseases* (Geneva: World Health Organization).

Table 5.3 and Figure 5.2 : Schmunis, G. A. (2007) 'Epidemiology of Chagas disease in non-endemic countries: the role of international migration', *Memórias do Instituto Oswaldo Cruz*, 102 Suppl. 1:75–85.

Tables 6.1 and 6.2, and Figures 6.1, 6.2 and 6.3: UNAIDS (2009) *AIDS Epidemic Update: November 2009* (Geneva: UNAIDS/World Health Organization).

Introduction

'*We've got the key to saving Grady!*', sang the protestors under the hot Atlanta sun. It was June 2007 – and the first Social Forum to be held in the United States. The march was peaceful, at times joyful. Music filled the air: along with the traditional drums that one hears at marches, protestors included a New Orleans marching band with tubas and trombones. The protestors were singing about Grady Memorial, the maligned and financially at-risk public hospital in Atlanta. One of the busiest trauma centres in the United States, the Grady serves a large population of low-income and uninsured people, as well as undocumented immigrants who otherwise would have little or no option for health care. The Grady's chief executive officer was looking to cut costs by closing services, including its much-needed outpatient dialysis clinic, and the protestors made sure that it was not done quietly.

Alongside the Grady protestors, others carried the People's Health Movement's banner proclaiming '*Health for all, now!*' I walked with protestors from Venezuela, who attended the Forum to describe their experiences with health care reform – where, with the help of thousands of Cuban doctors, they were providing free care to the poor. Their work brought health care to people who had been marginalized by the existing system. For many poor Venezuelans, this was the first time their diabetes, hypertension, and a host of otherwise undiagnosed conditions were being treated.

The protestors marching to save Atlanta's public hospital have a great deal in common with the Venezuelans and Cubans working to provide health care in marginalized and economically deprived communities. Yet, I suspect that they had never met before the Social Forum, and further suspect that they have not worked together since. Their struggles are rooted in similar causes, including poverty, inequality, and discrimination. Both groups share a deep awareness that living conditions and health are inextricably intertwined. And they work with similar objectives: ensuring that all people have access to the health care they need, that medical advances are shared across the socioeconomic spectrum, and that all people have the support they need in times of illness. But they work independently of one another, divided by language, geography, and politics.

The research literature on health inequities mirrors this division, with the struggle for Atlanta's public hospital being analyzed by researchers interested in 'health disparities' and the experiences in Venezuela examined by those in

1

'global health', those who study so-called 'developing' countries. Though there is certainly some overlap, research on these cases would usually be presented in different conferences and published in different journals.[1,2]

My work as a sociologist is centred on the idea that these struggles are not independent of one another, that the links between north and south must be reconsidered, as briefly embodied in that march down Atlanta's streets. 'Global health' matters not just because it tells us about patterns of disease around the world, but, more importantly, because of what analysis of global health can tell about the deep structural roots of health inequities. In order to develop this more layered analysis, we must first consider what is often meant in discussion of global health.

Recent years have seen the rise of two competing 'lenses', or ways of framing the global health conversation. One lens – closely tied to new ideas of globalization – sees an increasingly inter-connected world in which diseases spread from one place to another, from one population to another, with increasing frequency and with devastating effects. From this perspective, the new 'global era' may be marked not only by 'a newfound power for *individuals* to collaborate and compete globally' (Friedman, 2005: 10; emphasis in original), or an 'awareness of the world as a single place' (Cockerham and Cockerham, 2010: 3) – seemingly positive developments, but also by a new and extremely powerful capacity for the spread of disease, of contagion. This lens highlights the spectre of an influenza pandemic that would kill millions, along with the very real threats from ebola and other 'emerging' diseases like Severe Acute Respiratory Syndrome (SARS), or 're-emerging' diseases like drug-resistant tuberculosis. Linked primarily to the idea of *risk*, this discourse *securitizes* global health (Davies, 2010; Price-Smith, 2009) – and we come to see ever-increasing threats in the world around us.

This lens has significant implications not only for how we see the world and our place in it, but also for how we come to understand human suffering. From this perspective, what we might call the 'new global era' holds great promise and, at the same time, offers significant new dangers. Globalization has achieved great things, most notably, bringing distant populations together as never before; resulting in what the sociologist Roland Robertson calls 'the compression of the world' (1992: 8). But this brings with it possibly grave implications, as has been acknowledged at the highest levels of global health governance. Consider the following comments from Dr Margaret Chan, the Director-General of the World Health Organization:

> The world has changed dramatically since 1951, when the WHO issued its first set of legally binding regulations aimed at preventing the international spread of disease ... Since then, profound changes have occurred in the way humanity inhabits the planet. The disease situation is anything but stable. Population growth, incursion into previously uninhabited areas, rapid urbanization, intensive farming practices, environmental degradation, and the misuse of antimicrobials have disrupted the

equilibrium of the microbial world. New diseases are emerging at the historically unprecedented rate ... Airlines now carry more than 2 billion passengers annually, vastly increasing opportunities for the rapid international spread of infectious agents and their vectors ... These threats have become a much larger menace in a world characterized by high mobility, economic interdependence and electronic interconnectedness. Traditional defences at national borders cannot protect against the invasion of a disease or vector. Real time news allows panic to spread with equal ease. Shocks to health reverberate as shocks to economies and business continuity in areas well beyond the affected site. Vulnerability is universal. (WHO, 2007b: vi)

In describing vulnerability as universal, Chan urges us to grasp the very real threats that the 'compression of the word' has brought about. Yet, describing vulnerability as universal also erases important differences in susceptibility and actual lived experience.

I argue in this book that, rather than universalizing vulnerability, globalization has brought about its unprecedented segmentation. Contrary to popular accounts of the world becoming a 'smaller' place, and economics now being played on an 'even playing field' due to the rise of India and China (Friedman, 2005; Wolf, 2004), globalization's deleterious effects are concentrated among the poor – whether they be poor in an industrialized country losing its manufacturing base, or in a country of the global south that has struggled to maintain a semblance of a welfare state in the midst of structural adjustment programmes.[3,4]

The 'vulnerability is universal' lens, for many global health scholars, is correct but ultimately misguided. In universalizing vulnerability and the underlying risk of avoidable morbidity and premature mortality, this lens glosses over the striking patterns of inequality that characterize our world. The result, argues the anthropologist Tim Brown, is that a disease is prioritized in global health discourse only if it is a threat to the security of industrialized countries, to the point where 'the focus of current global health debate appears to be slanted towards the priorities of western nations' (2011: 324). And going further, one might argue that the current global health debate does not actually slant towards the priorities of western nations as seen from the perspective of social justice and health equity, but towards the needs of the 'worried well' (Morall, 2009).

For example, the central topic of debate in Canadian health care discourse is not the health crisis in Aboriginal communities – where life expectancy is 10–15 years lower than the national average (Statistics Canada, 2005), and where the risk of death from diabetes is five times higher (Young *et al.*, 2000). Neither is it the health of immigrants, which is known to deteriorate during the first ten years in the country (Beiser, 2005; De Maio, 2010b). Rather, the debate is focused on waiting times for elective surgeries and on a push for private for-profit medicine, testing the limits of Canada's public medicare system.

Very little is said in Canadian health journals about the country's practice of recruiting health professionals from the global south, although the 'brain drain' of new doctors from countries such as South Africa to countries such as Canada is a widely-recognized barrier to increasing access to health care services in some of the poorest countries in the world (Crush, 2002; Huish, 2009).

In the United States, the very politicized debate on President Obama's Affordable Care Act has centred on its effect on the budget deficit and its underlying constitutionality – and not on what David Ansell calls the 'caste system of health care' in the country which 'all but guarantees different health outcomes depending on the patient's insurance status' (2011: 212). Empirical research has shown that poor populations in the US have health indicators at the level of so-called 'Third World' countries (Barr, 2008; McCord and Freeman, 1990) – but that has not been part of the US health care debate. The only time that the health of the poor has featured in the discussion is when commentators raise concern over the exorbitant cost of providing first-line health care in the emergency room – which many poor, uninsured people in the United States rely on in the absence of a family physician. Along these lines, the health care needs of undocumented migrants in the United States were ignored from the early stages of deliberation, and the Affordable Care Act explicitly excludes them from benefits. But undocumented migrants do feature in media health reports when researchers raise the spectre of 'Third World' diseases such as Chagas posing a danger to the US population (Jauregui, 2012; McNeil, 2012).[5] Contagion, the transmission of disease or risk/cost of disease from the poor, is the central story.

The second lens that one might discern in the contemporary discourse on global health emphasizes global health inequities, seeing health as a human right (Kim *et al.*, 2000). From this perspective, vulnerability is not universal but, rather, highly-patterned along what the anthropologist and infectious disease specialist Paul Farmer (1999: 5) calls the 'fault lines of inequality'. While not denying the potential of an increased flow of infectious diseases from one place to another, this perspective acknowledges that the vast burden of avoidable morbidity and premature mortality falls on the world's poor, wherever they live.

We know from studies in the richest industrialized countries that the social determinants of health strongly shape patterns of population health; the wealthier one is, the longer one is expected to live (De Maio, 2010a; Marmot and Wilkinson, 2006). There is a well-documented 'social gradient', wherein the middle classes have better health than the poor and the rich have better health than the middle class.[6] Studies of US data have documented steep gradients for stroke, heart disease, and diabetes (Barr, 2008). These gradients – important in and of themselves as markers of morbidity, suffering, and disability – ultimately go on to produce inequitable patterns of mortality. The gap in life expectancy between African-Americans with a low level of education and white Americans with a high level of education, for example, currently stands at more than 14 years for men and at more than 10 years for women – with evidence that the gaps are widening over time (Olshansky *et al.*, 2012).

Other countries – even those with constitutional protections ensuring universal access to health care for their populations – also display social gradients in health. They are found, for example, in a wide range of health conditions in Canada (Raphael, 2004; Raphael *et al.*, 2006) and the United Kingdom (Acheson, 1998; Marmot and Wilkinson, 2006; Townsend and Davidson, 1982). Social gradients also exist in countries of the global south, including South Korea (Joshi *et al.*, 2008; Kim *et al.*, 2008), Mexico (Barraza-Llorens *et al.*, 2002), South Africa (Harling *et al.*, 2008; Mayosi *et al.*, 2009), Brazil (Moura *et al.*, 2009), and Chile (Vega *et al.*, 2001). A key question, which I explore in more depth in Chapters 2 and 3, relates to the extent to which social gradients are worsening over time in countries of the global south.

At the 'ecological' level of analysis, where we consider attributes of the places in which we live, income inequality has become a notable interest for epidemiologists and public health researchers.[7] Under the income inequality hypothesis, which I describe in Chapter 2, we expect that our health is influenced not just by our own income, but also by how income is distributed in the place in which we live (Wilkinson and Pickett, 2006, 2007). The most striking results have been published using data from the United States, Nancy Ross *et al.* (2000) finding that, for every 1 per cent increase in the proportion of income that was earned by the poorest half of households, mortality among working-age people in US cities would decrease by 21 per 100,000 every year. Both the gradient and the ecological-level inequality effect exist not only among the richest industrialized countries – even among those with universal access to health insurance, but also among populations in the global south (Biggs *et al.*, 2010; Moore, 2006), though the steepness of the gradient and the additional burden of inequality varies from place to place and group to group.

My work with colleagues in Argentina, for example, has highlighted the significant social gradients that exist in that country for diabetes and obesity (De Maio *et al.*, 2009). We found that women with low educational attainment are twice as likely as women with high educational attainment to have a body mass index of 30 or more, the World Health Organization's definition of obesity. They are also twice as likely to have been told by a medical professional that they have diabetes. Reflecting deep-rooted patterns of social inequality, gradients in health are both firmly entrenched and, nevertheless, dynamic – they can, and do, change over time. While our work with Argentina's 2005 and 2009 National Risk Factor Surveys illustrates that social gradients in physical inactivity – an important risk factor for many chronic diseases, including diabetes and obesity – are steepening (Linetzky *et al.*, 2013), we also found that social gradients for mammograms are decreasing (De Maio *et al.*, 2012a). All of this implies that patterns of inequality can change, influenced in part by a range of factors including local, national, and international policies.

Health researchers sometimes debate the philosophical differences between a health inequality and a health inequity. The former is generally accepted as describing a *difference*, while the latter is typically associated with differences that are deemed to be unnecessary, avoidable, and unfair (Kawachi *et al.*, 2002; Whitehead, 1992). In many cases, this becomes a *subjective* assessment based on empirical data. When does an inequality become an inequity? All of us may hold different ideas about this, and of course, the context matters. For me, most cases where a health *difference* emerges out of segmented access to socioeconomic resources is an inequity – for I believe that such health differences are indeed unnecessary, avoidable, and unfair. This is admittedly a moral/political stance, one based on the notion that social inequality is the result of political and economic decision-making – its level is not 'natural', neither is it beyond control.[8] In this book, however, I use these terms as reasonably interchangeable concepts. While I appreciate the nuance that their definitions can at times bring out, I am mindful that the usage of the terms is not entirely consistent in the literature. Blurring these concepts enables us to consider a broad range of literatures emerging out of different countries.

One of the arguments of this book is that global health should be conceptualized not as a security issue but, rather, as an equity issue. This brings into focus aspects of politics and economics – core elements of globalization – and how they shape the 'social gradient' in diabetes, obesity, and other risk factors for chronic diseases. These economic and political forces also influence one's exposure to neglected tropical diseases such as Chagas. From this perspective, the rapid development of global ties in the latest phase of economic globalization has brought about new threats of disease for populations around the world. But the burden of that threat pales in comparison with the burden of the real lived experiences of the poor – whose lives are cut short, whose existence is threatened by a lack of material resources. It is here that globalization has arguably had a stronger impact: it influences patterns of undocumented migration by workers seeking subsistence (Holmes, 2012; Huffman *et al.*, 2012; Larchanché, 2012) and it affects patterns of rural–urban migration in the global south (Bayer *et al.*, 2009; Bowman *et al.*, 2008). At the same time, globalization has effectively expanded restrictions to the manufacturing and distribution of life-saving medications (Bond, 1999; Havlir and Hammer, 2005) and its cultural and economic effects have promoted the spread of risk factors for chronic non-communicable disease (De Maio, 2011).

The result is a globalized world where the best-off countries have life expectancies of over 80 years, while the worst-off countries have life expectancies of 40 years, sometimes even lower; a world where the global pharmaceutical market is valued at US$650 billion (Smith *et al.*, 2009), spends hundreds of millions on marketing, and yet 2.5 million children die of diarrhoeal diseases every year for want of a simple salt water solution that would alleviate their condition and a safe water supply that would ensure it never became a life-threatening episode.

Seeing health as patterned along the fault of lines of inequality allows us to grasp the fundamental cause of disease and illness in the world: structural violence. In this book, I borrow a definition of structural violence put forth by Farmer *et al.*, and see structural violence as 'social arrangements that put individuals and populations in harm's way ... The arrangements are *structural* because they are embedded in the political and economic organization of our social world; they are *violent* because they cause injury to people' (2006: 1686, emphasis added).[9] A key argument of this book is that structural violence is a tool with which we may interpret empirical data and question theoretical arguments about global health inequities. It allows us to question, for example, 'cultural' explanations that ignore issues of power and inequality. Ill-framed cultural arguments often place the blame for a community's poor health on the community itself – their unscientific beliefs, their unhealthy lifestyles, or their high levels of political corruption, all of which limit how much can be done with scarce resources. From this perspective, health inequities – and we might be comparing the health of the rich and poor in a major city in an industrialized country, or the health of populations in rich and poor countries – are produced, in a significant way, by the beliefs and actions of the poor themselves. This approach inevitability holds individuals responsible: it is an individual who *chooses* to smoke tobacco, who *fails* to exercise as recommended by physicians, and who *exhibits* poor decision-making in their dietary habits. From this perspective, health is a personal responsibility and the unhealthy person is culpable for their plight.

Without negating personal agency, an analysis of global health inequities rooted in the concept of structural violence extends our explanatory model. Recognizing the existence of structural violence requires us to broaden and deepen our thinking about the causes of disease and illness; as Farmer argues: 'to explain suffering, one must embed individual biography in the larger matrix of culture, history, and political economy' (Farmer, 2003: 41). As a guiding theoretical concept, structural violence challenges us to see the complex interconnections between one's biography and society – a task that C. Wright Mills (1959) eloquently described as the 'sociological imagination'.

Too often, public health work has focused on individuals and communities in isolation from their geopolitical context, without adequately examining the economic and political constraints these populations face. For example, many Canadian studies of the health problems in First Nations communities have tended to ignore questions of colonialism and historical trauma (Samson, 2003). Similarly, in the United States, black–white infant mortality differentials have been attributed to the 'poverty of the culture' of the inner city, or to genetic differences between blacks and whites, and researchers are only beginning to acknowledge that what lies behind the significant black–white difference in infant mortality is actually the effect of racism and discrimination (Barr, 2008; Collins and David, 2009; Krieger, 2011). On a global level, we face the same challenge: identifying the 'generative mechanisms' (Scambler, 2001), which are often structural in nature, that lead to disease and manifest in patterns of health inequality.

The rise of these competing discourses in the global health literature has occurred at a time where the very definition of the field of global health has come into focus. Much of the research examined in this book could be described as 'public health' – a long-standing academic discipline characterized by its focus on improving the health of people through collective actions. Further, some of the work in this book may be defined as 'international health' – in that it seeks to better understand and, indeed, improve the health of populations around the world. But interestingly, recent years have seen a subtle shift in terminology, from 'international health' to 'global health' (Koplan *et al.*, 2009; Kruk, 2012). And the differences are beyond semantic. This new focus alters how we might go about research and what kinds of solutions we seek to develop.

Whereas international health in many ways was centred on health *out there*, in low- and middle-income countries, and while public health has historically been driven by a focus on populations and the idea of equity in health, neither of these perspectives adequately conceptualized the *interconnections* between policies and practices in the global north and the global south. Global health is increasingly not just about what happens *out there*, but is more concerned with how health/disease is shaped by global economic, political, and cultural forces that transcend national boundaries. In other words, 'global health' occurs *here* as well. When our health is influenced by international food processing regulations, we witness 'global health' in practice. When we work with or for companies with a global presence, we are part of a chain of events connected to global health; health 'there' is influenced by actions here. For Koplan *et al.*, 'global health':

> refers to any health issue that concerns many countries or is affected by transnational determinants, such as climate change or urbanisation, or solutions, such as polio eradication. Epidemic infectious diseases such as dengue, influenza A (H5N1), and HIV infection are clearly global. But global health should also address tobacco control, micronutrient deficiencies, obesity, injury prevention, migrant-worker health, and migration of health workers. *The global in global health refers to the scope of the problems, not their location.* (2009: 1994, emphasis added)

The shift from 'international health' to 'global health' has occurred at an important time: inequities in health outcomes are at their highest point in history. As noted earlier, the richest nations in the world currently have life expectancies of about 80 years. Yet, people born in the poorest nations in the world experience life expectancies of half that amount – about 40 to 45 years, with life expectancies in some sub-Saharan African countries now dipping below 40 as a result of the HIV/AIDS pandemic. And, as dismaying as these statistics may be, the picture is actually worse than they indicate, as national summary statistics (or what are also referred to as 'aggregate data') hide substantial within-country inequities based on gender, ethnicity, social class, and other factors that exist in all countries, even those with universal access to primary health care services.

Health inequities are produced by deep-lying structural forces. In other words, inequities in health are shaped by international, national and local phenomena – from international law and bilateral/multilateral trade agreements, to national laws and regulations governing not only health care systems but also the wide span of sectors that ultimately affect levels of population health, to seemingly individual 'choices' over tobacco use and physical activity. Understanding the complex interplay between these forces requires a nuanced appreciation of 'globalization'.

While the term 'globalization' is commonly used in the academic literature and the popular press, there is no general consensus on how it is to be defined (Bisley, 2007; Martell, 2010). And this is problematic, for, as the University of London's Andrew Jones argues, 'globalization has become so pervasively "known" that it is becoming taken for granted, and few people question what it really means or even why "it" is important' (2010: 1). In trying to understand global health inequalities, it is critical to open up debate of this fundamental concept.

How we define globalization is tied to how we might make sense of the structural forces that shape people's capacity to lead long and healthy lives. For example, a Marxist understanding of globalization privileges its fundamental economic properties, the liberated flow of capital, and the restricted flow of labour and families. A Marxist perspective on globalization emphasizes conflict, exploitation, and unjust global trade rules that limit the distribution of life-saving medicines. In contrast, a neoliberal position on globalization – illustrated most clearly in the journalistic accounts of globalization offered by Thomas Friedman (1990, 2005) and Martin Wolf (2004) – emphasizes the creation of new markets, new supply chains, and rising levels of prosperity in the world (though this tradition, betraying neoliberal dogma that benefits trickle-down in the long run, glosses over the unequal distribution of this prosperity). These perspectives lead to radically different emphases on the nature of global health inequalities, as well as to different ideas concerning what could be done to reduce them.

There is also debate surrounding the historical nature of globalization. Is it something fundamentally new? Is it a profoundly different era in human history, marked by technological innovation, cultural exchange, and economic potential? Or is it an extension – perhaps intensification – of existing capitalist structures and systems of commodity exchange? At least three different schools of thought can be discerned in the literature: the hyperglobalizer, sceptic, and transformationalist perspectives (Held *et al.*, 1999). The hyperglobalizer sees globalization as a whole new era in history; a fundamental break over what existed before. This position sees a truly 'borderless world', where individuals have a new-found freedom to engage with anyone across the globe. Often focused on the promise of communication technologies to enable people to work collaboratively across great distances, this is a fundamentally optimistic account of globalization, seeing it as route to global prosperity.

The sceptic position in this literature responds to the hyperbolic elements of these ideas, and argues that although globalization has indeed created new ties across the world, it does not represent a fundamental break in human history (Jones, 2010). Much of the research that we will see in this book concerned with neglected tropical diseases lends support to this position. Despite great advances in communication technologies, global networks, and other celebrated aspects of globalization, the majority of the world's poor will continue to live and die as they have in previous decades, often of treatable diseases and without any of the benefits derived from modern medicine, let alone communication technologies.

The transformationalist view argues that globalization may indeed offer something new but its effect on the world's poor is uncertain. From this perspective, globalization is an open-ended process offering many different possibilities for local, regional, national, and global connections. That is, rather than globalization marking a new distinct era in human history, it is best understood as an extension of pre-existing economic, cultural, and political processes. While something new many indeed be happening, it should be seen in deep historical terms. From this perspective, globalization offers hope for a more equitable world – but that result is by no means assured. Thus, we may emphasize that the current organization of global governance – dominated by non-democratic bodies such as the International Monetary Fund, the World Bank, and the World Trade Organization (WTO) – has resulted in the grossly unequal distribution of the benefits of globalization. This perspective links a variety of different thinkers, from the revolutionary ideas and actions of the Zapatistas to the 'reformist' perspective of the Nobel prize-winning economist Joseph Stiglitz.[10]

From the transformationalist perspective, the noted British sociologist Anthony Giddens offers an influential definition of globalization as 'the intensification of worldwide relations which link distant localities in such a way that local happenings are shaped by events occurring many miles away and vice-versa' (Giddens, 1990: 64). It is an open-ended definition, one which gives us great leeway in understanding globalization as comprising a number of complex (and, at times, contradictory) political, economic, and technological forces.[11]

In this book, I argue that the concept of globalization offers us a way of grasping how ill health – one of the most personal of all personal troubles – is explicitly social, how it is shaped by forces far removed from our bodies and our actions. Seeing health inequity from the perspective of globalization enables us to link our biology with global political economy, allowing us to see structural violence embodied as illness (Krieger, 2005, 2011; Krieger and Davey Smith, 2004). The end result is a nuanced sociological account of why some populations/subpopulations may live long and healthy lives, while others will not.

Structure of the book

In Chapter 2, I examine the general contours of the global health research literature, emphasizing aspects of optimism and pessimism in light of the most
recently available empirical data. I focus on the Millennium Development
Goals (MDGs) – the global objectives agreed to by world leaders in 2001
which have fundamentally shaped global health priorities. The MDGs have
spurred global efforts to reduce child mortality, improve maternal health outcomes, and diminish the burden of HIV/AIDS, malaria, and other diseases.
With clear targets, they have become the guiding mileposts for global health
action. Yet, the MDGs are not without limitations – they do not include targets for reducing the burden of chronic non-communicable diseases, neither do
they include targets for neglected tropical diseases. Moreover, the MDG
framework is blind to inequality; the targets focus on aggregate indicators, and
give no attention to inequalities *within* national averages. Perhaps most importantly, while clearly laying out targets that all who champion global health
rightfully value, the MDGs nevertheless perpetuate a 'development' paradigm
to global issues that largely neglect fundamental causes of global inequalities.
As such, there is much to be gained from evaluating the MDGs from a critical
perspective that is guided by principles of social justice.

After examining the health-related MDGs and reviewing the global epidemiological context, I examine the main approaches to studying global
health. I argue that traditional risk factor epidemiology is ill-suited to understanding global health inequalities, and outline what an interdisciplinary position drawing from epidemiology and the social sciences could achieve. In
developing this argument, I am mindful of the very real limitations that have
been exposed with respect to sociology's contribution to global health
(Cockerham and Cockerham, 2010). We have paid far too little attention to
global health – with, I think, negative effects on the real-world relevance of
our discipline. As a way to illustrate the need for a comprehensive approach
that draws insight from the wide range of disciplines working on health,
including sociology, I conclude Chapter 1 with an overview of the income
inequality hypothesis from a global perspective. Stemming from the work of
Richard Wilkinson (Wilkinson, 1996, 2000, 2005; Wilkinson and Pickett,
2007, 2008, 2009a, 2009b), the income inequality hypothesis has been one of
the 'big ideas' in social science and health research; yet its implications in relation to global health are just beginning to be acknowledged.

Chapter 3 examines epidemiological transition theory – a contested yet fundamental model that describes how a population's leading causes of death may
be expected to change from infectious diseases to chronic conditions as a
country undergoes economic development. The model underlies much of the
contemporary research on global health, yet studies from the global south
have increasingly challenged it by emphasizing issues of inequity, the result
being that the rich and poor may be better described as living in different 'epidemiological worlds' (Heuveline *et al.*, 2002; Martínez and Leal, 2003). The

classic formulation of this model posits that the transition is primarily associ-ated with a country's economic development, firmly reflecting its ideological roots in modernization theory in the style of W.W. Rostow (1960). Yet more recent research has questioned the assumptions of the model, often drawing insight from dependency and world-systems theories.[12] Empirical findings show that many countries of the global south experience a persistent 'dual burden' of disease with both infectious and chronic non-communicable dis-eases present in significant levels. These studies challenge the epidemiological transition theory's claim of progress through stages via economic development and, in doing so, offer an important window for understanding the growth of inequality in the new global era.

Chapter 4 provides a critical analysis of the burden of chronic non-commu-nicable diseases. These diseases (most notably cardiovascular diseases, can-cers, chronic respiratory diseases and diabetes) are the leading cause of death in the world. Yet, while traditionally depicted as being 'diseases of affluence', chronic diseases impose their greatest burdens among the poor, and thus con-tribute to the maintenance of patterns of social inequality in both advanced industrialized countries and in the global south. The burden of chronic dis-eases is expected to increase substantially in the coming decades, severely diminishing the economic potential of low- and middle-income countries and thwarting efforts to reduce poverty (Beaglehole *et al.*, 2007; Beaglehole and Yach, 2003; WHO, 2005).

The myths surrounding chronic diseases suggest that they mainly affect high-income countries, rich people, and men, and that they are diseases of old age. Perhaps more importantly, myths surrounding these conditions imply that they are the result of individual choices – so-called 'unhealthy lifestyles' – and therefore could be prevented, if only individuals would make better life deci-sions (WHO, 2005). Contemporary social science research, both at the empir-ical level and at the theoretical level, casts doubt on these myths. Along these lines, the globalization of obesity (itself a major risk factor for other chronic conditions, including diabetes and cardiovascular disease) may be understood in a more informative way. To what extent is obesity caused by individual choices? To what extent are these choices *constrained* by an individual's life chances, by the structure in which they live and work? Incorporating questions like these into our thinking about global health produces a richer, more nuanced, account of lifestyle choices made in the context of structural con-straints, generating awareness of how chronic diseases are linked to patterns of inequity.

Chapter 5 examines neglected tropical diseases (NTDs), a heterogeneous group of parasitic and bacterial diseases that afflict the poorest of the world's poor. NTDs are thought to affect a total of 1 billion people worldwide, with most cases occurring in sub-Saharan Africa. They also continue to exert a heavy toll in parts of Latin America and the Caribbean. Unlike infectious dis-eases such as tuberculosis and malaria (which have gained attention in the United Nations MDGs), NTDs receive relatively little attention, despite gener-

ating a substantial burden of disease, primarily through disability, disfigurement, stigma, and pain. Together with HIV/AIDS, tuberculosis, and malaria,
they may be seen as the product of the same underlying processes of structural violence. NTDs are both outcomes and key drivers of the profound
inequities that exist in the world today. Little has been written in the social science literature about NTDs, and what exists has not advanced an adequate
theorization of the links between global inequities, poverty, and structural violence (Mantilla, 2011).

NTDs include Chagas disease – a disease that is spread primarily by a 'kissing bug' that defecates into the bite wound and, in doing so, transmits a parasite (*Trypanosoma cruzi*/*T. cruzi*) into its victim. 'Kissing bugs' live in crevices
of the walls and roofs of very poor homes; they thrive in the crooks and gaps
left in mud-thatch construction and in walls made of precarious building materials. As I discuss in Chapter 5, Chagas infection is followed by two phases:
acute and chronic. The acute phase can last from four to eight weeks, and is
characterized by fever, swollen lymph glands, and, often, inflammation at the
biting site. Up to 40 per cent of infected people develop chronic Chagas disease (Reithinger *et al.*, 2009), which is characterized by cardiac and gastrointestinal complications. If left untreated, these can be fatal. In disease endemic
areas like Bolivia, Paraguay, and northern Argentina, Chagas is the leading
factor in cardiovascular deaths (Reithinger *et al.*, 2009). Almost one third of
patients develop Chagas-related heart damage, and 10 per cent develop damage to the oesophagus, colon, or nervous system (or a combination of these),
typically in the late chronic phase of the disease (WHO, 2010b). It is a quin-
tessential disease of poverty – one that poor peasants are at most risk of contracting, one that is largely undiagnosed, and one that has never been a priority for for-profit pharmaceutical research (only two pharmacological interventions for Chagas exist, and both are over twenty-five years old, with limited
effectiveness, toxic side effects, and complicated dosing regimens).

NTDs are life-limiting and life-threatening conditions that are largely ignored
by the research sector – although there are promising signs of change, particularly with the 2006 creation of the Global Network of Neglected Tropical
Diseases. Launched at the 2006 Clinton Global Initiative annual meeting, the
Global Network has spearheaded an unprecedented public awareness campaign
on the burden of NTDs. It has mobilized key global philanthropic organizations,
including the Bill & Melinda Gates Foundation, bringing badly needed funds to
the global campaign against NTDs. Another promising development in this area
is the Drugs for Neglected Diseases Initiative (DNDi), a not-for-profit partnership lead by *Médecins sans Frontières* (MSF). It brings together the capacities
and resources of a wide range of global partners, including Brazil's Oswaldo
Cruz Foundation, the Indian Council for Medical Research, the Kenyan Medical
Research Institute, as well as academic and drug industry partners. They are slated to deliver new treatments for some of the most prevalent NTDs by 2014, and
have already produced new treatments for malaria, sleeping sickness, and visceral leishmaniasis (also known as *kala arar*).[13]

In Chapter 5, I analyze the chronic nature of NTDs (Hotez *et al.*, 2007); for the most part, they debilitate, rather than kill, and expose millions of people to unnecessary morbidity. They are part of a vicious cycle of poverty, in that one's exposure to NTDs is driven by poverty, and NTDs themselves limit schoolchildren's performance in school and adults' capacity to work (Hotez, 2009; WHO, 2010b). They are, more than anything else, the bodily manifestation of structural violence.

Chapter 6 focuses on access to medicines and, in particular, access to antiretroviral therapy for HIV/AIDS. Low- and middle-income countries have overcome tremendous challenges in 'scaling' up access to HIV/AIDS medications for their populations ('t Hoen *et al.*, 2011; Bartlett and Shao, 2009). Analysis of their success and the challenges they have overcome offers us a sense of optimism that much can be done to address the burden of unnecessary morbidity and premature mortality. The experience of expanding access to HIV drugs after 2001 is a good news story of global health, though several challenges loom in the horizon ('t Hoen *et al.*, 2011). In Chapter 6, I discuss the implications of new global regulations governing the manufacture and distribution of antiretroviral medicines which have proven extremely valuable in the fight against AIDS. Countries of the global south (including Brazil, South Africa, Thailand, and India) have emerged as key players in challenging international patent regulations that restrict the availability of medicines for the poor. Their challenge did not go unaddressed by the pharmaceutical industry and the United States (Bond, 1999; Cockerham and Cockerham, 2010); analysis of their conflict draws us into the literatures on global health governance (Zacher and Keefe, 2008), intellectual property rights (Smith *et al.*, 2009), and global trade (Stiglitz, 2002, 2006) – literatures with vast implications for the health of populations around the world.

More specifically, in Chapter 6 I examine the question of access to antiretroviral medicines for people living with HIV amidst the restrictions placed on generic drug manufacturers in the global south that protect patents held by brand-name pharmaceutical companies. Central to that discussion is the WTO, its regulations on Trade-Related Aspects of Intellectual Property Rights (TRIPS), and the importance of the Doha Declaration, pushed by global south countries, emphasizing their legal standing in placing public health before corporate profits (Kerry and Lee, 2007). This has been an area of great conflict between patients, civil society organizations, non-governmental organizations, the generic and brand-name pharmaceutical industries, and governments around the world.[14] As Ellen 't Hoen, a researcher at MSF, points out:

> The global HIV/AIDS crisis has provided us with a magnifying glass under which the inequity in access to treatment has become painfully clear … Medicines cannot be treated as mere commodities. Often access to medicines is a question of life and death. Yet in international trade they are regulated very much the same as any other consumer good. ('t Hoen, 2000)

It is in this conflict that signs of the increasing negotiating power of the global south have been shown most clearly.

Chapter 7 explores contemporary efforts to improve global health and reduce inequities by examining two important Commissions launched by the WHO – the Commission on Macroeconomics and Health (also known as the Sachs Commission) and the more recent Commission on the Social Determinants of Health (CSDH). Both Commissions have been seen as central to a re-imagining of the potential to improve health around the world, and both have also been the source of much debate. The Sachs report, for example, has been questioned by Alison Katz, who notes: 'The Sachs Report: *Investing in Health for Economic Development* – or increasing the size of the crumbs from the rich man's table?' (2004: 751). As I discuss in Chapter 7, the Sachs Commission's focus on communicable diseases, malnutrition, and maternal/perinatal mortality greatly influenced the MDGs – which critics point out are entirely silent on chronic non-communicable diseases, the main causes of death in all areas of the world, save for sub-Saharan Africa. The Sachs Commission has also been heavily critiqued for focusing almost exclusively on *medico-technological* solutions to problems that are best solved in the realm of *public health*, and for ignoring the *macroeconomic* determinants of both poor health and poverty. In contrast, the CSDH, headed by Sir Michael Marmot, took a far more progressive posture, and concluded that 'reducing health inequalities is ... an ethical imperative. Social injustice is killing people on a grand scale' (WHO, 2008a: iix). The CSDH describes the forty-year gap in life expectancy from the poorest to the richest as four decades that are 'denied' (WHO, 2008a: 166). At the same time, it documents *within* country inequities based on a variety of factors – economic, political, and gender-based. The Commission calls for a refocusing of much of the global discourse on heath; it calls for a shift in focus from development to equity.

In analyzing these two major WHO Commissions, and in considering contemporary efforts to improve global health and reduce inequities, I invoke the Latin American tradition of social medicine (Barreto, 2004; Waitzkin *et al.*, 2001) and synthesize its core tenets with contemporary ideas on structural violence. Although largely ignored in the English-language literature, it is the tradition of social medicine that has done the most to conceptualize disease as a product of both biological and socio-political processes. This tradition shares many similarities with the social determinants of health literature – yet, it expands the frame of the discussion and thereby opens up the 'solution space' in substantial ways. According to the Latin American Social Medicine Association's Rafael Guzmán, the Latin American tradition of social medicine does not:

> see the main problem as *limited to health inequalities* ... Rather we must examine the source of social inequity, recognizing that it arises and takes its specific forms from a system of appropriation of power and wealth ... while supporting the [WHO Social Determinants of Health]

Commission in its call for social policies that reduce inequality in health, [this tradition] does not limit itself to such policies. It will also seek to overcome the social inequities that produced said inequality in the first place. *This is not a minor difference.* If health care is presented by the ruling classes as a way of 'equalizing' things within a society marked by exploitative and oppressive social relations, we must ask whether this proposal is part of a social program aimed at the causes, that is, the forms of capitalist oppression, or whether it is merely one more resource to maintain the hegemony of the powerful and wealthy. (2009: 117; emphasis added)

The Latin American tradition of social medicine is not something that we can simply learn *about*, but rather, something that we can learn *from*. Many of its key ideas have now been adopted by social determinants of health researchers in the global north – yet, the lineage of these ideas is seldom acknowledged. One can read the social determinants of health literature and never come across citation of works from the global south – as if health inequities in the global south are either a separate field of study (for 'development' studies), or as if those health inequities, and the efforts already made to understand and overcome them, do not offer lessons for the rest of the world.[15]

Today, social medicine offers us a way to engage theory with practice; it calls for research on global health that integrates biomedicine and the social sciences, including sociology and political economy (Waitzkin *et al.*, 2001). It focuses our attention on structural violence – to the deep-lying social determinants of health; to not only health inequalities, but also the underlying social inequalities that generate them. Above all, the social medicine tradition reminds us that health inequities are the *embodiment* of unequal power relations in society.

Global health inequities

Richard Smith (2002), while editor of the *British Medical Journal*, argued that globalization 'is on trial', and that it will be judged on whether it allows further deterioration in the health of the world's poor, or if its lauded openness and interconnectedness will lead to direct improvements in their lives. Smith observed that globalization:

> may mean the rich continuing to neglect and exploit the poor, spending huge amounts on their own defences to keep out the poor, and allowing deterioration in global health ... In that case, riots will continue at the meetings of global leaders, and the world may become steadily more unpleasant for all of us, rich and poor. Alternatively, globalization through increasing openness and recognition of interdependence could lead to dramatic reductions in poverty and improvements in health.

Finding political commitment to use the best of modern science and technology and the huge wealth of the rich world to improve health would ... inspire and unite peoples all over the world. (2002: 55)

Understanding how this will play out requires acknowledging that globalization is not a new process. Indeed, the globalization literature emphasizes the historical dimensions of the concept (Jones, 2010), and is replete with typologies contrasting various types of stages in 'global' ties between nation-states and populations around the world (Martell, 2010). Along these lines, it is clear that disease has had global implications for thousands of years; for as long as humans have migrated, diseases have spread (Cockerham and Cockerham, 2010; Porter, 1997). But arguably, something new *is* happening now, in this strengthened and qualitatively different form of globalization that the world has experienced in the past twenty years (and whose pace is perhaps even increasing). The very nature of globalization has changed – and it is now, more than ever, an integral component of the structure in which human lives play out. It is this new globalization that pulls migrant workers, and pushes communities from the places where they have lived for generations. It is this globalization which offers new treatments and medical interventions that were unfathomable even just twenty years ago, but also displaces traditional foods and customs with processed high-fat, high-sugar food and sedentary lifestyles.

Because globalization directly influences patterns of global health inequities, we need to understand its contours. For inequities in health are not 'natural'; they are socially produced. And they are not static – but dynamic and developing. They change over time, and they are influenced by both government policy and private actions. As the Canadian sociologist David Coburn notes: 'degrees of inequality are clearly influenced by international, national and local political policies which are amenable to change. We can either ignore these processes or seek to understand and begin to change them' (2000: 144). The historical record of sociology, unfortunately, reflects the first of these options – with medical sociologists in particular paying scant attention to matters of global health inequities.

It stands to reason that if patterns of inequities change over time, they can be *reduced* over time. A range of 'action points' exists, from improving early childhood education and living conditions, to better housing policies and work legislation, to policies that strengthen public health care systems, as shown most clearly by the WHO's (2008a) Commission on the Social Determinants of Health. It is in this task that sociology and the other social sciences are most needed – for the social determinants of health ultimately bring 'risk' into the 'body'; they, along with the health care system, influence the well-being of all of us. And while sociology has largely been a weak voice in the global health literature, there are signs that this may be changing – and this not only helps to sustain the real-world relevance of the discipline, but brings the promise of a more holistic/structural approach to thinking about health and illness. Such a paradigm moves us away from blaming individuals and communities for their plights, and enables us to use the notion of structure with sensitivity – highlighting, as appropriate, the structural constraints under which everyday choices are made.

WHO Director-General Chan is right – there are new threats in the world, and integrative aspects of globalization have spread the risk of disease in unprecedented ways. Yet, analysis of the evidence suggests that the securitization of global health – becoming preoccupied with the threats posed to the industrialized rich countries from new and re-emerging infectious diseases, and losing sight of the very real burden of disease experienced by the poor in the global south – would be an injustice. It is the poor, those whose agency that is most constrained by structural violence, who are at most risk of preventable illness and premature mortality. It is their lived experience now; it is our charge to alleviate that burden and, at the very least, stop contributing to it.

Understanding Global Health

The past fifty years have seen remarkable progress in aggregate health indicators in most regions of the world. Globally, life expectancy has increased substantially. Whereas a child born in 1955 could expect to live only 48 years, a child born in 2000 could expect to live 66 years (CDC, 2011). Current projections suggest that the average life expectancy in the world may reach 73 years by the year 2025. Similarly, the world's under-five mortality rate, often seen by global health researchers as the most important of all population health indicators, stood at 108 in 1980 but diminished to 58 by 2009 (UNDP, 2012). However, these overall global improvements hide the more important story – the differences that exist *between* as well as *within* regions of the world in terms of how long and how healthy our lives are expected to be.

Never before has there been as much technological capacity to treat disease, alleviate suffering, and extend human life. The achievements of medical science are indeed awe-inspiring: from heart surgeries that are now routine in many hospitals, to organ transplants that extend and improve quality of life, to neonatal technologies that nurture the lives of extremely premature babies. Medical science's capacity to *intervene* is impressive and developing every day. Population-level achievements are also very much worth celebrating: smallpox has been eradicated, and the Global Polio Eradication Initiative reports that the end of polio – a disease that killed or paralyzed more than half a million people worldwide every year during its peak the 1940s and 1950s – is in sight. Many other infectious diseases are controlled, if not eradicated – at least, for some populations.[1] For example, expansion of coverage with measles vaccine since 2000 is thought to have averted 12.7 million deaths (CDC, 2011). Further, the WHO Framework Convention on Tobacco Control (FCTC), the WHO's first global health treaty, holds promise to reduce the number of premature deaths that are attributable to tobacco use (currently estimated at more than 5 million per year) (Wipfli and Huang, 2011).[2]

There is, therefore, much to praise. But health experts have been unduly optimistic before. For example, the University of British Columbia's Mark Zacher and Tania Keefe argue that, in the 1960s and 1970s, 'many health officials genuinely believed that humans were on the verge of eradicating infectious diseases once and for all' (2008: 2).[3] This was before HIV/AIDS reminded the world of its epidemiological fragility, and before researchers showed that only by ignoring the diseases of the poorest of the poor could we ever believe that we were on the verge of eradicating infectious diseases 'once and for all'.

We should celebrate the advances of medical science – but when we focus on inequalities, as I do in this book, we see that the benefits derived from scientific advancements are highly fragmented. The result is that poor and rich live in radically different 'epidemiological worlds'. Why should this concern us? To the extent that you look through the 'global health as threat' lens I described earlier in this book, you are most worried about the permeability of the border between these epidemiological worlds; you are most concerned about contagion. For what are perhaps understandable reasons, the central concern of this position is one of protection from 'external' pathogens. However, to the extent that you choose to look through the second lens, where global health is not *securitized* but, rather, seen through the prism of inequity, you are dismayed by the fact that the great advances of medical science have not been shared more fairly in this promising age of globalization. Reflecting fundamental inequalities in economic and political power, the great advances in medical science have not been shared across the globe. This is also true of advances in living conditions, including sewage systems, clean water, safe housing, and electricity. And these inequalities manifest in health outcomes, including preventable infant mortality, adverse pregnancy outcomes, and vastly unequal life expectancies.

Rebuking claims that 'class is dead' in the post-industrial era, epidemiological research clearly shows that health follows a social gradient within countries (Marmot, 2002, 2004). And contrary to premature claims that the 'world is flat', with the economic rise of rapidly developing countries like India, China, and Brazil, we also see different 'epidemiological worlds' across and within national borders (Skolnik, 2008). The global burden of avoidable morbidity and premature mortality is immense. In consequence, yes, there are very real reasons to feel a sense of optimism in relation to global health – and, as I will show, there are important signs that, on aggregate, the global health picture is improving. Yet, there are very real and substantial warning signs against any undue triumphalism – while overall indicators such as life expectancy and infant mortality have indeed improved in most areas of the world over the past fifty years, the *inequities* between the worst-off and best-off are increasing.

In this chapter, I examine the general contours of the global health research literature. I focus on the MDGs – the global objectives agreed to by world leaders in 2001 which have fundamentally shaped global health priorities. After examining the health-related MDGs and reviewing the global epidemiological context, I examine the main approaches to studying global health. The discussion features the discipline of epidemiology, and raises the very real limitations that have been exposed with respect to sociology's contribution to global health. As a way to illustrate the need for a comprehensive approach that draws insight from the wide range of disciplines working on health, including sociology, I conclude the chapter with a discussion of the income inequality hypothesis – one of the 'big ideas' in the past fifteen years in population health research. Perhaps more than any other area of the literature, work on the income inequality hypothesis has brought to the fore how structural factors affect the health of populations, how our biology is inextricably intertwined with our political economy. Yet, the literature on the hypothesis has been unduly limited in its approach, and only recently have researchers begun to examine the hypothesis from the perspective of global health.

Life and death in the era of globalization

Much of the global health discourse in the past fifteen years has revolved around the MDGs (UNDP, 2008). The MDGs, each with a measurable target, are overarching global objectives to reduce poverty, discrimination, and disease, and were agreed upon by world leaders in 2001, building on the United Nation's Millennium Declaration (Ollila, 2005).[4] There are eight MDGs, three of which are directly focused on health outcomes:

1. Eradicate extreme poverty and hunger – by halving, between 1990 and 2015, the proportion of the world's population that lives on less than \$1 per day.
2. Achieve universal primary education – by ensuring that by 2015 boys and girls alike can complete primary schooling.
3. Promote gender equality and empower women – by eliminating gender disparities in education.
4. Reduce child mortality – by reducing the number of children who die before age 5 by two thirds between 1990 and 2015.
5. Improve maternal health – by reducing maternal mortality by three quarters between 1990 and 2015.
6. Combat HIV/AIDS, malaria and other diseases – by halting and reversing the spread of HIV/AIDS, and ensuring universal access to treatment, together with halting and reversing the incidence of malaria and other major diseases.
7. Ensure environmental sustainability – by reducing biodiversity loss and reducing the proportion of the world's population without sustainable access to safe drinking water and basic sanitation.
8. Develop a global partnership for development – addressing the special needs of the least developed countries. (United Nations, 2011)

All of the MDGs impact population health – from MDG 1 (the goal of eradicating extreme poverty and hunger) to MDG 8 (the goal of developing a global partnership for development). MDGs 4–6 offer explicit targets of improving *aggregate* indicators of population health; importantly, however, they are silent on the question of inequality. The MDGs focus on overall – or *average* – targets, and say nothing about inequalities within those averages (Pande and

Yazbeck, 2003). This is a critical limitation, for aggregate improvements can be achieved without benefiting the worst-off (De Maio *et al.*, 2008). A country can, for example, reduce its aggregate infant mortality rate without reducing infant mortality of its poorest and most marginalized families.

Before examining the latest data on the world's progress towards the MDG targets, I first offer some remarks to contextualize the MDGs themselves. It is difficult to overstate the significance of the MDGs with respect to their influence on the global health agenda, for the whole UN system has adapted the orientation of their programmes to meet the MDG objectives (Ollila, 2005). They have structured global health activism and global health governance. Global philanthropy has embraced the MDGs, and they have served to concentrate the focus of academic research. For many activists, scholars and NGOs, the MDGs are the fundamental tool for championing development in the global south. However, there are also some strong concerns over the MDGs.[5] Some of the critique, as noted above, rests on the MDGs' neglect of inequalities within national averages, a notion that I will pick up in Chapter 3, when discussing epidemiological transition theory.

Other points of critique are based on the MDGs' reliance on what some see as inappropriate models of charity and 'development' assistance. For example, Gorik Ooms *et al.*, in a critical essay on the charitable foundations of development thinking, argue:

> It is commonly thought that the major reason why countries cannot achieve improved health or social wellbeing is that they are simply too poor: poverty traps communities into a vicious cycle of inadequate capital to build schools and businesses, and such communities never have enough money to fund sustainable services needed for health, education, or other basic community infrastructure, which in turn is needed to have healthy workers and business development that would produce capital. (Ooms *et al.*, 2010)

Ooms *et al.* point out that, on the surface, this seems like a very reasonable position. Yet, at the same time, they point out that this way of thinking misses the big issues; the reasons *why* some populations are poor. If we limit our thinking to the surface-level analysis, we come to think that development requires a charitable contribution of aid, rather than a reorganization of the global economic playing field. The MDG framework is premised on the notion that a huge influx of capital, defined as development aid, will be sufficient to overcome the poverty that marginalizes a high proportion of the population in countries of the global south. Ooms *et al.* describe this as a 'Big Push' against poverty: 'the thinking of decision-makers in global health and development has been permeated by a heavy emphasis on a short-term increase in financing; in short, their view is that with a brief but large injection of capital, we can 'help people help themselves' (Ooms *et al.*, 2010). Debates over the long-term sustainability of the MDG efforts have focused on the feasibility of transferring costs to developing countries. That is, once progress was kick-started by a massive influx of funds associated with the MDGs, developing countries would be in a position to better look after their own populations. Very little has been said within the MDG literature to acknowledge the need for more radical reform in global politics and economics to improve the health of populations in the global south, for example, by dismantling agricultural subsidies in the United States and the European Union that undermine the global south's capacity to export foodstuffs to those markets.[6]

Paul Farmer, in *Pathologies of Power*, draws a relevant distinction between charity, development, and social justice. While there are commendable aspects of each, he ultimately argues that charity and development – as paradigms, as ways of thinking and acting – are flawed. With respect to charity, he observes:

> Those who believe that charity is the answer to the world's problems often have the tendency – sometimes striking, sometimes subtle, and surely lurking in all of us – to regard those needing charity as intrinsically inferior. This is different from regarding the poor as powerless or impoverished because of historical processes and events ... There is an enormous difference between seeing people as the victims of innate shortcomings and seeing them as victims of structural violence. (Farmer, 2003: 153)

There is an important element of charity as underlying philosophy in much of the MDG work. In this sense, the failure of countries in the global south to deal with HIV/AIDS, or to control diseases such as Chagas, comes to be seen as being derived from their 'inferior' status; they lack the technological capacity and/or the resources to prevent unnecessary morbidity among their populations. Solutions derived from the charity paradigm may very well achieve some short-term success, but their long-term effectiveness is questionable. For example, should global health focus on generating charitable donations of pharmaceuticals? Should we seek to expand access to products designed, patented, and manufactured in the richest industrialized countries, and bring them to the countries in the global south? Or, perhaps simultaneously, should we work to reform global trade regulations, so generic manufacturers in Brazil, India, Nigeria, and Thailand can produce life-saving medicines for sale at a fraction of their patent-protected costs? The first option is rooted in the notion of charity, while the latter, a far more structural intervention, may yield the more substantial long-term results. Similarly, should efforts to control Chagas disease focus on the large-scale spraying of insecticides? Or should Chagas *prevention* and control programmes take the form of large-scale improvements in housing quality?

Along with charity, ideas of *development* are central to the MDGs. Strongly rooted in *modernization* theories made popular in the 1950s, this position sees development occurring in a linear-like process over time. Farmer argues that:

this perspective seems to regard progress and development as almost *natural processes*. The technocrats who design development projects ... plead for patience. In due time, the technocrats tell the poor, if they speak to them at all, you too will share our standard of living. (After a generation, the reassurance may be changed to 'if not you, your children'). (Farmer, 2003: 155, emphasis added)

This paradigm inherently characterizes the MDGs: they are – more than anything else – based on the notion that, over time, things will get better. And at the level of aggregate data, there is a certain appeal to this. But looking at the inequities that hide behind national averages reveals both charity and development as flawed ways of thinking and working. In their place, Farmer urges us to work from the perspective of social justice – from a position wherein we understand, where we emphasize, that 'what happens to poor people is never divorced from the actions of the powerful' (Farmer, 2003: 158).

A social justice perspective on the MDGs' health targets would not be satisfied with aggregate targets. Yes, reducing the overall burden of disease is critical. However, what is really needed is a nuanced epidemiological account of the inequalities that are hidden by national averages. A 10 per cent reduction in infant mortality may be shared relatively equally across a country, or it may hide substantial differences by region, ethnicity, socioeconomic status, and other factors. A 10 per cent reduction may, in fact, be generated by large improvements in some groups and no improvements, or even worsening outcomes, in other groups. This pattern is perhaps most clearly seen in Orsi *et al.*'s analysis of black–white mortality differentials in the United States. Using nationally representative data, they observed that mortality from breast cancer decreased substantially from 1990 to 2005. But when they compared outcomes for non-Hispanic whites and non-Hispanic blacks, a significant inequality hidden by the overall improvement emerged: breast cancer mortality (age-adjusted and expressed per 100,000 women) among non-Hispanic whites dropped from 32.1 in 1990 to 25.8 in 2005 but remained stagnant for non-Hispanic blacks, with mortality rates of 35.9 in 1990 and 35.5 in 2005 (Orsi *et al.*, 2010). In other words, aggregate-level progress hid a remarkable inequity, with non-Hispanic black women experiencing almost no improvement in age-adjusted mortality rates from breast cancer in twenty-five years in the United States. The empirical evidence suggests that a similar 'fragmentation' of the benefits of medical care is occurring in the global south, with those best positioned in the socioeconomic hierarchy being more likely to take advantage of cancer screening, preventive health care checks, and other health promoting activities.

There are therefore very real reasons to believe that the MDG framework will not break the pattern of poverty and inequality that leads to global health inequities. As it reflects charity/development paradigms and rarely reaches the point of focusing on social justice, the MDG framework leaves the structural conditions in which global health inequities grow intact. Along these lines,

Ooms *et al.* (2010) decry that the MDG system perpetuates, rather than breaks, the global poverty trap. And, in practice, the world's capacity to meet the MDG targets is questionable; the latest data show that most of the world's countries are not on track to meet their MDG targets, and concern exists that inequalities are actually increasing around the world (United Nations, 2011a).

Let us take a closer look at the health-focused MDGs: MDG 4 (dealing with child mortality), MDG 5 (maternal health), and MDG 6 (HIV/AIDS, malaria, and other diseases).

We saw that MDG 4 calls for the world to reduce the under-five mortality rate (measured as number of deaths among children less than five years of age per 1,000 live births) by two thirds between 1990 and 2015. It is here where the most remarkable gains have been made – but also where the world's striking patterns of inequity are clearest. According to the latest data from the WHO, under-five mortality declined by 35 per cent between 1990 and 2010 – from an estimated 88 deaths per 1,000 to 57 deaths per 1,000. Globally, fewer and fewer children die in their first five years of life. Sub-Saharan Africa – the worst-off area of the world for childhood mortality – has experienced declines in this time period, but is not on track to meet the MDG target of a two-thirds reduction of 1990 levels in under-five mortality levels by 2015. Table 2.1 illustrates the percentage reduction in under-five mortality rate by sub-region.

All areas of the world have experienced improvements over this twenty-year period. But the worst-off region (sub-Saharan Africa) remains far behind other regions of the global south, let alone the developed regions. The under-five mortality rate in sub-Saharan Africa stood at 180 (deaths per 1,000 live births among children aged less than five years), and declined to 129 by 2009; this amounted to a decrease of just over 28 per cent (United Nations, 2011a) – an important decrease, to be sure. But it is far lower than the over 50 per cent reductions seen in Central, South-Eastern and Western Asia, Northern Africa, and the Latin American and Caribbean nations. The latter, for example, saw its

Table 2.1 Under-five mortality rate by sub-region, percentage change 1990–2009

Region	Change in under-5 mortality, 1990–2009 %
Sub-Saharan Africa	−28.3
Southern Asia	−43.4
Oceania	−22.4
Central Asia	−52.6
South-Eastern Asia	−50.7
Western Asia	−52.9
Northern Africa	−67.5
Latin America and the Caribbean	−55.8
Eastern Asia	−57.8
Developed regions	−53.3

Note: Author's own table based on United Nations (2011a).

Table 2.2 Maternal death by sub-region, percentage change
1990–2008

Region	Change (1990–2008) %
Sub-Saharan Africa	−26.4
Southern Asia	−52.5
Oceania	−20.7
Caribbean	−46.9
South-East Asia	−57.9
Northern Africa	−60.0
Latin America	−38.5
Western Asia	−50.0
Central Asia	−22.9
Eastern Asia	−62.7
Developed regions	−34.6

Note: Author's own table based on United Nations (2011a).

under-five mortality rate drop from 52 in 1990 to 23 in 2009. Even developed regions experienced a greater relative decline than the sub-Saharan region (from 15 to 7, amounting to a 53 per cent reduction in under-five mortality) (United Nations, 2011a).

The global picture of maternal health (assessed as deaths per 100,000 live births) is similar. According to the latest WHO figures, the global picture is improving. However, the rate of improvement is slower than is needed to meet MDG 5, which called for a three-quarters reduction of maternal mortality between 1990 and 2015 (WHO, 2012b). This is particularly striking in sub-Saharan Africa: while maternal death data are improving, they are nowhere near the level needed to meet the MDG reduction target (see Table 2.2).

Maternal death rates (per 100,000 live births) have dropped in all regions, but the rate of decline has varied significantly from region to region. The greatest gains have occurred in Eastern Asia (which saw a drop from 110 to 41 – a 62.7 per cent reduction – between 1990 and 2008) and Northern Africa (which experienced a decrease from 230 to 92 – a 60 per cent reduction) (United Nations, 2011a). Several other regions experienced declines of over 50 per cent. Sub-Saharan Africa, the worst-off region in terms of maternal health, has shown the smallest reduction, of just over 26 per cent (from 870 to 640). Maternal death rate in that region is more than twice the amount in Southern Asia, the next worst-off region (which saw a decrease from 590 to 280 during this period) (United Nations, 2011a). And if one compares the worst-off country to the best-off country, the level of inequity is staggering: the lifetime risk of maternal death is 1 in 8 in Afghanistan; it is 1 in 17,400 in Sweden (WHO, 2008a).

Malaria, tuberculosis, and HIV/AIDS are some of the biggest worldwide killers. Malaria alone is thought to threaten half of the world's population, and significant advances have been made against it since the year 2000.

Around the world, deaths from malaria are down about 20 per cent, and wide-spread improvements in the use of insecticide-treated bed nets are reported across sub-Saharan Africa (United Nations, 2011a). The WHO projects that, in 2010, of the estimated 216 million cases of malaria, 655,000 ended in death, with over 85 per cent of deaths occurring in children under the age of five (WHO, 2012b). Yet, there is a general sense of optimism with anti-malarial efforts, undoubtedly related to the attention given to the disease by the Global Fund. Funded by donations from the G8 countries, the Bill & Melinda Gates Foundation, and a number of pharmaceutical companies, the Global Fund has contributed greatly to the scaling up of treatment for not only malaria (both in terms of treatment as well as prevention, via insecticide-treated bed-nets), but also HIV/AIDS and tuberculosis (Feachem and Sabot, 2006).[7]

The situation with tuberculosis is more complex, as tuberculosis surged along with the HIV/AIDS pandemic beginning in the 1990s.[8] The WHO estimates that the annual number of new cases of tuberculosis in the world has fallen slowly since 2006 – though the number of new cases was still almost 9 million people. Since 1990, deaths from tuberculosis have fallen worldwide by one third – and, worldwide, countries are on target to meet MDG 6, which called for countries to 'have halted by 2015 and begun to reverse the incidence of malaria and other major diseases'. However, tuberculosis remains a major killer – and, although in 95 per cent of cases it is treatable with antibiotics that have been available for more than 25 years, tuberculosis is still thought to kill 1.7 million people every year.

The greatest success has been seen in the area of HIV/AIDS. The number of new cases of infection has decreased over the past ten years – from 3.1 million new infections in 2001 to 2.7 million new infections in 2010 (United Nations, 2011a). But when we consider the level of activity devoted to prevention efforts worldwide, this reduction is perhaps better seen as a very modest accomplishment, in that almost 3 million new infections still occur every year. And while the fact that incidence is decreasing is celebrated as a success story in the global health literature, one is struck by the high number of new infections that continue to develop worldwide and, in particular, in sub-Saharan Africa, a region that accounts for 70 per cent of HIV cases worldwide (WHO, 2012b). Moreover, the number of people living with HIV/AIDS continues to increase across the world – though in some ways this can also interpreted as good news, as it means that more and more people are accessing life-saving antiretroviral therapy and fewer people die from AIDS-related causes.

There are, therefore, important improvements in the global health landscape in recent decades. And these are worth celebrating. Yet, amidst these improvements, the past twenty years have seen a growth in what we might call global health inequities – inequalities that are 'avoidable, unnecessary, and unfair' (Whitehead, 1992). More than 1 billion people are exposed to 'neglected tropical diseases', representing unnecessary morbidity, social exclusion, and, in some cases, premature mortality (Hotez *et al.*, 2008b; Hotez and Kamath, 2009) – and these diseases are absent from the MDG framework.

Millions of people die every year from preventable diseases, including 2.5 million children who die every year from diarrhoeal diseases. It is these deaths that should cause us to pause when confronted with calls to increase biomedical research capacity, to spend billions on new and more drugs: these deaths do not call for more *biomedical* research. After all, we already have the capacity to deal with life-threatening diarrhoeal diseases – a simple salt water solution, and, in the long-term, a clean water supply and healthy living conditions. Millions die every year from conditions that do not call for advanced biomedical technologies but, rather, improvements in living conditions. And millions more suffer from inadequate access to existing treatments, with, for example, only one third of people thought to be in need of antiretroviral therapy actually receiving this life-saving HIV treatment (WHO, 2010c).

Ways of studying global health

Questions of population health have been primarily seen as the domain of epidemiology; the branch of science that specializes in studying the causes of disease, its distribution, and ways of controlling its spread in populations (Krieger, 2011). Epidemiological work looks for patterns to the distribution of health – not only in terms of infectious and non-infectious diseases, but also in terms of behaviours, attitudes, and knowledge. Epidemiological research seeks to understand the causes and determinants of health and illness. Its focus is on populations, rather than individuals; it has sought to illustrate the *social patterning* of disease. In doing so, epidemiological research has usually taken a macro, rather than micro, perspective. In contrast to clinical medicine – with its focus on an individual and their physical ailments – epidemiology looks at the health of populations broadly defined.

Much of modern epidemiology is concerned with identifying the prevalence of individual-level *risk factors* for disease. This approach to epidemiology highlights the importance of *compositional* factors (characteristics of individuals), such as whether one smokes, or the type of diet one consumes, or whether one uses a seat belt when driving a car. Although these recommendations help to maximize the health of any given *individual*, it is a fallacy to assume that, at a population level, they are the most important things that must be done to promote health. There are some things that influence an individual's health that cannot be measured at the level of individuals, and cannot be 'changed' at the level of individuals – for example, the type of welfare regime that is in place in your country, or the level of income inequality in your region, or the type of anti-tobacco legislation in effect in your community. There is therefore good reason to pursue a *multilevel* strategy, where our health is influenced not only by our own characteristics and our own choices and actions, but also by the characteristics of the places in which we live. The income inequality hypothesis, which I shall examine in some detail, is characteristic of this school of thought.

As noted, the epidemiological approach has been criticized for focusing too much on individual-level risk factors, and for ignoring the social and political processes that lead to disease. For some critics, the way in which epidemiology is practised limits its true potential as a source of knowledge for improving the health of populations (Bezruchka, 2006; Davey Smith, 2001). For example, Dennis Raphael *et al.* argue that 'epidemiology has been the primary tool wielded by the medical profession in quest of the causes of disease and illness. Its application, however, has been narrow, with little appreciation of the complex of political, economic, and social factors that set the stage for the onset of disease and illness' (2006: 5). The question here is one of *framing* – what do we include as causal agents in our theories? To what extent do we track 'upstream' and examine *causes of the causes*? For example, do we focus solely on the type of diet an individual follows, or do we also consider the availability of healthy food in their area? Do we consider the regional and global trade policies that influence the availability and pricing of food in that individual's market? Alternatively, do we focus solely on an individual's consumption of tobacco? Or do we use a wider frame and integrate into our research questions macro factors, such as the extent to which that individual's city has enacted tobacco control legislation? This line of questioning also easily applies to risk behaviour related to HIV infection, as well as anti-malarial practices such as using an insecticide-treated bednet.[9] In arguing that epidemiology has been narrow in its application, critics such as Raphael *et al.* emphasize the discipline's preoccupation with 'proximal' risk factors, and its neglect of the more 'distal' factors. From this perspective, the epidemiological literature, as a whole, has failed to grasp fully the fundamental causes of disease (Raphael *et al.*, 2006).[10] A growing literature on the social determinants of health suggests that in order to more fully understand the fundamental causes of disease, researchers need to expand their theoretical models of causality to also large-scale social factors such as income inequality.

An even more radical critique has developed from political economy, which suggests that researchers need to examine a society's system of commodity production and distribution (Muntaner, 2003; Muntaner *et al.*, 2001). From this perspective, health, as income inequality, is a consequence of macro-economic forces governed by the structure of the economic system. These macro-economic forces are an integral component of structural violence, which we defined in Chapter 1 as 'social arrangements that put individuals and populations in harm's way . . . The arrangements are *structural* because they are embedded in the political and economic organization of our social world; they are *violent* because they cause injury to people' (Farmer *et al.*, 2006: 1686, emphasis added). The integration of a multifaceted term such as this, one that has no clear unit of measurement, into a largely quantitative area of research remains a daunting task – but one that must be met, if we are to grasp the forces that manifest in health inequities around the world.

Arguably, epidemiology has succeeded in its focus on individual risk factors but has neglected the underlying structural forces that shape our exposure to risk factors. This has been described most eloquently by the Australian epidemiologist Anthony McMichael, who noted that 'modern epidemiology is thus oriented to explaining and quantifying the bobbing of corks on the surface waters, while largely disregarding the stronger undercurrents that determine where, on average, the cluster of corks ends up along the shoreline of risk' (1995: 634). In other words, epidemiology has focused too much on individuals and their attributes (the bobbing of corks in McMichael's analogy), and should re-focus on the mechanisms by which risk is generated. McMichael's undercurrents – acts of structural violence – have only recently come into focus in global health research.[11]

Re-focusing epidemiology so that it engages with generative mechanisms is entirely possible. This would enable us to give not only *descriptions* (for example, whether a country or region is on track to meet an MDG goal), but also *explanations* (identifying aspects of social structure that increase/decrease social gradients). Indeed, a growing body of literature within the discipline has called for a new social/global epidemiology that seeks to do just that (Berkman and Kawachi, 2000; Cwikel, 2006; Kawachi and Wamala, 2007). For example, Neil Pearce urges that 'a "global" approach should not ignore the importance of individual-level risk factors – ultimately, most of us die from easily preventable proximal causes such as tobacco, occupational exposures, diet, car accidents, etc. – but should indicate the importance of studying such proximate causes in their social and political context' (2004: 1129). Following calls such as Pearce's, we have seen significant developments in epidemiological practice. Increasingly, researchers include both compositional variables (reflecting the characteristics of people) and contextual variables (reflecting the characteristics of the places in which people live) into their analyses – paving the way for a richer, more sociologically meaningful account of the social determinants of health, analyses that see the 'causes' of disease operating both at distal and proximal distances. Such work is part of what we might call a 'turn' in health research towards fundamental causes: racism and discrimination (De Maio, 2012; De Maio and Kemp, 2010; Krieger, 2011), inequality (Wilkinson and Pickett, 2007, 2008, 2009b), the 'intersection' of race, class, and gender (Schulz and Mullings, 2006) – in general, structural violence and its effects on the health of populations.

To understand health in a global context, we need to also grasp related approaches to the study of disease in populations, including the contributions from sociology and anthropology. These disciplines share a concern with inequities, but have traditionally used differing methods and theories for studying health and illness. Sociology has had a strong engagement with health concerns, at least formally starting with the work of Talcott Parsons in the 1950s. His was a 'structural-functionalist' approach to understanding how society came to sanction some conditions/behaviours as legitimate illness; he sought to understand the social mechanisms that distinguish illness from deviant behaviour. His main conceptual contribution – the sick role – remains in use in medical sociology (Shilling, 2002; Williams, 2005), but it has not contributed in substantial ways to questions of inequality, let alone global health. The 1960s and 1970s saw increased attention to health and illness from symbolic interactionism and conflict paradigms, with sociologists studying the socialization of physicians, the medicalization of everyday life, and patient-physician interaction (De Maio, 2010). However, no major sociologists of the time worked on questions of health inequality, or global health in general. Sociological contributions to the study of health inequalities research showed promise in the early 1980s, with Peter Townsend's work on the UK Black Report, and in the 1990s and 2000s, sociology engaged with debates on social capital, income inequality, and social determinants of health (Bartley, 2004; Bartley *et al.*, 1998).

Glaringly absent in all of this, however, is engagement with global health. Sociologists have made scarce contributions to the global health literature, and are only now beginning to turn their attention to health and globalization. Along these lines, Geoffrey Cockerham and William Cockerham note that 'the study of globalization in medical sociology has been slow to develop, but the topic is growing in importance with the increased realization that health and disease have global connections' (2010: 21). Readers from outside the discipline may well wonder why it has taken sociology so long to come to this realization – after all, the discipline is grounded in concerns over social justice (Feagin, 2004; Feagin and Vera, 2008) and all of the classical sociologists integrated cross-national data into their most important works. Yet, contemporary sociology have not seen global health inequalities as integral to understanding societies.[12] Sociologists, surprisingly, have not made structural violence a core concept of the discipline, despite a long-standing debate in the discipline over the interaction of social structure and personal agency.

In contrast to sociology, anthropology has a longer tradition of engaging with global concerns – clearly emerging from its traditional focus on 'less developed' societies. Anthropology developed side by side with tropical medicine, and historically focused on understanding cultural beliefs and traditional healing practices in colonial settings and among indigenous communities. However, more recently, anthropological work on global health inequalities has offered a great deal of insight into questions of structural violence, particularly in the now-classic books *Death Without Weeping: The Violence of Everyday Life in Brazil* (Scheper-Hughes, 1992), *Stories in the Time of Cholera: Racial Profiling During a Medical Nightmare* (Briggs and Mantini-Briggs, 2003), as well as the more recent *When Experiments Travel: Clinical Trials and the Global Search for Human Subjects* (Petryna, 2009) and *The Republic of Therapy: Triage and Sovereignty in West Africa's time of AIDS* (Nguyen, 2010). Paul Farmer's *AIDS and Accusation: Haiti and the Geography of Blame* (1992), *Infections and Inequalities: The Modern Plagues* (1999), and *Pathologies of Power: Health, Human Rights, and the New War on the Poor* (2003) are, for many people in these disciplines, the strongest statements on the links between structural violence and global health inequalities.

Farmer calls for a new approach to global health, and openly questions the existing weaknesses of our disciplines – from anthropological work that focuses solely on 'culture' while obscuring inequality and structural violence, to research based on assumptions of epidemiological transition, to medical ethics that dwells on end-of-life decisions while ignoring large-scale violations of human rights. He urges us to examine how structural violence acts to worsen the health of individuals and populations, and asks: 'By what mechanisms, precisely, do social forces ranging from poverty to racism become *embodied* as individual experience?' (Farmer, 2003: 30; emphasis in original). To accomplish this, Farmer describes the need for our work to be *historically deep* and *geographically broad*, arguing that only in this way can we begin to see that 'what happens to poor people is never divorced from the actions of the powerful' (Farmer, 2003: 153).

Farmer's work emphasizes the pathogenic effects of inequality. He concludes: 'societies riven by social inequality have poorer health indices than societies in which comparable levels of wealth are more evenly distributed' (Farmer, 2003: 20). And it turns out that, at the same time that Farmer published his major works, a parallel line of investigation blossomed in social epidemiology on income inequality as a social determinant of health. Most closely tied to the work of Richard Wilkinson, the debate over the income inequality hypothesis is in many ways a quantification of Farmer's central thesis. Almost exclusively a statistical research area, the income inequality hypothesis illustrates many of the critiques levelled against epidemiology and has, thus far, been unable to live up to Farmer's vision of historically deep and geographically broad analysis. In the next section, I outline some of these critiques in relation to the hypothesis, and conclude with an analysis of the hypothesis from the perspective of global health inequality.

Income inequality as a global determinant of health

Perhaps the most promising perspective to study global health inequalities draws from epidemiology, sociology, and anthropology – along with other related disciplines, including economics and political science. It is just such a mixture of disciplines that have featured in the debate over the income inequality hypothesis. The idea that our health depends not only on our own income, but also on *how income is distributed in the place in which we live* has generated intense debates – with disagreements often yielding productive exchanges on methodological, theoretical, and epistemological issues (Coburn, 2004; De Maio, 2010a; Muntaner and Lynch, 1999; Subramanian and Kawachi, 2003). Much of this research has been positivist in its approach – it is based on the epistemological notion that *to measure* is *to know*. There certainly are appealing aspects of this approach, and researchers have had some success in measuring inequality and population health, along with other phenomena that are seen as intertwined with these factors, including 'social capital'. However, some critics have charged that the reliance on positivist methods has limited the study of income inequality as a social determinant of health, with increasing calls for a critical realist approach that would focus, above all, on the *generative factors* that lead to both income inequality and poor population health. This is a rapidly evolving area of research, and many central issues remain contested, to the point where a consensus on the hypothesis is far from clear. In particular, what the hypothesis looks like from a global health perspective is just beginning to be sketched out (Bernburg, 2010; De Vogli *et al.*, 2009; Deaton, 2002; Starfield and Birn, 2007; Subramanian and Kawachi, 2007).

More than 200 statistical studies have examined the relationship between income inequality and population health, and approximately 90 per cent of these have found at least some support for the hypothesized relationship. However, once control variables are taken into account, this figure drops to approximately 40 per cent (Wilkinson and Pickett, 2009a). That is, only a minority of studies conclude with full support for the hypothesis, and others give mixed results, with the hypothesis being supported only under some conditions. It is here where the statistical issues pertaining to testing the hypothesis become quite complex and contested, with little agreement in the literature surrounding what kind of variables should be included in statistical models as 'control' variables to isolate the effect of inequality itself (and, in turn, whether the statistical practice of 'controlling' for the effects of independent variables gives us an evidence base from which to establish causality). There is also no consensus on the geographical level at which the hypothesis should be tested, with some studies being carried out with national data, and other studies being carried out at state/provincial, city, and municipal levels.

Most importantly for our discussion, there is no clear consensus with respect to the regions of the world where the hypothesis might apply (Lynch *et al.*, 2003; Lynch *et al.*, 2004; Subramanian and Kawachi, 2003). Wilkinson's early formulation of the hypothesis focused on the advanced industrialized countries of the Organisation for Economic Co-operation and Development (OECD) – and his rationale for choosing countries was based on the notion of epidemiological transition. From Wilkinson's perspective, countries which have 'undergone' epidemiological transition, and where non-communicable diseases (cancer, cardiovascular disease) are the leading cause of death, are places where we may detect a pathogenic effect of inequality. Since Wilkinson's initial formulation of the hypothesis, it has become widely accepted that non-communicable diseases are actually the leading cause of death everywhere in the world, except for some countries in sub-Saharan Africa. As I discuss in Chapter 3, the notion of epidemiological transition has itself been criticized for ignoring the socioeconomic segmentation we see in population health data.[13] There is therefore a very real reason to examine the income inequality hypothesis in the global south – areas of the world that experience *higher* levels of inequality than do the richest industrialized countries.

Among the most unequal countries in the world are India and South Africa. In both places, income inequality has been linked to adverse health outcomes. In India, statistical analysis has shown that income inequality is associated with both under- and over-nutrition, to the point where a one standard deviation increase in state income inequality is linked to a 19 per cent greater odds ratio for underweight and a 21 per cent greater odds ratio for being obese (Subramanian *et al.*, 2007). In South Africa, high levels of community income inequality are linked to higher prevalence rates for tuberculosis, even after statistically controlling for demographic and behavioural risk factors, including a person's educational attainment, their employment status, and their household wealth (Harling *et al.*, 2008).

The bulk of literature suggests that income inequality is associated with poor health outcomes, at least in the United States (Backlund *et al.*, 2007; Ross *et al.*, 2000; Wilkinson and Pickett, 2009b), with some contested exceptions (Deaton and Lubotsky, 2003; Muntaner, 2003; Subramanian and Kawachi, 2007). The extent to which this model applies in within-country analyses in other parts of the world, including the relatively more equal countries of Scandinavia (Böckerman *et al.*, 2009) and Central and Eastern Europe (Bobak *et al.*, 2007), has been called into question. Also, non-significant findings have been published using data from other relatively equal countries, including Germany (Breckenkamp *et al.*, 2007), Denmark (Osler *et al.*, 2002; Osler *et al.*, 2003), Canada (Auger *et al.*, 2009; Veenstra, 2002), and Japan (Shibuya *et al.*, 2002).

One explanation for the 'null findings' in some countries is that there is a 'threshold' effect, where income inequality does have a detectable effect on health, but only at or above a certain level of inequality. Supporting this idea, statistically significant relationships between income inequality and population health have been detected in the relatively unequal countries of China (Pei and Rodriguez, 2006), Italy (De Vogli *et al.*, 2005), Brazil (Cavalini and de Leon, 2008), Chile (Subramanian *et al.*, 2003), and Argentina (De Maio, 2008; De Maio *et al.*, 2012b). At the same time, recent multi-country analyses (Dorling *et al.*, 2007; Moore, 2006; Pickett *et al.*, 2005; Pickett and Wilkinson, 2007) have generated renewed support for the hypothesis, although this has been disputed in work using self-rated health measures (Jen *et al.*, 2009).[14] The net result of the empirical work in this area is deeply nuanced.

The literature on the income inequality hypothesis is impressively interdisciplinary, drawing from biomedical research on stress pathways (Brunner, 1997; Wilkinson, 2000c) to sociological work on social capital (Mansyur *et al.*, 2008; Moore *et al.*, 2006; Poortinga, 2006), economic research on the measurement of inequality (De Maio, 2007), philosophical discussion of inequality versus inequity (Asada, 2007; Daniels *et al.*, 2000), and debates on class (Muntaner and Lynch, 1999). The field has shown an active engagement with social theory – drawing at times from Durkheim (Turner, 2003), as well as Marx, Bourdieu, Veblen, and others (De Maio, 2010a). Throughout this literature, a dominance of quantitative methods is clear. What is less clear, however, is the epistemological basis of this research area – with contributions from positivist and critical realist positions (De Maio, 2010a). Related to this, the geo-political 'frame' of this area of study needs to be re-considered (Labonté and Torgerson, 2005), with calls for a global perspective on the income inequality hypothesis increasingly being raised.

Most studies have been bounded by nation-state boundaries – with relatively few projects harmonizing data across countries. This is an important limitation: while our studies are bounded by political boundaries, both financial capital and disease are not. The starting point in a critical realist account of the health effects of income inequality (almost certainly an analysis of financial capital, trade flows, and economic integration with the global capitalist economy) flows across political borders (Coburn, 2000, 2004). In other words, the independent variables are ontologically positioned *outside* the empirical frame of studies using national datasets. The result is that the 'historically deep and geographically broad' type of analysis that has been called for by scholars such as Farmer (2003) remains difficult to carry out.[15]

However, there are certainly promising signs in this area. Spencer Moore's (2006) analysis of global patterns in life expectancy is indicative of the importance of a global approach informed by political economy. His analysis suggests that global trade patterns and world-system role (peripheral or non-peripheral) are critical dimensions of the health effects of income inequality. His analysis of 107 countries compared four typologies:

- high/low income
- OECD membership/non-membership
- core/non-core (based on a country's level of exchange in capital-intensive commodities)
- non-periphery/periphery (based on world systems theory).[16]

Using a regression analysis with an interaction effect between inequality and global position, Moore demonstrates that inequality actually has a stronger negative effect on life expectancies in peripheral populations, rather than non-periphery countries, contrary to what had been emphasized by Wilkinson. Furthermore, Moore observed significant differences by typology used to classify countries, concluding that the prevailing practice of classifying countries simply by income group was not adequately capturing levels of global stratification. These findings have given a renewed impetus to the notion that global health research needs to be informed by and engaged with political economy.

Most recently, Brian Biggs et al. (2010) have demonstrated that income distribution plays a significant role in the relationship between GDP per capita and population health among the countries of Latin America. These findings, combined with analyses illustrating a health effect of income inequality in Brazil (Cavalini and de Leon, 2008), Argentina (De Maio, 2008; De Maio et al., 2012b), Chile (Subramanian et al., 2003), and South Africa (Harling et al., 2008), suggest that Wilkinson's initial focus on the countries of the OECD was unduly limited. Indeed, with statistical indication that income inequality is associated with population health in the global south and with an understanding that the diseases linked to allostatic load (the physiological basis by which Wilkinson argues inequality is linked to health) are the leading causes of death in these countries (Banatvala and Donaldson, 2007; Horton, 2007; Nabel *et al.*, 2009), a shift towards a truly global analysis of the health effects of income inequality is needed. Yet, this type of analysis is pushed aside by an excessive focus on MDG targets – which, after all, say nothing about the causes of the targeted health outcomes.

A new wave of work is examining the hypothesis in the global south, and more work is needed, with better data and over longer periods of time.[17] What is most needed, however, is a re-focusing of the hypothesis to account for structural violence, to situate income inequality in a larger chain of events that ultimately lead to preventable morbidity and premature mortality. David Coburn, drawing on the political economy tradition of Vicente Navarro (2002), notes that:

> income inequality is itself the consequence of fundamental changes in class structure which have produced not only income inequality but also numerous other forms of health-relevant social inequalities. Welfare measures in turn reflect basic social, political and economic institutions tied to the degree to which societies take care of their citizens or leave the fate of citizens up to the market, i.e., neo-liberalism. Income inequality is a consequence, not the determinant. (2004: 43)

Coburn has forcefully criticized the trend in medical sociology (and the literature on the health effects of income inequality in particular) not to question the origins of social inequalities:

> While numerous researchers have explored methods of ameliorating the effects of poor social conditions on the health of the underprivileged ... hardly any have asked about the possible causes of inequality itself. Yet, examining the causes of social inequalities, and not simply their effects, changes our understanding of the causal sequences involved in the income inequality/health status relationship. (Coburn, 2001: 50)

For Coburn, the health effects of income inequality are important but should be examined through the wider lens of political economy, rather than epidemiology; he calls for an increased role for critical realism and a diminished role for positivism as guiding epistemology. The importance of a global approach is echoed in Farmer's description of his experiences in treating HIV and tuberculosis patients in rural Haiti:

> [t]he cost of modern inequality is even greater than that calculated by Wilkinson and others who define 'societies' as nation-states ...

Wilkinson misses the worst of it ... The sick of rural Haiti, urban Peru, and sub-Saharan Africa may be invisible to those tallying the victims of modern inequality, but they are, in many senses, casualties of the very same processes that have led to crime and decreased social cohesion 'at home'. (1999: 281)

Can an expanded global perspective – a view that focuses not just on the effects of inequality, but also its causes – be incorporated into global health research? There are signs that the literature is shifting towards this – but it is a fundamental break with our traditional practice, and calls for an unprecedented level of cooperation and dialogue among the various disciplines that work on global health. This, at times, is frustratingly beyond our reach, as I show in Chapter 5, when discussing neglected tropical diseases. In one of the latest WHO reports on the prevention and control of neglected tropical diseases, we find an important notion: 'for most NTDs, sustained elimination is possible only with full access to safe water, waste disposal and treatment, basic sanitation and improved living conditions' (WHO, 2012a: 1). Yet in that very same paragraph, the WHO notes: 'However, *since this area of work is related to development and not directly to the work of WHO's Department of Control of Neglected Tropical Diseases, it is not discussed in the roadmap*' (WHO, 2012a: 1–2; emphasis added). The statement, in effect, moves discussion of poverty, of inequality, of structural violence off the table – and leaves room only for technical cures such as insecticides and what the WHO calls 'mass drug administration' (MDA), an effort to distribute mass quantities of pharmaceuticals in the global south as a way of preventing and controlling NTDs (Spiegel *et al.*, 2010). If we are to account properly for the health effects of inequality, and if, following Coburn and Farmer, we see a larger canvas that illustrates the relationships between inequality, structural violence, and health, we must go beyond these artificial and self-imposed barriers to interdisciplinary work.

The task may not be as difficult as it may at first appear. I take some inspiration from a different WHO report – this time, their 2005 document 'Preventing Chronic Diseases'. In particular, I take inspiration from a relatively simple graphic they included in the report, reproduced here in Figure 2.1.

At the right of the figure, we have health outcomes – the main chronic diseases: heart disease, stroke, cancer, chronic respiratory diseases, and diabetes. It is these conditions that account for the majority of the world's deaths, as we shall see in Chapter 4. The WHO argues that these conditions are caused by a range of factors – the most 'proximal' being raised blood pressure, raised blood glucose, abnormal blood lipids, and overweight/obesity. The connection between these risk factors and chronic disease outcomes is well-established, as is the connection slightly more 'upstream', toward the factors that shape blood pressure, blood sugar, and so on. Here, we see unhealthy diet, physical inactivity, and tobacco use – the main 'targets' of health promotion. And just focusing on these three elements of the framework, we have a good descrip-

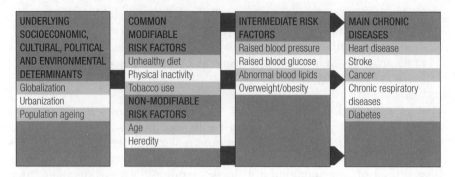

Figure 2.1 'Causes of the causes' framework
Source: WHO (2005) (used with permission).

tion of a traditional approach to population health. What can we do to improve people's diet? To promote physical activity? To reduce tobacco consumption?

The column on the left of the framework is where the promise of an interdisciplinary approach to global health inequality begins to manifest. How does 'globalization' relate to the more proximal risk factors? How does globalization connect to disease outcomes? My reading of this literature is that it is exactly here that Wilkinson's income inequality hypothesis is most relevant – as a way of explaining how large-scale processes that manifest in income inequality come to affect our health. This calls for understanding the global political economy that underlies tobacco consumption, working conditions, food production and distribution, and living conditions (urbanization). This type of work may proceed by developing theoretical models expanding the 'explanatory sphere', combining nuanced measures of income distribution with alternative indexes of socio-economic inequality.[18] For example, such measures could incorporate measures of gender inequality and racism, vastly improving how researchers in this area conceptualize inequality itself. This area of work may also be developed by a stronger engagement with ideas emerging in the political science literature on welfare regimes (Esping-Andersen, 1990; Starfield and Birn, 2007), enabling a more nuanced contextualization of the political economy of income inequality. Clearly, success of this endeavour relies on our collective ability to bring down disciplinary borders and work collaboratively across the broad spectrum of disciplines that engage with questions of politics, economics, and health.

Conclusion

Global health research is at a critical crossroads. On one hand, it is firmly engaged with UN-led work on the MDGs. Indeed, several MDGs offer health-specific targets pertaining to under-5 mortality, maternal mortality, and the incidence of HIV/AIDS, malaria, and other diseases. These targets have radically increased public attention towards some of the major indicators of population health, and philanthropic foundations such as the Bill & Melinda Gates Foundation have responded with unprecedented funds for research. On the other hand, global health research – if it relies too much on the MDGs as a guiding analytical framework – risks glossing over inequalities as a central topic of study. Re-focusing global health research so that its gaze is firmly centred on inequality is possible – and, from my perspective, badly needed. We saw in this chapter how an inequality lens that privileges structural violence may be particularly useful in relation to the income inequality hypothesis. In Chapter 3, I turn our attention to one of global health's core conceptual tools, epidemiological transition theory. It is one of our most important tools – but, like the MDGs, it comes with a risk of focusing too much on national averages, with a resulting neglect of inequalities. Epidemiological transition theory is also one of the pillars of Wilkinson's original formulation of the income inequality hypothesis. It is a fundamental model – yet much contested; one that is very influential in global health, yet often criticized in studies published by researchers from the global south.

The Epidemiological Transition

The epidemiological transition is one of the core tenets of the global health research literature. It is a theory that seeks to explain a society's population health profile, and how it changes over time. First developed by the Egyptian-born demographer Abdel Omran, epidemiological transition theory describes a change in a country's leading causes of death from infectious (or communicable) to chronic (or non-communicable) diseases (see Omran, 1971, 1983). The classic formulation of this model posits that the transition is primarily associated with a country's economic development. It describes how countries transition over time from an 'era of pestilence and famine', characterized by brutally low life expectancies and outbreaks of infectious pathogens, to an era of 'man-made and degenerative' diseases, where life expectancy is high and mortality relatively predictable from one year to the next.

As a theoretical framework, the epidemiological transition is often implicit in global health thinking. It is often taken for granted that the model works, and that it describes with some degree of precision the development of global health over time. Yet, researchers have also paused to 'unpack' the model, sometimes developing ways of extending the theory to better fit contemporary epidemiological profiles in specific countries and regions (Cook and Dummer, 2004; Gaylin and Kates, 1997; Heuveline *et al.*, 2002; Waters, 2006). Other researchers, as I show in this chapter, have been critical of the theory's underlying assumptions, critiquing it as part of a larger ideology of oppression and structural violence (Avilés, 2001). For example, Carolina Martínez and Gustavo Leal, from Mexico's Autonomous Metropolitan University, analyzed historical mortality data from Mexico, and reached the conclusion that the model is an *illusion*, ultimately charging that 'health ministries in the *so-called low- and middle-income countries* would do well to abandon the illusion of *epidemiological transition* in order to deal with the difficult yet unavoidable task of caring for their populations' (2003: 542; emphasis in original). From their perspective, epidemiological transition fails in its objective as a useful tool with which to evaluate changes in population health. Their critique, as I discuss in this chapter, aims to move questions of inequality from the margins to the forefront.

Along these lines, Mauricio Barreto from Brazil's Universdidade Federal de Bahia critiques the model of epidemiological transition:

this so-called theory was derived from the conservative idea of inex-
orable phases of social and economic development in peripheral countries, which reproduced the phases of development experienced in core
countries. ... it was believed that modernization meant precise, linear
phases that would lead us to a world free first of all from infectious diseases and later perhaps from disease in general. The peripheral countries
would merely follow the core countries in these supposedly fixed and
unavoidable steps. (Barreto, 2004: 1134)

Barreto's comment highlights epidemiological transition theory's relationship
to the much maligned modernization approach that characterized development thinking in the 1950s. As I discuss in this chapter, critiques of epidemiological transition theory by Latin American researchers, in particular, has
instead been aligned with dependency and world-systems theoretical
approaches, now understood by many to inform 'critical' theories of globalization (Jones, 2010).

The most recent research in this area has questioned the assumptions of epidemiological transition theory, and empirical findings show that many countries of the global south experience a persistent 'dual burden' of disease, something that the original theory did not foresee. The coexistence of chronic diseases such as cancer, cardiovascular disease, adult-onset diabetes, and arthritis
with infectious diseases such as tuberculosis and malaria presents formidable
challenges to fragmented and under-funded health care systems.
Understanding epidemiologic transition, or what we might instead see as epidemiological *overlap*, is therefore critical to gauging the pressures on health
care systems in the global south, as well as to thinking about strengthening
those health care systems.

A traditional view of the transition emphasizes discrete stages, or true
turning points, in a country's economic and epidemiological development.
For example, Richard Wilkinson – who we saw in Chapter 2 as the central
figure behind the income inequality hypothesis – argues that the epidemiological transition:

marks a fundamental change in the main determinants of health and
seems to indicate the point in economic development at which the vast
majority of the population gained reliable access to the basic material
necessities of life. The impact of medical science is not reflected in the
epidemiological transition. In fact, the transition would have happened
(and largely did happen) without it. (1994: 65)

Here, Wilkinson emphasizes a traditional view of the epidemiological transition (as a 'fundamental change in the main determinants of health') and identifies an important foundational element of the theory – that medical science
was not responsible for the epidemiological transition, at least not for the
advanced industrialized countries.

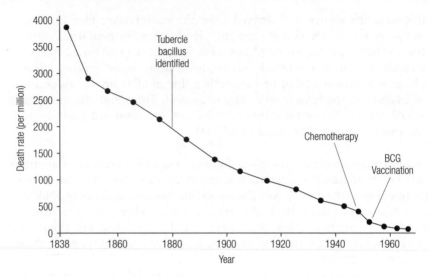

Figure 3.1 Death rate in England and Wales from tuberculosis, 1838–1960s
Source: McKeown (1979) (reprinted by permission of Princeton University Press).

This is perhaps now best supported by work published by the physician and demographic historian Thomas McKeown. Using historical records, he observed that the largest reductions in death rates from tuberculosis occurred *before* knowledge of its underlying biology and far before effective medical interventions were developed (McKeown, 1976). McKeown's main finding is illustrated in Figure 3.1.

Using historical data from England and Wales, McKeown shows that death rate (per million) declined very steeply before *mycobacterium tuberculosis*, the bacillus that causes tuberculosis, was first identified in 1882 by Robert Koch (who went on to receive the Nobel Prize for his discovery). Death rates in England and Wales continued to decrease throughout the late 1800s and early 1900s, and were only a small fraction of their historical level when effective treatments for tuberculosis, including the antibiotic *streptomycin*, were used after World War II. The English and Welsh tuberculosis records illustrate an important notion: historical declines in mortality rates from infectious diseases are not associated with medical intervention but, rather, with overall improvements in living conditions.

John McKinlay and Sonja McKinlay's (1977) analysis of US death rates for infectious diseases very much support McKeown's assertion. They found a similar pattern not only with tuberculosis death rates in the US, but also among other major infectious diseases, such as diphtheria, scarlet fever, and measles. Death rates for all of these infectious killers declined dramatically before the development of effective interventions. For some researchers, this amounts to one of the great heresies of our time: medical intervention was not responsible for the great declines in mortality rates from infectious diseases seen in the past 150 years in the industrialized world.[1] In its place, demographers like Omran cite economic development as the key catalyst for the decreasing mortality rates.

As we will see in this chapter, economic development is at the core of epidemiological transition theory. In this regard, epidemiological transition theory is much like other 'stage' theories of development – whether a capitalist model (such as the stages of economic growth devised by W.W. Rostow (1960), which begins with 'traditional' societies that transition through five stages leading to the age of 'high-mass consumption'), or a communist model such as that of Karl Marx (which predicted capitalist societies transforming, via their own internal contradictions, into communist societies). 'Stage' thinking is also present in many of the classic sociological ideas of Emile Durkheim, who saw progression from 'mechanical' to 'organic' solidarity occurring in industrializing societies. Similarly, Omran's stage model attempts to reveal how a society's population health patterns change over time.

Development of the model

Omran's model describes important shifts in a society's patterns of fertility and mortality, along with changes in the underlying causes of death. Omran summarized the theory of epidemiological transition as follows:

> evolutionary changes in different societal settings from a situation of high mortality, high fertility, short life expectancy, young age structure, and predominance of communicable [infectious] diseases; especially in the young, to one of low mortality, low fertility, increasing life expectancy, aging, and predominance of degenerative and man-made diseases, especially among the middle and old ages. (1996: 5)

Describing it as an evolutionary process, a key feature of Omran's thinking is revealed; for epidemiological transition occurs not as abrupt changes but, rather, as gradual shifts. For Omran, the factors driving the transition are complex, but they revolve around the socioeconomic, political and cultural development of a society, as reflected in a population's standards of living, habits, hygiene, and nutrition. He did not see medical intervention as a central factor in Western Europe's epidemiological transition, noting – in a way that foreshadows the findings of McKeown and those of McKinlay and McKinlay – that 'the influence of medical factors was largely inadvertent until the twentieth century, by which times pandemics of infection had already receded significantly' (Omran, 1971: 520). For Omran, the epidemiological transition is shaped by changing levels of mortality and fertility and, importantly, by the fact that mortality patterns change before fertility patterns change.[2] The theory is illustrated in Figure 3.2.

On the x-axis is time, reflecting a country's 'progression' with regard to economic development. The y-axis reflects a country's crude birth and death rates

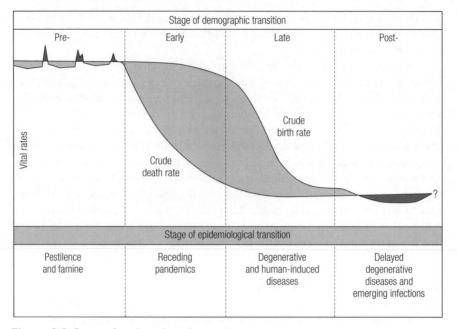

Figure 3.2 Stages of epidemiological transition

Source: McCracken and Phillips (2005) (reprinted by permission of Routledge).

(expressed as rates per 1,000 population), which aggregate to its population growth. To explain the theory, Omran put forth five propositions, which I now discuss.

Proposition 1: *Mortality is the fundamental factor in population dynamics.*

This is now a basic and widely-accepted tenet of demography (Caldwell, 2001; Jones and Moon, 1992). Declines in mortality rates precipitate increases in population growth, and changes in fertility rates have historically been tied to previously experienced decreases in mortality. The temporal order of these changes is important, and Omran's model changed thinking in demography at the time, which had placed more emphasis on changing fertility rates than on changing mortality rates. Omran argued that patterns of fertility are more limited in their fluctuation, with an upper bound generated by biological and social limits to female reproduction and a lower bound influenced by female survival during reproductive years. Patterns of mortality, in contrast, show more marked 'peaks and valleys', showing the effect of infectious disease epidemics. Omran illustrated this proposition with vital statistics from Sweden, shown in Figure 3.3.

Sweden's vital records go back to the early 1700s. Omran used these data to illustrate the dramatic peaks and valleys in mortality levels at early stages of the epidemiological transition – with the peaks reflecting outbreaks of dev-

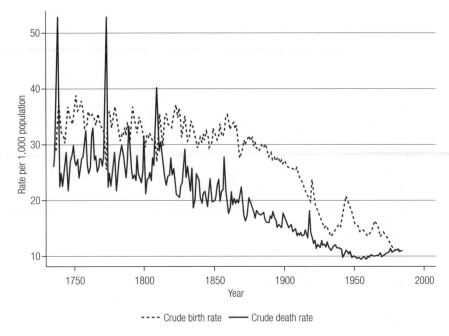

Figure 3.3 The epidemiological transition in Sweden
Note: Author's own analysis of data from Chesnais (1992).

astating infectious diseases. The death rate is shown (generally) in the lower end of the data, and the birth rate on the upper end of the data. A decline in general mortality rates, combined with a 'levelling' of the peaks and valleys (clear by the 1870s onwards in Figure 3.3, with the exception of 1914, when death rates peak as a result of the influenza pandemic), was a clear-cut signal that a country was undergoing the early phase of epidemiological transition.

> **Proposition 2**: *The transition is marked, above all, by a long-term shift in morbidity and mortality patterns. Infectious epidemics are gradually displaced by 'degenerative and man-made diseases as the chief form of morbidity and primary cause of death'.* (Omran, 1971: 516)

In many ways, this proposition is the most important one of the entire theory. Omran described this long-term shift as occurring in three stages:

- the age of pestilence and famine
- the age of receding pandemics
- the age of degenerative and man-made diseases.

The age of pestilence and famine is characterized by very high and fluctuating levels of mortality. In Figure 3.3, this age would characterize the period in

Sweden before the 1850s. Omran describes the age of pestilence and famine in these terms: 'Caught between the towering peaks of mortality from epidemics and other disasters and the high plateaus of mortality dictated by chronic malnutrition and endemic diseases, life expectancy was short and human misery was assured' (Omran, 1971: 512). Societies in the age of pestilence and famine experience very low levels of life expectancy, typically ranging from 20 to 40 years, and are burdened by very high levels of infant mortality (with infants particularly prone to infectious epidemics and the effects of malnourishment). For Omran, 'the *age of pestilence and famine* is, for all practical purposes, an extension of the pre-modern pattern of health and disease which continued in the Western societies until the middle of the 18th century, or sometimes thereafter' (1983: 306; emphasis in original). In global terms, Omran described the age of pestilence and famine extending to less-developed countries until the early part of the twentieth century.

The major causes of death in this age are reminiscent of Thomas Malthus' 'positive checks' on population growth: epidemics, famine, and war. This age is characterized by what are now termed 'diseases of poverty', including tuberculosis and cholera. These diseases thrive in settings of poverty and inequality – they are clear pathological manifestations of structural violence, in that they are nurtured and spread by living conditions and economic systems that marginalize the poor.

The age of pestilence and famine can be seen in the world today. For example, it is seen in Haiti, where more than 75 per cent of the population lives below the poverty line and where only 51 per cent of the rural population has reasonable access to a clean water source. There, life expectancy at birth is 62, a full 12 years fewer than the average for the rest of Latin America and the Caribbean (World Bank, 2012). Infant mortality amounts to 70 deaths for every 1,000 live births, far higher than other countries in the region. Following the devastating earthquake of 2010, when an estimated 300,000 are thought to have perished, Haiti has experienced a significant outbreak of cholera,[3] adding to the infectious disease burden which has plagued the country, particularly as a result of tuberculosis and HIV/AIDS (Farmer, 2011). Since the earthquake, the birth rate in Haiti has tripled, reflecting the 'peaks' and 'valleys' integral to Omran's analysis.

The second stage in Omran's theory is described as the age of receding pandemics. This stage witnesses progressive declines in mortality – seen in Figures 3.3 and 3.4. Peaks in mortality rates characteristic of the age of pestilence and famine become less frequent and less severe; they eventually disappear and, subsequently, average life expectancy at birth increases and can range from 30 to 55 years. This was the observed experience in eighteenth- and nineteenth-century Western Europe. Omran used historical data from New York City to illustrate this aspect of the transition, as shown in Figure 3.4.

The peaks and valleys seen in the period 1800–1900 are indicative of the age of pestilence and famine. In particular, outbreaks of yellow fever, cholera, and smallpox cause high fluctuations in mortality in the city. But around 1890,

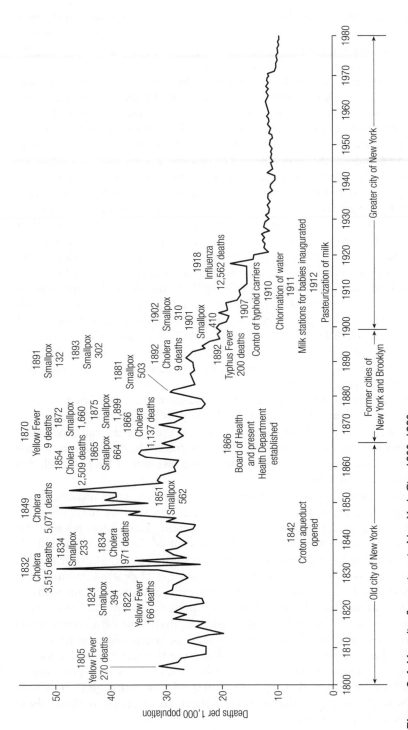

Figure 3.4 Mortality fluctuations in New York City, 1800–1980s

Source: Omran (1983) (reprinted by permission of Oxford University Press).

mortality rates begin to decline, and there is a marked smoothing of the year-to-year levels, with substantially fewer peaks and valleys. The period from 1920 onwards is marked by a relatively flat and low plateau of mortality, and year-to-year levels become more predictable.

The age of receding pandemics sees a gradual decline in infant and adult mortality, and is also followed by subsequent declines in fertility rates. Overall, this is a period of significant population growth. In global terms, Omran described most of the non-Western world as being in this phase of epidemiological transition as of 1983, when he published his major update on the theory. And, indeed, this was a period of profound population growth in the global south, despite the ongoing pressures from communicable diseases.

The final phase of Omran's model is the age of degenerative and man-made diseases. This stage sees a continued decline in mortality rates, to the point of stability at a relatively low level. Life expectancy at birth rises to exceed 70 years, and the leading causes of death are cardiovascular diseases, cancers, stroke, diabetes, and 'diseases introduced by man such as radiation injury, accidents, occupational hazards, carcinogens in the environment and in industry, and food additives' (Omran, 1983: 307). In the original formulation of epidemiological transition theory, this was the last stage in the model but subsequent 'extensions' of the theory have proposed additional new stages (Cook and Dummer, 2004; Olshansky and Ault, 1986), including an age of *delayed* man-made and degenerative diseases, where the leading causes of death are the same as in Omran's third stage, but they strike populations aged in their 80s, rather than in their 60s and 70s.

Most reflective of Omran's notion of epidemiological transition is Chile. When Omran developed the theory, he described Chile as a so-called 'transitional' case, a country whose transition was not the same as was experienced by the Unites States and the Western European countries, but whose transition was very much under way. Chilean data for the last half of the twentieth century is presented in Table 3.1

Chile's epidemiological transition is reflected in the large increase in the percentage of the population aged 65+ years, as well as the substantial reductions in general mortality and infant mortality rates. Most telling is the data on causes of death – whereas 12.0 per cent of deaths in Chile in 1970 were attributable to malignant tumours, this figure rose to 20.9 per cent by 1995, an increase of 74.2 per cent. The percentage of deaths attributable to cardiovascular diseases rose by over 20 per cent, and deaths from parasitic and infectious diseases dropped from 10.9 per cent to only 2.7 per cent, a decrease of over 75 per cent. Notice, however, that these data do not reveal anything about the social patterning of these aggregate figures; we do not know the shape of the social gradients that underlie these national statistics, neither do we know if the burden of infectious diseases falls primarily in marginalized rural populations.[4] As critics of epidemiological transition theory would point out, the data (and the theory) reveal nothing about inequities within countries.

Table 3.1 Chile's epidemiological transition

	1970	1995	Change 1970–95 %
% population aged 0–14 years	39.2	29.4	−25
% population aged 65+ years	5.0	6.6	+32
General mortality rate	8.7	5.5	−36.8
Infant mortality rate	82.2	11.1	−86.5
% deaths from cardiovascular diseases	22.3	26.8	+20.2
% deaths from malignant tumours	12.0	20.9	+74.2
% deaths from infectious and parasitic diseases	10.9	2.7	−75.2

Source: Vio and Albala (2000) (reprinted by permission of Cambridge University Press).

> **Proposition 3**: *The epidemiological transition appears first in health and disease patterns among children and women. But it does not alter the social class differential in mortality.*

Often neglected in contemporary adaptations of epidemiological transition theory, this proposition emphasizes Omran's 'generalist' view that the transition does not substantially alter social divisions in populations. That is, the transition may first appear among children and women, as mortality rates are very much shaped by infant deaths and pregnancy-related mortality among women. But the transition is not thought to impact health inequalities significantly. For Omran, 'the epidemiologic transition usually favors the young over the old, and females over males. While the transition benefits all social classes, the class differential in mortality is usually maintained, notwithstanding that the pace of change is faster and the takeoff is earlier for the affluent and the more privileged than for the poor and the disadvantaged members of a population' (Omran, 1983: 308). As we will see, this has been a point of significant criticism of the theory. Omran did analyze differences in mortality rates between whites and blacks in the United States, and argued that the data showed a gradual convergence, with a diminishing level of inequality between whites and blacks. And that *is* what the data showed in the 1960s. However, the period since then has seen an increase in white–black mortality differentials in that country, something that Omran's model did not predict (Gaylin and Kates, 1997). Indeed, the most recent work analyzing white–black health inequities in the United States shows either no progress over the past fifteen years or, for some conditions, actual increases in the gap (Margellos *et al.*, 2004; Orsi *et al.*, 2010).

> **Proposition 4**: *Changes in patterns of health and illness are most closely tied to changes in demographic and socioeconomic conditions – described by Omran as the 'modernization complex'*

With this proposition, epidemiological transition theory reveals its foundation as a development theory and, in particular, as a 'public health' manifestation of modernization theory in the style of Rostow (1960). From this perspective, development followed five distinct steps:

- traditional (a largely agrarian society with limited productivity)
- preconditions to take-off (characterized by the development of state apparatus and investments in education, science, and banking)
- the take-off (marked by industrialization)
- the drive to maturity (involving a shift in industrialization from textiles to more technologically advanced industries)
- mass consumption (marked by increased urbanization and a shift in employment from blue-collar to white-collar occupations).

Gross domestic product per capita would be expected to increase in each stage, and a country's standard of living would improve in a uni-dimensional path towards development. Rostow's model was built on the development experience of the United States, and he believed that country was a model that could be followed by the rest of the world.[5]

Dependency theorists such as André Gunder Frank (1969) and Fernando Henrique Cardoso (1972) criticized the modernization model of economic development on the grounds that it did not reflect Latin American empirical realities, and for its Eurocentric and pro-capitalist ideological bias. According to dependency theorists, modernization ignored the historical and political factors associated with development and inappropriately assumed that development was primarily a function of factors internal to each country (Connell, 2007; Kay, 1991). Instead, factors external to each country, including its relation to the world economic system, were seen to be crucial factors that shaped development trajectories. This tradition described the *development of underdevelopment*, arguing that imbalances in economic power unjustly tilted the global economy in favour of already industrialized countries, relegating the so-called 'third world' to the role of basic raw commodity exporters.

Immanuel Wallerstein's world-systems theory – itself a refinement of dependency models – illustrates the ideological foundations of modernization/ epidemiological transition theories (Jones, 2010). Under Wallerstein's model, the countries of the world are identified as forming part of the core, the semi-periphery, and the periphery. The core is formed by rich nations at the centre of the capitalist world economy; these are countries that primarily import raw materials and commodities from other countries. Low-income countries form the periphery. Many of these countries were formally colonized in earlier periods and continue to exist in quasi-colonial relationships with the core; they provide inexpensive and dispensable labour markets, raw materials, and, in some cases, markets for finished industrial and commercial products. Semi-periphery countries have closer ties to the core. Wallerstein argued that the world economy shapes this state of dependency by imposing particular characteristics onto low- and middle-income countries:

- a narrow, export-oriented economy tailored to the production of raw commodities and foodstuffs
- a lack of industrial capacity, which forces low- and middle-income countries to purchase expensive goods from the core
- high levels of foreign debt, which provide leverage by which core countries can control trade agreements.

As I discuss later on in this chapter, Luis Avilés' (2001) important critique of epidemiological transition theory is rooted in a dependency/world-systems analysis.

Omran's theory is clearly a product of its time; steeped in modernization theory and lacking the critiques raised by the approaches of dependency – and, later, world-systems. Omran saw development naturally occurring over time, though the pacing of that development could vary from place to place. But the notion of progress, of development through stages, was nevertheless fundamental to Omran's theory. On this issue, epidemiological transition is incompatible with more critical approaches to understanding development or the lack thereof. Martínez and Leal argue, for example, that the model 'was based on the scientific, social perspectives that prevailed at the time, governed by gradualistic conceptions of the economy and linear visions of *social time*' (2003: 540). It is an *optimistic* theory, one that sees epidemiological and economic improvement occurring over time. Critics argue that it is an *overly* optimistic theory – about both economic development (which dependency and world-systems theories suggested are not inevitable) and about infectious diseases (with HIV/AIDS being the clearest rebuke to the idea that infectious diseases could no longer threaten 'post-transition' populations).

The fifth and final proposition put forth by Omran states:

Proposition 5: *There are 4 basic models of epidemiological transition.*

Omran initially outlined three different models of transition, but revised it to four in his subsequent 1983 paper, as shown in Table 3.2.

Omran's theory relied on the historical experience of the advanced industrialized countries of the West. He drew, above all, from US, English/Welsh, and

Table 3.2 Types of epidemiological transition

Transition type	Example countries/regions
'Classical' or Western	England, Wales, Sweden, United States
Accelerated	USSR, Japan, Eastern Europe, Chile and parts of Latin America
Delayed	Most of the 'Third World'
Transitional variant of delayed type	South Korea, Singapore

Note: Author's own table based on Omran (1983).

Swedish historical records. Other countries and regions were compared with this 'classical' transition; with the USSR, Japan, and some countries of Eastern Europe showing what Omran called an 'accelerated' transition, with a later but faster drop in mortality and fertility. While medical technology did not play a fundamental role in the classical transition, Omran did see it playing a key role in the accelerated transition. Importantly, Omran defined this as the large-scale importation of medical technologies from the richest countries – a process rooted in the charity and development paradigms critiqued in Chapter 1. A 'delayed' model reflected a late drop in mortality with persistently high birth rates (amounting to rapid population growth), and Omran saw this model reflecting most of the 'third world'. Lastly, in his revision to the original theory, Omran added a fourth model, which he deemed a 'transitional variant of the delayed model', fitting the experiences of countries such as South Korea and Singapore, which he saw as converging with 'classical' countries, but not as rapidly as the 'accelerated' countries.

Revision of the theory

Omran was careful to note that the classic transition model may not map onto the experiences of countries in later historical periods. He noted that 'because the dynamics of the Western transition were closely related to the unique characteristics of the industrial and social revolution in the West, it is clear that the experience in this model is not automatically transferable to the less developed countries of today' (Omran, 1983: 313). Yet, this caveat in his 1983 update has not stopped the theory from taking on a positivist law-like image. Defenders of epidemiological transition theory have revised and expanded Omran's model to account for a growing number of developments that diverge from the 'classic' transition – from an extension to a fourth, delayed, era of 'man-made and degenerative diseases' (where such causes of death would still overwhelmingly drive patterns of population health, but would do so later in life) (Olshansky and Ault, 1986), to alternative models of 'reversed' and 'overlapped' transitions (Salomon and Murray, 2002) to account for ever more diverging patterns observed in global health research.

In one of the most important developments of Omran's model, Patrick Heuveline et al. (2002) examined what they dubbed the 'uneven tides' of the epidemiological transition. Their analysis of global patterns of economic development, poverty, and mortality largely confirmed the general shift envisioned by Omran. At the same time, their analysis emphasized the persistent inequalities that are glossed over by the model. Heuveline et al. begin by noting that the WHO's 1996 *Global Burden of Disease* study (see Murray and Lopez 1996) surprised many experts in the world by showing, for the very first time, that non-communicable diseases had come to be the leading cause of death, even in most developing countries. They note that 'many experts did not expect the "developing world" in 1990 to have reached the stage of transition at which non-communicable diseases dominate' (2002: 314). They go on to give a critical examination of the implications of this finding – and of the potentially premature conclusion, raised by many commentators in global health, that it was time to reassess current priorities so that they matched the new global burden. Heuveline *et al.* poignantly 'caution against some possible consequences of a policy shift based solely on global estimates and argue that international assistance, in particular, should be guided by equity considerations' (2002: 314). In other words, epidemiological transition could be easily used to mistakenly reduce attention to communicable diseases, as they could be seen as being replaced by non-communicable causes of death.

Heuveline *et al.* point out that 'Group 1' causes of death (comprising communicable diseases, maternal, and perinatal causes, as well as nutritional deficiencies) still account for the majority of deaths in sub-Saharan Africa and parts of India – meaning that the WHO's finding that the aggregate burden of disease tilting towards non-communicable diseases is not particularly generalizable to the whole world. Looking across the world's population, non-communicable diseases are thought to account for the majority of deaths, as shown in Table 3.3, at least at a macro level. Yet, among the world's poorest quintile, it is Group 1 causes that account for the majority of deaths (58.6 per cent). In contrast, only 7.7 per cent of deaths among the world's richest quintile are associated with Group 1 causes. It therefore matters whether we look at national aggregated data, or whether we look at the socio-economic patterning of populations.

Moreover, their analysis highlighted the importance of local level analysis. Heuveline *et al.* argue: 'In spite of the common view that the world population is fast converging toward the low mortality and cause-of-death structure of the most developed nations, we continue to find at a more local level of analysis, a strong, persistent income gradient in the relative importance of different causes' (2002: 314). Their findings begin to break down the 'global' model of epidemiological transition and urge us to think about local differences, about local inequalities.Above all, their analysis adds nuance to the 'universal' model developed by Omran. Heuveline *et al.* note that:

declines in mortality throughout the developing world constitute arguably the most salient achievement of the latter part of the twentieth

Table 3.3 Distribution of deaths by group of causes among different world groups, 1990

Causes of death	World	World's poorest 20%	World's richest 20%
Group I	34.2	58.6	7.7
Group II	55.7	32.0	85.2
Group III	10.1	9.4	7.1
All causes	100.0	100	100

Source: Adapted from Heuveline et al. (2002) (reprinted by permission of Elsevier).

century. These undeniable successes have led some to view all parts of the
world as converging towards the mortality levels and patterns exhibited
by the industrialized countries. While on average, the demographic gap
between developed and developing regions appears to be closing, pro-
gresses have been achieved at a variable pace resulting in an increasing
heterogeneity among the developing countries. (Heuveline *et al.*, 2002:
318)

In essence, they find support for Omran's theory on a very general level, yet
caution that it is hardly a comprehensive model for changes in population
health, as it hides 'heterogeneity' – what we might call 'inequities' – within and
between developing countries.

A similar argument was made by Daniel Gaylin and Jennifer Kates, who critiqued epidemiological transition theory as a 'universalizing concept', and
argued that the theory 'eclipses key epidemiologic differences between population subgroups based on socioeconomic status, race, and sex' (1997: 609).
They question the 'generalized' version of the theory, which, in their view,
uncritically connects modernization, economic progress, the decline of infectious disease, and overall declines in mortality rates. They call for a more
refined approach to epidemiological transition, one that brings inequality
from the margins to the centre of the analysis, with the objective of creating 'a
more complete and accurate representation of population morbidity and mortality' (1997: 609).

In the view of Gaylin and Kates, Omran's model was overly optimistic
about the demise of infectious diseases and ignored social inequalities – aspects
of population health in any country that inevitably lead to the theory lacking
real-world relevance. And, indeed, Omran's model was developed before we
knew of HIV/AIDS and before we had experienced multidrug-resistant tuberculosis, and his theory did not foresee any new infectious disease pandemic,
particularly among populations in 'post transition' countries. Rather than as a
'universalizing concept', something applicable to all countries in all times,
Gaylin and Kates put forth a version of epidemiological transition as something more specific: they argue for the need to 'particularize' the theory and
hold that 'the epidemiologic transition is much less uniform and consistent a
process than widely held notions would suggest' (1997: 614).

Martínez and Leal's (2003) analysis of the epidemiological transition in
Mexico is particularly insightful. From a position of critique reminiscent of
dependency and world-systems positions, they argue that epidemiological
transition theory assumes that economic development takes place in sequen-
tial stages. Moreover, they argue that the theory by definition assumes that the
transition is a 'natural destiny' of societies. To explore these notions, Martínez
and Leal examined population health trends in Mexico over the period
1895–1995. An important part of their analysis is illustrated in Table 3.4.

Over this period, we see the dramatic declines in general mortality rate that
form the basis of Omran's theory. In 1900, Mexico's general mortality rate

Table 3.4 Population health indicators, Mexico, 1895–1995

Year	Population	General deaths	Deaths in infants under 12 months	General mortality rate per 1,000	Child mortality rate per 1,000
1895	12,632,427	391,177	N/A	31.0	N/A
1900	13,565,942	456,581	N/A	33.7	N/A
1910	15,160,369	N/A	N/A	N/A	N/A
1921	14,333,082	364,832	99,783	25.5	220.0
1930	16,552,722	441,712	107,921	26.7	131.6
1940	19,653,552	458,906	110,039	23.3	125.7
1950	25,779,254	418,430	113,032	16.2	96.2
1960	34,923,129	402,545	119,316	11.5	74.2
1970	48,225,238	485,686	146,028	10.1	68.5
1980	66,846,833	434,465	94,116	6.5	38.9
1990	81,249,645	422,803	65,428	5.2	23.9
1995	91,158,290	430,278	48,023	4.7	17.5

Source: Martínez and Leal (2003) (reprinted by permission of Elsevier).

was 33.7 per 1,000 inhabitants whereas, by 1995, this figure had dropped to only 4.7 per 1,000 inhabitants. We also see a very substantial decrease in child mortality, in line with Omran's third proposition. The earliest data is available for 1921, when 220 infants per 1,000 live births died before their first birthday. By 1995, this figure had dropped to 17.5 deaths per 1,000 live births. And both of these elements constitute part of the very good news story that we can tell in global health – in most countries of the world, there have been significant improvements in macro-indicators of population health, and, in particular, substantial decreases in general mortality and infant mortality. Combined with a general decrease in Mexico's fertility rate beginning in the 1970s, these data signal the general outline of Omran's model. But Martínez and Leal go further, noting that: 'calling this process *epidemiological transition* is undoubtedly one way of describing it ... However, it says nothing of the complex balance between morbidity and mortality, or of their relationship to the specific constellations from which they have arisen, or of the role they played in medical and health interventions' (2003: 543–4). That is, building on the critique raised by Heuveline *et al.* (2002), Gaylin and Kates (1997) and others (Caldwell, 2001; Frenk *et al.*, 1989; Gómez, 2001; Rivera *et al.*, 2002), Martínez and Leal urge us to move our thinking about epidemiological transition forward by re-examining the model's core properties and by incorporating a more nuanced perspective that highlights within- and between-country inequalities in health.

Among the issues they raise for re-examination is epidemiological transition's focus on mortality over morbidity. And this is critical, for many communicable diseases do not necessarily lead to mortality, at least in the short-term. Many communicable diseases – including all of the major neglected tropical diseases – cause long-term suffering instead. Their burden is therefore hidden if we focus exclusively on death rates. Martínez and Leal emphasize that:

> a look at *morbidity* shows that communicable diseases are still very much in evidence. Low-cost, high-yield preventive measures managed to stop many of these from proving fatal, yet the conditions of lack of sanitation and poverty in which large groups of people live, in both increasingly atomized rural and the ever more crowded urban space means that this aspect of the *burden of disease* is unlikely to be eliminated from the health scenario in the near future. (2003: 544)

Looking behind the national aggregates, they note the spatial concentration of mortality and morbidity in specific areas of the country (for example, Chiapas), and the clustering of communicable as well as non-communicable diseases (and accidents plus violence) among the most disadvantaged segments of Mexican society. They recall the earlier observation of David Phillips: 'the rich and the poor, urban and rural dwellers and other sub-groups of populations of many countries effectively live in different 'epidemiological worlds'; a focus on national averages does a disservice to virtually all people' (1994: viii). As such, Martínez and Leal urge the abandonment of epidemiological transition as a technical tool for health care planning and question its validity as a theory. Their analysis leads them to conclude that, at least in the case of Mexico, epidemiological transition is an 'illusion', and they call for health researchers and policy-makers to abandon the seeming comfort of a pre-determined destiny. In its place, they call for detailed epidemiological assessments that aim to detect, not gloss over, social inequalities.

Other researchers have critiqued the theory, but instead of calling for its abandonment, have tried to develop ways of incorporating nuance into its general framework. A case in point is Ian Cook and Trevor Dummer's (2004) attempt to apply the model to China's experiences in the post-revolution period. They document an early (pre-1949 revolution) period of infectious disease and mortality spikes attributable to flooding and drought, an era akin to Omran's age of pestilence and famine. Beginning in the 1990s, China experienced an important overall decline in infectious diseases, with diminishing incidence of cholera, dysentery, hepatitis, and typhoid – some of the major diseases of poverty. Concurrently, China has experienced increases in death rates from chronic diseases, including cancers and heart disease. These shifts coincide quite well with the general parameters of Omran's model. At the same time, Cook and Dummer suggest that China's experience also refines epidemiological transition theory:

> We would argue that the health situation in China reflects a new, late stage, epidemiological transition phase, where the transition from diseases of poverty to diseases of affluence has not reflected smoothly the economic and development transition. Consequently, China faced health

issues related to an aging and increasingly affluent population, combined with problems caused by rapid urbanization, emerging and re-emerging infectious diseases and widening inequalities in health and health care. (2004: 341)

For Cook and Dummer, the Chinese experience in the past twenty years does not invalidate the model of epidemiological transition. Unlike critiques such as that of Martínez and Leal, they do not call the model an illusion, neither do they call for its abandonment. Yet, they do offer a similar refinement, and find that the contemporary epidemiological scene in China is highly segmented, with rural/urban, poor/rich populations living in different epidemiological worlds.

We have seen thus far that Omran's overall model may be true – but only in very general, aggregate terms. For critics such as Martínez and Leal, Gaylin and Kates, and others, however, the aggregate-level story is too superficial to warrant use as a way of evaluating a country's epidemiological position. Along these lines, John Caldwell's critique of the epidemiological transition model rests on both empirical and theoretical grounds. Noting that 'there are probably as many models as there are societies' (2001: 160), Caldwell criticizes the model for focusing on the changing causes of death at the expense of the 'changing causes of patterns of illness' (2001: 160). Extending that line of critique, Heuveline *et al.* (2002), Gaylin and Kates (1997) and others argue that reliance on this model may do more harm than good. This has been expressed most powerfully by Farmer, who also questions the theory:

> this model masks interclass differences *within* a particular country. For the poor, wherever they live, there is, often enough, no health transition. In other words, wealthy citizens of 'underdeveloped' nations (those countries that have not yet experienced their health transition) do not die young from infectious diseases; they die later and from the same diseases that claim similar populations in wealthy countries. In parts of Harlem, in contrast, death rates in certain age groups are as high as those in Bangladesh; in both places, the leading causes of death in young adults are infections and violence. (Farmer, 2003: 156–7)

An inequality lens, therefore, fundamentally alters how we conceptualize a population's epidemiological as well as economic situation. The greatest danger in the model is that it gets us to think that progress is simply a matter of time, of further *development*. In contrast, a critical perspective tuned to the question of equity would highlight that the increased risk of disease comes not from a lack of development in 'third world countries' but, rather, from political neglect, economic exploitation, and resource withdrawal from marginalized communities (Avilés, 2001). While Omran's model has some validity in aggregate terms, it is in disaggregated terms that health analyses are most fruitfully carried out, and where policies may be implemented with most benefit.

Before concluding this chapter, I want to raise one final critique of epidemiological transition. This time, I draw on the work of Luis Avilés, from the University of Puerto Rico. His critique offers us important insight on the role of science as *ideology*, and on the notion of epidemiology *as discourse*. Avilés describes his analysis as an exploration of epidemiological practice, and the tension between epidemiology as a science and epidemiology as a way of engaging in advocacy and social activism. In doing so, he critiques Omran's model of epidemiological transition, identifying the discourse of epidemiology as a discourse of development – a discourse that Avilés describes as embodying 'the colonizer's model of the world' (2001: 165). Drawing on the work of James Blaut, Avilés sees this perspective as holding a Eurocentric position, wherein the European experience is the standard, and the rest of world's experiences are to match up to that model. Avilés criticizes this worldview for implicitly (or, at times, explicitly) arguing that the non-European world is stagnant, traditional, and backwards, and that it is that backwardness that prevents global progress. To improve the lot of the 'developing world', more *diffusion* of technology and capacity from the developed world is needed; in other words, more development *aid*. Avilés points out that this is firmly in line with modernization theory, and remains a key characteristic of development discourse. Perhaps most importantly, he argues that 'the discourse of development shapes the way problems are perceived and defined, and, therefore, frames the strategies considered (and not considered) to solve them' (2001: 164–5). He critiques the implications of Omran's model: 'epidemiological transition theory legitimizes the dominance of development institutions by presenting them as authoritative and benevolent organizations and worthy of support, as – according to the theory – only through their advice and interventions can Third World nations move to another epidemiological stage' (2001: 166). From this basis, he provides a case study of El Salvador's *Epidemiological Profile* – a report published in 1994 under the sponsorship of the United States Agency for International Development (USAID).

Avilés emphasizes that the report features all of the standard aspects of Omran's model – rate of population growth, fertility rate, causes of death, child mortality, and overall mortality rate by age and gender. The report presents only aggregated statistics, ignoring inequalities. Avilés observes: 'the particular aversion of the report to deal with issues of poverty as a public health concern is consistent with its general framework based on the epidemiological transition theory, a theory that is characteristically silent about (if not sightless to) health inequalities within each individual country' (2001: 165). He argues – as do other critics, such as Heuveline *et al.*, that Omran's epidemiological transition model leaves 'the problem of social class inequalities unnamed, unanalysed, and invisible' (2001: 165). Ultimately, Avilés concludes that 'the epidemiological transition theory, as it applies to the countries of the periphery of the global economy, has no other purpose but to reinforce current patterns of domination' (2001: 167). In line with other critics, he urges us to move away from epidemiology as a discourse of development, and towards epidemiology as social justice. He sees this possible through 'critical epidemiological profiles', which would feature three inter-connected lines of investigation:

- heterogeneity
- universal interconnections
- historicity.

Interestingly, these lines of investigation dovetail with Farmer's call for geographically broad and historically deep analysis discussed in Chapter 2.

With a guiding principle of heterogeneity, Avilés urges epidemiologists, and others working on questions of global health to highlight the social patterning of disease, to move away from seeing populations as undifferentiated units and to move towards working with populations as heterogeneous groups. Only by comparing health outcomes across social class, geographical area, ethnicity, and other socially meaningful categories can we identify and, over time, track patterns of population health. Unfortunately, this is not a principle accepted in the MDG targets, which focus exclusively on national aggregates.

Second, Avilés calls for epidemiological work that is grounded in universal interconnections, which he defines as follows: 'going beyond the multicausal paradigm of risk factor epidemiology, it is essential to explore the fundamental causes of disease distribution as rooted in the organization and dynamics of society at the local, regional, and global levels' (2001: 169). Fundamental causes of disease – be it income inequality, following Wilkinson's hypothesis, or aspects of global economics and politics that influence patterns of inequality, following Coburn's development of Wilkinson's model – are, indeed, absent from Omran's epidemiological transition theory. One of the most important challenges in global health is to develop a holistic research paradigm that not only values biomedical insight on disease processes, but also integrates empirical and theoretical contributions from the social sciences. Only in this way can we come to understand disease in its biological and political aspects. A new theory of global health is needed – and it must, I think, be focused on the fundamental question of health inequality; it must go beyond national aggregate data and, instead, use locally-salient markers of class division. At the same time, a new theory of global health must be grounded in what Avilés calls universal interconnections – it needs to go beyond traditional risk-factor epidemiology to take a holistic, structural perspective on the determinants of health.

Last, Avilés calls for work guided by historicity, which he defines as having two aspects: the history of the disease or problem under study, *and* the history of scientific thinking about that disease or problem. He urges us to think about both elements whenever we carry out research. The first element is akin to Farmer's call for health research that is 'historically deep'; analysis that not only acknowledges how historical patterns of class conflict and other forms of oppression shape current-day patterns of health, but also places these historical factors within explanatory models of health outcomes.

Is this possible? For example, can contemporary research on health inequalities in Mexico acknowledge and bring to the centre of the analysis the historical trauma and current-day political and economic marginalization experienced by indigenous peoples? Can research on health outcomes among Canadian First Nations do the same? Or will we be limited by 'risk factor' epidemiology, and continue to focus only on the behaviours of individuals, blaming them for unhealthy diets and for not following the latest health promotion dictum? There certainly are promising areas of work in epidemiology and related fields which signal that this may be possible (Krieger, 2011), though much of this work has not engaged with questions of global public health.

The second element – pertaining to the history of scientific thinking about the disease or problem in question – urges us to remain critical and reflexive about our theories and method, including a central model such as epidemiological transition.[6] Using the model without critical reflection over its effects distorts our work, and, as critics like Avilés point out, would result not only in a mistaken view of health problems facing the global south, but also mistaken ideas for strategies to improve health around the world.

The Latin American tradition of social medicine stands as a stark contrast to epidemiological transition theory.[7] Rather than glossing over inequality and neglecting the social, political, and economic drivers of changing morbidity and mortality, this tradition seeks to integrate these and other aspects of structural violence into its gaze. It has done so, in the words of Mauricio Barreto *et al.*, 'through the denunciation and opposition to all forms of social or health inequalities towards the construction of equity oriented health policies' (2001: 158). I return to this tradition in Chapter 7, when discussing contemporary global efforts to reduce health inequities.

Conclusion

It is important to emphasize that there are different ways of doing epidemiology, and different ways of conceptualizing global health. Epidemiological transition gives us one approach – but, as with all approaches, it has important weaknesses. Some researchers are trying to refine the model, and thereby bring questions of inequality from the margin to the centre. Others have called for its abandonment, and urge us to move towards more detailed accounts of social inequalities in population health indicators.

Epidemiological transition theory was entirely too optimistic about the demise of infectious diseases – and HIV/AIDS is a testament to that hubris, as is the persistence of neglected tropical diseases in the global south. The theory is also problematic to the extent that it generalizes across different social groups; it glosses over social inequality and the different 'epidemiological worlds' that the poor and rich, wherever they are, inevitably inhabit. Perhaps the promise of epidemiological transition theory rests not as a universalizing concept, applicable to all societies across time, but as a tool for comparing particular groups in specific settings. In this way, epidemiological transition theory's utility rests not on its universality but, rather, on its capacity to enable comparisons, becoming a tool for understanding inequalities that may well be avoidable, unnecessary, and unfair. Chapters 4 and 5 examine the social patterning of the two sides of the transition: Chapter 4 examines chronic noncommunicable diseases, and Chapter 5 focuses on neglected tropical diseases.

The Burden of Chronic Non-Communicable Diseases

We have seen that epidemiological transition theory predicts a gradual shift in a country's causes of death – from communicable to non-communicable – with countries progressing from the age of 'pestilence and famine' to the age of 'receding pandemics' to, finally, the age of 'man-made and degenerative diseases'. And while there are very important reasons to view this model with great scepticism – primarily because it glosses over the inequalities that exist *within* national averages – the theory has, by most accounts, some validity at a very macro-level of analysis (Mathers and Loncar, 2006). One of the most important predictions of the model pertains to the growth of chronic non-communicable diseases; on this issue, epidemiological transition has significant implications for population health in the global south.

In this chapter, I examine the global burden of chronic diseases, in terms of both national averages (aggregate data) and social gradients (disaggregated data). I begin with some observations on the 'emerging crisis' of chronic diseases in India and South Africa. Building on those examples, I then examine the burden of chronic diseases in Latin America, highlighting some of the work I have recently carried out with colleagues in Argentina's Ministry of Health. I conclude the chapter with an analysis of the latest development in this area: a milestone United Nations high-level meeting held in September 2011, which many in the global health community heralded as a tremendous opportunity to raise the social justice agenda in relation to chronic non-communicable diseases (Beaglehole *et al.*, 2011b; Mamudu *et al.*, 2011).

Global health research indicates that chronic non-communicable diseases are the most important drivers of population health in the world (Alwan and MacLean, 2009; Greenberg *et al.*, 2011; Magnusson, 2009; Nabel *et al.*, 2009). Indeed, the data are clear in showing that chronic diseases are the leading causes of death in most areas, save for sub-Saharan Africa and parts of India. The latest global estimates, published by the World Health Organization in 2005, indicate that 35 million people died from heart disease, stroke, cancer, and other chronic conditions in that year (Lim *et al.*, 2007; Strong *et al.*, 2005). These WHO data suggest that chronic diseases (including heart disease, stroke, cancer, respiratory diseases, and diabetes) account for 60 per cent of the world's deaths, and that close to 80 per cent of these deaths occur in low- and middle-income countries (WHO, 2005). An estimated 30 per cent of deaths from chronic diseases occur before the age of 60 (Alwan *et al.*, 2011), a testament to their effect on potential years of life lost around the world. The burden is clearly immense; according to the WHO figures, chronic diseases account for 'double the number of deaths from all infectious diseases (including HIV/AIDS, tuberculosis and malaria), maternal and perinatal conditions, and nutritional deficiencies combined' (WHO, 2005).[1,2]

This burden is projected to increase substantially in the decades to come (Beaglehole *et al.*, 2007; Horton, 2007; Mathers and Loncar, 2006; Stevens *et al.*, 2007), severely diminishing the economic potential of low- and middle-income countries, and thwarting efforts to reduce poverty. By the year 2030, the leading causes of death in the world are projected to be ischaemic heart disease (a condition where fatty deposits in coronary arteries ultimately reduce blood flow to the heart), cerebrovascular disease (including strokes), and chronic obstructive pulmonary disease (COPD).[3] The leading infectious diseases – HIV/AIDS, tuberculosis, and malaria – are expected to decrease in their standing relative to chronic conditions such as diabetes mellitus and lung cancer (WHO, 2008).[4] Diabetes alone is now estimated to afflict between 285 and 350 million people worldwide, with significant increases in its prevalence in low- and middle-income countries over the past few decades (Danaei *et al.*, 2011; Shaw *et al.*, 2010).[5]

While traditionally depicted as being 'diseases of affluence', chronic diseases impose their greatest burdens among the poor and thus contribute to the maintenance of patterns of social inequality in both advanced industrialized countries and in the global south. Along with being considered diseases of affluence (perhaps as they constitute the end point in Omran's model of epidemiological transition), chronic diseases have been associated with a number of myths or half-truths, and much of the recent WHO scholarship has aimed to dispel these. Among these myths is that chronic diseases mainly affect high-income countries, rich people, and men, and that they are diseases of old age. Perhaps more importantly, myths surrounding these conditions imply that chronic diseases are the result of individual choices – so-called 'unhealthy lifestyles' – and therefore could be prevented, if only individuals would make better life decisions (WHO, 2005). The danger in all of this, of course, is that we begin to place complete responsibility on sick people, arguing that if only they had stopped smoking, or if only they have exercised more often and followed a better diet, they would not be in the position they find themselves in.[6] These myths dovetail with the personal responsibility ethos of neoliberalist policies, further reducing the capacity for collective solutions to public health problems.

Along these lines, the globalization of obesity (itself a major risk factor for other chronic conditions, including diabetes and cardiovascular disease) may be understood in a more informative way. Empirical work has demonstrated that a 'nutrition transition' associated with increased consumption of foods high in fats and sugars is occurring in many countries of the global south (Finucane *et al.*, 2011; Hawkes, 2006). This is particularly pronounced in Latin America, where researchers have also documented diminishing levels of physical activity and generally more sedentary lifestyles (Webber *et al.*, 2012). But the 'obesity epidemic' is truly global, affecting countries across regions (Martorell, 2002; Sobal and McIntosh, 2009; Wang, 2001).

To what extent is obesity caused by individual choices? To what extent are these choices *constrained* by an individual's life chances, by the structure in which they live and work? One way to measure this 'constraining' of choices has been developed by welfare regime scholars, who use various typologies to categorize countries with respect to their level of 'commodification' of basic commodities and services. One of the latest studies in this area has found that economic inse-curity is a particularly powerful predictor of obesity in 'market' economies such as the United Kingdom, Canada, Australia, and the United States – but not in 'social democratic' countries such as Norway (Offer *et al.*, 2010).[7]

Incorporating globalization as a key concept in obesity research is clearly warranted – for the factors that are associated with obesity are themselves global in nature. Jeffery Sobal argues, for example, that 'Global increases in the incidence and prevalence of obesity are grounded in the globalization of Western post-industrial food systems and consumer culture that has increas-ingly penetrated all societies of the world' (2001: 1137). He urges us to think of obesity as a socio-political product, rather than a characteristic of individ-uals. From this perspective, obesity is to be studied not simply as a biomedical fact (someone is obese or they are not, based on body mass index cut-off val-ues) but, rather, obesity should be studied through the analysis of markets and cultures. According to Sobal:

> Globalization involves more than internationalization or cross-national, cross-cultural, or cross-population linkages. Achievement of globality makes nations components of a common global whole rather than sepa-rate units of analysis to be compared independently. Global govern-ments, global corporations, global media, global food systems, and glob-al diseases become the new units of analysis rather than separate nation-al, local, or individual cases. To the extent that obesity represents a worldwide epidemic, it constitutes a global pandemic rather than a set of independent occurrences in various nations … global conditions have underlying global causes. (2001: 1137)

Conceptualizing obesity in this way leads us away from the traditional health promotion literature based on individual-level behaviour change and towards a new perspective that values multi-level thinking, with individuals making decisions within the constraints of their environments. A new wave of research in social epidemiology is doing that under the concept of 'obesogenic' environ-ments (Kirk *et al.*, 2010).

Incorporating these ideas into our thinking about global health produces a richer, more nuanced, account of lifestyle choices made in the context of structural constraints, generating awareness that chronic diseases are interwoven with patterns of inequity. In this chapter, I highlight contemporary social science research which casts doubt on these myths, enabling us to better understand the social patterning of the chronic diseases.

The emerging crisis of chronic diseases: evidence from India and South Africa

India is experiencing a sharp increase in the burden of chronic diseases. Already, chronic diseases account for 53 per cent of mortality and 44 per cent of disability-adjusted life years lost in that country (Srinath Reddy et al., 2005). India has the largest number of people with diabetes in the world, with an estimated 19.3 million in the mid-1990s, and an estimated 57.2 million by 2025 (King et al., 1998). Tobacco-related cancers already account for a majority of all cancers in India, and tobacco consumption – particularly through chewing tobacco – is common.[8] More than 50 per cent of males aged 12–60 years report currently using tobacco products (Srinath Reddy et al., 2005). The latest estimates from the country suggest that tobacco is related to 1 in 5 deaths among men aged 30–69 years and 1 in 20 deaths among women of the same age group (Jha et al., 2008). This is a clear indication of the tremendous benefits that concerted anti-tobacco programmes could achieve. Hypertension – one of the most important 'modifiable risk factors' for cardiovascular disease – is also on the rise in the country, where it is already estimated to affect 20–40 per cent of urban adults (Kearney et al., 2005).

These statistics may appear to be consistent with what is often reported in the advanced industrialized countries. However, in contrast to the advanced industrialized countries, chronic disease-caused deaths occur at relatively early ages in countries such as India. In the global south, chronic diseases are not diseases of old age but, rather, of middle age – they strike among working-age populations. Srinath Reddy et al. note, for example, that 'India suffers the highest loss in potentially productive years of life, due to deaths from cardiovascular disease in people aged 35–64 years (9.2 million years lost in 2000). By 2030, this loss is expected to rise to 17.9 million years – 940% greater than the corresponding loss in the USA, which has a population a third the size of India's' (Srinath Reddy et al., 2005: 1744). Along with the cost associated with potential years of life lost, we see the burden of cardiovascular disease in India rising in prevalence estimates: 'The estimated prevalence of coronary heart disease is around 3–4% in rural areas and 8–10% in urban areas among adults older than 20 years, representing a two-fold rise in rural areas and a six-fold rise in urban areas over the past four decades' (Srinath Reddy et al., 2005: 1744). Clearly, the burden of cardiovascular disease is rising in India, a situation that will stress the country's primary health care sector and continue to lead to the potential years of life lost among its population.

Srinath Reddy *et al.* emphasize that, while the advancing epidemic of chronic disease is occurring throughout the country, its effects are marked by social inequality: 'the poor are increasingly affected by chronic diseases and their risk factors. Low levels of education and income now predict not only higher levels of tobacco consumption, but also increased risk of coronary heart disease' (Srinath Reddy *et al.*, 2005: 1746). Moreover, the presence of chronic disease in a family exposes households to an increased risk of catastrophic spending and impoverishment (Engelgau *et al.*, 2012).[9] Treatment of diabetes, for example, costs a person in India with average income 15–25 per cent of their household earnings (Ramachandran *et al.*, 2007). While India continues to face tremendous challenges with communicable diseases, including tuberculosis, and faces a growing burden associated with HIV/AIDS, it is already engaging with an emerging crisis of chronic non-communicable diseases. And it is taking important actions, including enacting the Indian Tobacco Control Act in 2003, which, among other things, banned smoking in public places, limited direct and indirect advertisements of cigarettes and other tobacco products, limited the sale of tobacco products near educational institutions, and strengthened regulations over the use of health warnings on all tobacco packaging. India's National Cancer Control Programme has also received acclaim for emphasizing that cancer affects the poor (Srinath Reddy *et al.*, 2005).

The South African literature reports a similarly rapid transition towards chronic diseases. But, instead of a displacement of communicable diseases by non-communicable diseases, the University of Cape Town's Bongani Mayosi *et al.* describe the South Africa epidemiological profile as consisting of a *quadruple burden*, where non-communicable diseases exert a growing burden on the population, alongside non-communicable diseases, perinatal and maternal complications, and injury/violence-related outcomes (Mayosi *et al.*, 2009). And this multiple burden of disease raises intractable challenges for policymakers: what should a health system focus on? What should the priorities for prevention and treatment be? Mayosi *et al.* note that, in South Africa, the bulk of resources have been devoted to the major communicable diseases: 'prevention and treatment of non-communicable diseases are marginalized in South Africa because of the overwhelming prevalence of communicable diseases such as HIV/AIDS and tuberculosis' (Mayosi *et al.*, 2009: 934). The catastrophic implications of these diseases are evident in life expectancy data from South Africa: in 1970, life expectancy at birth was 52.8 years. This figure rose steadily during the 1980s, and reached 61.5 years in 1990 (although I would emphasize that these national data hide the inequities in health that were generated by the country's system of apartheid). The HIV/AIDS epidemic wiped 10 years from life expectancy in South Africa. By 2005, life expectancy stood at 51.1, and only rose modestly back to 52.8 by 2011, the latest available data point from the United Nations (UNDP, 2012).

WHO estimates indicate that non-communicable diseases account for almost 30 per cent of the total burden of disease in South Africa (WHO, 2008d).[10] That burden is expected to increase substantially in the coming decades, particularly with respect to diabetes, kidney disease, and some cancers. Already, the combined toll of heart disease, diabetes, and stroke comprises the second most important cause of death among adults in South Africa, behind only HIV/AIDS (Bradshaw *et al.*, 2003). South African health researchers have warned of an impending epidemic of cardiovascular and metabolic disease (Opie and Mayosi, 2005).

Importantly, this 'impending epidemic' is generated *from* significant social gradients (Ataguba *et al.*, 2011). Discussing the burden of chronic diseases in South Africa, Mayosi *et al.* emphasize that 'the distribution of non-communicable diseases displays socioeconomic disparities, with the heaviest burden for poor communities in urban areas' (Mayosi *et al.*, 2009: 935). They offer, for example, age-standardized mortality rates in Cape Town, which show a clear social gradient 'in which people living in the poor subdistrict of Khayelitsha have 856.4 deaths per 100,000 attributable to such diseases compared with rates of 450–500 per 100,000 in the wealthy northern and southern subdistricts of Cape Town' (Mayosi *et al.*, 2009: 935). Not only is South Africa experiencing a rapid growth of the burden of chronic disease, but the evidence is clear in indicating that this increased burden will likely increase the substantial inequalities in the country, as it is it the poor who will experience the highest increases of disease and who, paradoxically, have the least capacity to modify lifestyles and diet in accordance with the latest risk factor recommendations. In the next section, I explore this notion in further detail, in relation to Latin America.

The burden of chronic diseases in Latin America

A basic prediction of epidemiological transition theory holds that non-communicable diseases *displace* communicable diseases as a population's leading causes of death. And, on a very general level, that is true. But the experience of countries such as India and South Africa indicate that this shift is not so much a displacement as an *epidemiological overlap* or *segmentation*, with different socio-economic classes in a population effectively living in different epidemiological worlds.[11] This co-existence of both communicable and non-communicable diseases is also clear in Latin America, and it represents a formidable challenge. As Nicholas Banatvala and Liam Donaldson note, '[t]he coexistence of a substantial burden of cancer, vascular disease, diabetes mellitus, and arthritis with HIV, tuberculosis, and malaria would challenge even the most mature and well-resourced health-care system' (2007: 2076). Across Latin America and the Caribbean, chronic non-communicable diseases (most notably cardiovascular diseases and cancers) account for the majority of deaths, and infectious diseases account for one quarter of total deaths (Perel *et al.*, 2006).

Table 4.1 The burden of chronic diseases (selected Latin American countries)

Country	Distribution of years of life lost by broader causes (% of total)			Age-standardized mortality rates by cause (per 100,000 population)			
	Communicable diseases	Non-communicable diseases	Injuries	Non-communicable diseases	Cardiovascular	Cancer	Injuries
Argentina	18	66	17	521	212	142	52
Bolivia	55	34	11	824	260	256	80
Brazil	30	50	20	712	341	142	81
Chile	17	64	19	453	165	137	50
Colombia	25	35	40	511	240	117	141
Ecuador	37	42	21	576	244	129	89
Paraguay	45	39	16	598	291	141	57
Peru	43	42	15	584	190	175	69
Uruguay	12	72	15	518	208	170	55
Venezuela	24	45	32	496	241	107	90
Income group (worldwide)							
Low income	70	20	10	754	418	114	116
Lower-middle income	34	48	18	668	324	136	81
Upper-middle income	30	51	19	728	436	138	102
High income	8	77	15	419	173	136	42

Source: Adapted from WHO (2008b) (used with permission).

Health care systems in Latin America struggle to meet the challenges of this wide range of disease; they face a persistent burden from infectious diseases and a growing pressure from chronic diseases. This dual burden of disease is perhaps best understood by a comparison of the years of life lost in specific countries by type of cause (see Table 4.1).[12]

A close reading of the data in Table 4.1 reveals important differences within the region. In some countries, including Argentina, Brazil, and Chile, non-communicable diseases result in the greatest number of years of life lost, in comparison with communicable diseases and injuries. In other countries, including Bolivia, Paraguay, and Peru, communicable diseases exert the more prominent influence on years of life lost. This reflects underlying patterns associated with economic development as modelled by the epidemiological transition. As shown in Table 4.1, the balance of the burden between communicable and non-communicable diseases varies greatly by income group classification (these data reflecting the situation worldwide, not just in Latin America). In low-income countries, communicable diseases exert the most important influence on years of life lost, and this balance changes quite quickly – even in lower-middle income countries, non-communicable diseases amount to a heavier toll, again reflecting the epidemiological transition. Age-standardized mortality rates by cause also reveal important within-region differences, with cardiovascular diseases extolling a particularly heavy burden in Brazil and Venezuela.

Along with the pressure that chronic diseases bring to the health care system, they are also troubling due to their significant macro-economic effects, particularly because the available epidemiological data points to cardiovascular diseases striking younger working-age people in low- and middle-income countries (Fuster and Voûte, 2005). We saw earlier, for example, that cardiovascular diseases place a particularly high burden on working-age people in India (Srinath Reddy *et al.*, 2005). This pattern is repeated elsewhere in the global south, with devastating economic effects. A WHO analysis of the disease burden and loss of economic output associated with chronic diseases in 23 selected countries (including Argentina, Brazil, Colombia, and Mexico) suggests that, between 2006 and 2015, chronic diseases will result in a lost economic productivity of US$84 billion (with approximately US$47 billion of this loss occurring in China, India, and Russia), an incredibly high burden that undoubtedly will limit the feasibility of large-scale poverty alleviation efforts (Abegunde *et al.*, 2007). Table 4.2 presents the results for the Latin American countries in their study. Mexico, Brazil, Argentina, and Colombia are all expected to experience substantial reductions in potential GDP as result of the main chronic diseases in the next ten years.

Building from the WHO's *Global Burden of Disease* study (Murray and Lopez 1996), and acknowledging that much uncertainty remains concerning the quantification of the comparative burden of diseases around the world, their analysis suggests that chronic diseases can be expected to result in the loss of approximately US$13.5 billion in Argentina, Brazil, Colombia, and Mexico alone. Abegunde *et al.* point out that 'two major factors account for the grim forecasts on the economic effect of chronic diseases: the lost labour units because of deaths from chronic disease and the costs of treating chronic disease, which continue to increase annually' (2007: 1936).

Table 4.2 Projected forgone national income due to heart disease, stroke and diabetes

	Foregone GDP (US$ billions)		Cumulative GDP loss
	2006	2015	(US$ billions) by 2015
Argentina	0.13	0.16	1.40
Brazil	0.33	0.50	4.18
Colombia	0.07	0.10	0.82
Mexico	0.48	0.89	7.14

Source: Adapted from Abegunde *et al.* (2007) (reprinted by permission of Elsevier).

Despite this burden, we have seen that chronic diseases are not explicitly addressed in the MDGs (Fuster and Voûte, 2005; Horton, 2005). Yet, they are a critical challenge facing the global south, one that must be understood not only from the perspective of forgone national income and 'lost labour units', but also from the perspective of social justice.[13]

Common myths surrounding chronic diseases

Many of the WHO's advocacy efforts have been dedicated to combating the commonly-accepted myths and 'half-truths' surrounding chronic diseases, presented in the following list:

- Chronic diseases mainly affect high-income countries
- Low- and middle-income countries need, first, to focus their attention on infectious diseases and, second, chronic diseases
- Chronic diseases are diseases of affluence; they mainly affect rich people
- Chronic diseases are diseases of old age
- Chronic diseases mainly affect men
- They are the result of individual choices – 'unhealthy lifestyles'
- Nothing can be done to prevent them
- Prevention and control, when possible, is too expensive. (WHO, 2005)

In fact, the best recent data support none of these myths. As the WHO argues, four out of every five chronic disease deaths occur in low- and middle-income countries. The burden of these diseases is therefore a particular concern in the so-called 'developing' world; they are not the exclusive problem of high-income countries. We have already seen, for example, that chronic non-communicable diseases account for the majority of deaths across Latin America and the Caribbean, while infectious diseases account for less than one quarter of total deaths. The second myth (that low- and middle-income countries need to focus their attention, first, on infectious diseases and, second, chronic diseases) is based, at least in part, on concern for scarce resources – the argument being that, in the context of limited funds, infectious diseases need to be addressed as a public health priority. This position also clearly reflects the 'global health as a threat' lens described earlier in this book, with infectious diseases being transmissible from one setting to another, and therefore a potential threat to the security of populations in other countries. Such a view clearly prioritizes infectious over non-communicable diseases. However, this ignores the on-the-ground complexity; both infectious and chronic diseases shape patterns of population health and the overwhelming burden of disease – as measured in terms of the proportion of total deaths – is from chronic diseases. Even in countries where each individual non-communicable disease is thought to be relatively uncommon, their *combined burden* is now seen as substantial (Bukhman and Kidder, 2011).

The challenges of epidemiological overlap were discussed in 2006 by William Waters of the Universidad San Francisco de Quito using data from Ecuador, a country near the middle of the economic and health ranking in Latin America. Waters describes epidemiological overlap as a 'double bind', wherein infectious and communicable diseases are not completely controlled and, at the same time, opportunities to detect and treat non-communicable diseases are fragmented by socioeconomic status. However, this does not suggest that chronic conditions should be seen as a second-line priority in the region (Boutayeb, 2006), for these are the conditions that lead to the majority of premature deaths and hamper the quality of life of large segments of the working-age population. Instead, Waters' analysis of the situation in Ecuador indicates that the complexity of the epidemiological overlap needs to be an integral component of health system planning in the region.

The third myth suggests that chronic diseases are diseases of affluence, that they mainly affect the rich. Rejecting this myth, the WHO states that, in all but the least developed countries of the world, chronic diseases actually run along lines of social inequality. That is, they affect the poor more than the rich, following what medical sociologists and epidemiologists refer to as the social gradient. According to Norman Daniels *et al.*, 'the fact is that health inequalities occur as a gradient: the poor have worse health than the near-poor, but the near-poor fare worse than the lower middle class, the lower middle class do worse than the upper middle class, and so on up the economic ladder. Addressing the social gradient in health requires action above and beyond the elimination of poverty' (2000: 29). These gradients are firmly documented in the industrialized world. Research published in recent years supports the social gradient model in Latin America – with, for example, clear gradients for both men and women in chronic disease risk factors by educational attainment in Brazil (Moura *et al.*, 2009) and Chile (Koch *et al.*, 2010). The latest global analyses of obesity and smoking behaviour indicate increasing, or *steepening*, social gradients (Fleischer *et al.*, 2012). My work with colleagues in Argentina, using data from the 2005 National Risk Factor Survey, has shown this gradient pattern with obesity, unhealthy diet, and diabetes (De Maio *et al.*, 2009).[14]

Understanding how these inequalities change over time is a critical goal in public health. There is a need to monitor the evolution of inequalities in order to evaluate possible actions to tackle them. Indeed, the WHO Commission on the Social Determinants of Health concluded with a strong call to action for the routine monitoring of health inequalities (CSDH, 2008). Until recently, this has not been possible at the national-level of analysis in many Latin American countries. However, recent developments in surveillance systems for chronic diseases in the region – and in Argentina, in particular, the availability of data from nationally-representative risk factors surveys from 2005 and 2009 – have now enabled analyses of changing gradients in health.

My colleagues in Argentina and I have focused on better understanding the dynamics of the social gradient. Our work with Argentina's 2005 and 2009 National Risk Factor Surveys illustrates that social gradients in physical inactivity – an important risk factor for many chronic diseases – are steepening (Linetzky *et al.*, 2013), while social gradients for mammograms are decreasing (De Maio *et al.*, 2012). In particular, we found that the direction of the gradient in physical inactivity – as measured either by household income, or by a person's educational attainment – shifted, and lower socioeconomic status groups now experience a higher likelihood of this important risk factor. In contrast, socio-economic gradients for obesity show signs of increasing for women but not for men. Gradients for diabetes show signs of increase for men and have remained significant for women over the period 2005–09.[15] All this implies that patterns of inequality can change – even over a relatively short period of time – and that they are influenced by a range of factors including local, national, and international policies.

The notion that chronic diseases affect mainly the elderly is also misleading: 'almost half of chronic disease deaths occur prematurely, in people under 70 years of age. One quarter of all chronic disease deaths occur in people under 60 years of age' (WHO, 2005). In the case of low- and middle-income countries, the leading category of chronic disease – cardiovascular diseases – strikes particularly hard among working-age people. Tobacco use and obesity – two of the major risk factors for chronic disease – threaten the health of children and young adults (Fuster and Voûte, 2005). According to the WHO, in low- and middle-income countries 'middle-aged adults are especially vulnerable to chronic disease. People in these countries tend to develop disease at younger ages, suffer longer – often with preventable complications – and die sooner than those in high income countries' (WHO, 2005: vii). Alongside the myth that chronic diseases are diseases of old-age, the myth that chronic diseases mainly affects men also ignores the significant burden these diseases pose for women. The most recent data indicate that chronic diseases affect men and women about equally (WHO, 2005) and, in some cases, the effects of 'emerging' gradients are seen most clearly in women. My work with colleagues in Argentina has shown that the overall prevalence of low physical activity, obesity, and diabetes increased from 2005 to 2009 and, while increases occurred in most of the income and education groups, women with the lowest socioeconomic status generally showed the highest increases (Linetzky *et al.*, 2013).

Victim-blaming, or the notion that chronic diseases are the result of individual choices in favour of unhealthy lifestyles, is particularly common. Itself a reflection of epidemiology's traditional focus on individual-level risk factors (Davey Smith, 2001), this myth ignores social context; it ignores the social dimensions that underlie exposure to health-related risks that shape patterns of morbidity and mortality in all populations. This position lays blame, for example, on the obese, seeing their bodies as a sign of moral failure, which Stuckler *et al.* (2011) describe as a 'weakness of will'. In sociological terms, this amounts to a denial of the sick role, wherein a person is not culpable for their condition. For the WHO, '[t]he truth is that individual responsibility can have its full effect only where individuals have equitable access to a healthy life, and are supported to make healthy choices. Governments have a crucial role to play in improving the health and well-being of populations, and in pro-viding special protection for vulnerable groups' (2005: 16). In reality, the poor not only face significant constraints in maximizing the health benefits of their everyday behaviours, they also experience, as Stuckler *et al.* (2011) emphasize, 'powerful pressures' to adopt unhealthy behaviours through structural arrangements that limit the availability of healthy food, exercise facilities, and other health-enhancing resources. Above all, this myth ignores the very real constraints placed upon individual agency by structural violence (Farmer 2003). The last two myths – that nothing can be done to prevent chronic dis-eases, and programmes for their control are too expensive for low- and mid-dle-income countries – are particularly damaging to efforts to improve popu-lation health in Latin America, and neglect, for example, the documented effects of smoke-free legislation in the region (Ferrante *et al.*, 2012; Schoj *et al.*, 2010).

Chronic disease and health inequity

In order to fight the myths surrounding chronic diseases, we need high-quali-ty data and theoretical frameworks with which to analyze it. Above all, we need research that places utmost importance on health inequities – inequali-ties, or differences, that are avoidable, unnecessary, and unfair (Whitehead, 1992), and we need to ground our work on the notion of structural violence. This constitutes a central component of a holistic approach to global health, one that can use the idea of social structure with sensitivity to better under-stand the patterning of disease; an approach that recognizes the very real restraints people face in trying to make healthy lifestyle choices. Moreover, such an approach can integrate globalization and its many manifestations into a multifaceted image of the social patterning of preventable morbidity and pre-mature mortality.

Overall, a sociological perspective on population health brings our research gaze to two inter-related issues: the social determinants of health *and* a focus on inequity. Both issues are central to understanding the social dimensions of chronic diseases. The social determinants of health emphasize that health is produced largely outside the formal health care system (Daniels *et al.*, 2000). While the formal health care system is undoubtedly crucial in improving the quality of life of people with illness, and ensuring access to health care servic-es remains one of the pressing challenges facing all countries, the social deter-minants of health bring our attention to the very organization of society and the quality of social relations as a source of health (or illness). This approach enables us to see structural violence as an epidemiological issue.

A concern for inequities in health brings to light the social patterning of dis-ease. Morbidity and mortality are not randomly distributed in a population; contextual factors (e.g., qualities of the places in which people live) as well as compositional characteristics (i.e., characteristics of individuals themselves)

Table 4.3 The 'average/deprivation/inequality' framework

Period	Average perspective	Deprivation perspective	Inequality perspective
One period (cross-sectional)	– What is the national average?	– Who shows the highest level of risk factors?	– What is the disparity between the least healthy and healthiest?
Over time (longitudinal)	– How has the national average changed over time?	– Has the situation of the most deprived improved over time?	– Has the difference between the least healthy and the healthiest narrowed or increased over time?

Source: UNDP (2000) (reprinted by permission of Oxford University Press).

are important determinants of health. Research from this perspective attempts to overcome the limitations of a narrow individual-level analysis, but simultaneously emphasizes that recognizing the aggregate burden of chronic diseases is not enough (De Maio *et al.*, 2008; Evans *et al.*, 2001). This perspective says that data on the social patterning of chronic disease outcomes and risk factors are needed in order to develop effective policy responses. Such data could be used to identify regions, communities, and groups that have a high prevalence of risk factors or suffer from particularly high rates of specific disease outcomes. The 'average/deprivation/inequality' (ADI) framework – first described by the United Nations Development Programme (UNDP) in its 2000 *Human Development Report* is useful in this task (see Table 4.3).

The first phase of the ADI framework focuses on national or subnational averages, and how these change over time. The second phase examines deprivation, identifying the group(s) with the highest level of risk factor or burden of disease. Over time, we can study whether the conditions of the worst-off groups improve. The third phase of the ADI framework identifies not only the worst-off, but quantifies the gap between the worst- and best-off groups.

Much of the literature on risk factors for chronic non-communicable diseases currently falls into the 'average' phase of the framework by reporting national prevalence rates. We study, for example, to determine whether the national rate of tobacco use has increased in country A or country B from one year to the next. And this is clearly very important, and represents a crucial aspect of any attempt to evaluate relevant public policies. However, to understand the social patterning of chronic disease outcomes and risk factors, the second and third steps of the ADI framework are needed. The deprivation perspective seeks to break down the national average by relevant socioeconomic and demographic factors in order to identify the groups that experience either the poorest levels of health or the highest levels of risk. In other words, the deprivation perspective seeks to disaggregate national summary statistics by meaningful sociological and/or geographical levels in order to identify the segments of society experiencing the heaviest burden.

Analyses based on the ADI framework hold tremendous policy potential; they allow us to develop programmes aimed to serve the worst-off and, in a way, foster principles of social justice. The inequality perspective takes this one step further, not only identifying the worst-off, but also considering the *difference* between the worst-off and the best-off groups. This is particularly important when it comes to public health interventions, which have an unfortunate history of sometimes increasing inequities as an unintended consequence of its actions (Bartley, 2004; Lorenc *et al.*, 2013). This would enable analyses of health inequities grounded in the pursuit of social justice. It would also enable researchers to evaluate policies, model the costs/benefits of interventions, and assess the progressive realization of health as a human right.

The need to re-frame the burden of chronic non-communicable diseases as a social justice issue is receiving progressively more attention, most recently with world leaders holding a high-level meeting at the United Nations in September 2011. The meeting was a significant opportunity for action, a chance to raise the visibility of the burden of chronic non-communicable diseases in the global south and, perhaps most importantly, a chance to strengthen the WHO's role as a leader in global health advocacy (Mamudu *et al.*, 2011).[16] Heads of state and senior diplomats convened, and global health researchers hoped this would generate a collective response to the growing global burden of chronic non-communicable diseases. In particular, WHO-lead efforts pushed for the meeting to generate international cooperation in five so-called 'priority intervention' areas: tobacco control, salt reduction, improved diets and physical activity, reduction of unhealthy patterns of alcohol consumption, and access to essential medicines and health services (Beaglehole *et al.*, 2011b).

The meeting held tremendous potential to galvanize political attention on chronic diseases and, in particular, on the global forces that are acknowledged to be root causes. For, while all chronic diseases have proximal causes – including unhealthy diet, lack of physical activity, and tobacco use, the growing consensus in global health research is that these causes must be understood as being part of a much larger chain of events. As Hadii Mamudu *et al.* state, chronic non-communicable diseases

> must be addressed not only through individual lifestyle changes (tobacco use cessation, limiting alcohol use, healthy diet and physical activity), but also through public policy interventions to modify societal and environmental factors that affect the context within which individuals make behavioural choices. These include interventions such as requiring food companies to eliminate trans-fats, improving community access to healthy foods, restricting marketing of unhealthy foods and tobacco, and transforming health systems to assure application of clinical prevention strategies. (2011: 348)

Many in the global health community saw the high-level meeting as a critical juncture, a point at which global leaders would address the neglect of chronic diseases in the MDGs, and move forward by agreeing on new quantifiable targets and new binding international agreements.

In the end, the meeting was primarily symbolic in its achievements; it failed to generate firm global targets, there are no new binding agreements, and there is no chronic disease-focused development goal on the horizon. Critique has been swift from many quarters of the global health community. Sara Reardon, for example, writes in *Science* that the meeting 'produced a watered-down document that is long on talk and conspicuously short on actions, with little guidance on who should do what to combat noncommunicable diseases' (2011: 1561). Lisa Rosenbaum and Daniela Lamas write in the *New England Journal of Medicine* that the meeting's concluding statement 'was notably silent with regards to deadlines or explicit targets for member nations to meet. And despite a general call for evidence-based interventions, there is no accompanying requirement for ongoing data collection to track outcomes' (2011: 2346). Moreover, critics have decried the influence of food, tobacco, and drug industries on the meeting and have accused the high-income countries of hypocrisy, as many countries who blocked firm commitments on tobacco control and salt reduction, for example, have enacted anti-tobacco and salt reducing legislation *for their own populations* (Lincoln *et al.*, 2011; Stuckler *et al.*, 2011).[17] A more optimistic assessment is offered by Robert Beaglehole *et al.*, who note that while 'it would have been ideal for the Declaration to have included time-bound goals and targets ... [The Declaration nevertheless] opens up new opportunities to move the non-communicable disease agenda forward' (Beaglehole *et al.*, 2011a: 1283). Overall, there are signs of a promising new global movement emphasizing the burden of chronic non-communicable diseases, but pressure will need to be exerted from many fronts to make sure that work in this area moves in the direction of identifying and overcoming inequalities in health, seeing structural violence – in all its aspects – as the root cause of preventable morbidity and premature mortality.

Conclusion

A focus on inequities would greatly advance our understanding of the burden of chronic diseases in the global south. The aggregate-level indicators published by the WHO, disturbing as they are, take on a higher degree of urgency if we recognize that they *hide* the substantial inequities that exist in all countries. It is imperative that we move from seeing chronic non-communicable diseases as a growing burden towards seeing these conditions, and the population health patterns they establish, as the manifestation of structural inequalities in society.

We are faced with a unique opportunity not only to develop policies to improve aggregate-level health indicators, but also to contribute to the alleviation of the social inequality around the world. Without significant action to address the growing burden of chronic non-communicable diseases, the countries of the global south – and, particularly, the poor of the global south – will experience growing levels of preventable morbidity and premature mortality. Research into chronic non-communicable diseases in low- and middle-income settings is just beginning – but the available evidence is unambiguous in signalling the need for urgent action.

In Chapter 5, I move 'backwards' through the epidemiological transition and examine neglected tropical diseases, conditions that afflict the poorest 1 billion people in the world today. They are, more than anything else, the bodily manifestation – the embodiment – of structural violence, and expose the most marginalized people on earth to a suffering of which most of us in high-income countries are not even aware.

Neglected Tropical Diseases

Neglected tropical diseases (NTDs) are a heterogeneous group of parasitic and bacterial diseases that afflict the poorest of the world's poor (Holveck *et al.*, 2007; Hotez *et al.*, 2008b; Mathers *et al.*, 2007). They are 'ancient' diseases; in contrast to 'emerging' diseases such as Ebola, West Nile fever, or even HIV/AIDS, NTDs have been around for thousands of years (WHO, 2003). Descriptions of schistosomiasis, hookworm, and other NTDs featured in this chapter are found in ancient texts, including the Bible and the writings of Hippocrates (Grove, 1990). Much is known about how NTDs work and how they spread; for some NTDs, medical science offers effective treatment, often costing less than fifty cents per day (Hotez and Pecoul, 2010).[1] Yet, NTDs are estimated to cause more than 500,000 deaths annually – that is, *every year* NTDs kill as many people as were killed in the 2004 Christmas tsunami (Hotez *et al.*, 2006), but they do not make the news, as their victims are almost entirely confined to the poorest classes in poor countries. NTDs have been largely ignored by the pharmaceutical industry, and until recently, NTDs have also been ignored by social scientists.

It is important to note that the reference to NTDs as 'neglected' does not imply that they are of secondary importance behind other infectious diseases such as HIV/AIDs, tuberculosis, and malaria – diseases that have gained attention in the MDGs. Indeed, global health researchers have established that the combined burden of NTDs ranks as high as those of other better-known afflictions in many places, even if their death toll is lower. Rather, *'their neglect reflects their epidemiology*: they are prevalent among the poorest and most marginalized of the world's population' (Manderson *et al.*, 2009: 1; emphasis added). NTDs are burdens of what Chris Beyrer *et al.* refer to as 'forgotten populations,' emphasizing that because NTDs do not generally affect so-called developed countries, they have been 'largely ignored by medical science' (2007: 619). For Peter Hotez, NTDs are the 'forgotten diseases afflicting forgotten people' (2008a: 6). But, while forgotten, they are very real in their impact on the lives of those affected.

Globally, NTDs are estimated to affect more than 1 billion people, with a further 2 billion potentially at risk (Ault, 2008). As noted above, they are thought to cause more than 500,000 deaths every year, with an additional burden in terms of preventable morbidity, disability, and suffering (Conteh *et al.*, 2010). All told, they entail a significant constraint on people's agency and represent a strong rebuke to premature triumphalism over poverty alleviation in the global south. Their very presence in countries such as India and Brazil – countries heralded in popular accounts highlighting the promise of globalization – gives us pause when considering global health inequities in the twenty-first century (see Hotez, 2008b; Lindoso and Lindoso, 2009; Lobo *et al.*, 2011).

NTDs differ in their etiology, biological mechanisms, and clinical symptoms, but they share a series of social features; above all, they are bound together by poverty. It is poverty that exposes people to the parasites and bacteria that cause the major NTDs, and it is poverty, along with a lack of global political will, that keeps NTDs underdiagnosed, under-researched, and under-treated. The WHO expresses this point clearly: 'the most profound commonality is their stranglehold on populations whose lives are ravaged by poverty' (2010b: 2). Indeed, NTDs are a *proxy* for poverty and disadvantage (Hotez and Ferris, 2006); NTDs are prevalent *only* in settings of poverty and they thrive in zones of military or paramilitary conflict.[2] It is clear that NTDs form a part of a vicious circle: poverty nurtures the risk of contracting an NTD, and NTDs, in turn, severely diminish the economic capacity of individuals and communities, thereby nurturing poverty and inequality. Importantly, this is recognized at the highest levels of global health governance. For example, the WHO proclaims that NTDs 'constitute a serious obstacle to socioeconomic development and quality of life' (2010b: 5). Yet, despite this burden, few international resources have been devoted to research on NTD treatment, control, and prevention, although as will be shown, there are some positive signs that this is changing (WHO, 2012a).

NTDs affect mostly marginalized populations with low political visibility and little economic power. They are driven by inadequate access to clean water and modern housing. Yet, NTDs do not travel widely – for example, in comparison to the highly contagious tuberculosis, they are not seen as much of a danger in non-endemic areas.[3] Most NTDs are chronic in nature; they work slowly, often afflicting their victims over decades. As Hotez poignantly argues: 'In some cases, poor people can suffer from NTDs for their entire lives' (2008a: 6), and their affliction will not garner the attention of the mass media, or even the biomedical and social science research communities. NTDs have not been seen as a 'global threat' but, rather, just as part of life in the poorest areas of the global south.

I began this book contrasting different 'lenses' which can be discerned in the global health literature. These lenses have critical implications for how we come to understand the global burden of NTDs and, indeed, how we might move forward with NTD research. The first lens is focused on the idea of *contagion*, of *risk*, and *securitizes* global health, prioritizing the health needs of the advanced industrialized countries. From this perspective, global health matters because globalization has greatly eroded the boundaries between the 'developed' and 'developing' worlds, and diseases from poor parts of the world can be transmitted to the rich parts of the world with frightening ease.

In *Global Politics of Health*, Sara Davies (2010) describes this 'securitized' perspective as the *statist* position (see also Labonté *et al.*, 2009; Labonté and Torgerson, 2005; Lee, 2003; Price-Smith, 2009). The position invokes a state's need to defend itself from external threats. It frames disease as an enemy, much like a foreign army that must be defeated. In this light, 'global battles' against HIV/AIDS and, through the Global Fund, against tuberculosis and malaria, are waged to protect advanced industrialized states from contagion. According to Davies, 'powerful actors still only see a health crisis as worth responding to when it threatens them. Massive national expenditure on disease control can only be justified when governments can draw a link between the threat, infectious disease, and national security' (2010: 22). The problem in all of this, of course, is that a 'securitized' discourse on global health leaves the social conditions wherein disease flourishes intact. From this position, unless NTDs are framed as a threat to the industrialized countries, they will never be a priority.

Opposing the statist position, Davies (2010) defines the globalist tradition. This perspective is more strongly tied to the global discourse on human rights and social justice. From this position, disease is seen from the perspective of individuals and marginalized populations. Chagas disease, from the globalist position, is not important merely because it may spread to non-endemic countries, tainting their blood supplies and requiring specialized costly treatments for those affected, but also because it continues to burden poor populations in the global south, causing unnecessary morbidity and premature mortality. From this perspective, NTDs need not threaten the industrialized countries to be deemed a priority. One of the challenges in contemporary global health research, in my opinion, is to strengthen the globalist position on NTDs, to make it – rather than the statist perspective – the normative lens.

Another notable characteristic of NTDs is that they are heavily stigmatized (Weiss, 2008). Many NTDs cause disfigurement – perhaps most graphically in the case of lymphatic filariasis, which causes elephantiasis of limbs - and this results, in many countries, in the routine discrimination of infected girls and women in particular (Allotey and Gyapong, 2005; Hotez, 2008c, 2009). Some NTDs have been associated with adverse pregnancy outcomes; this, too, generates stigma and discrimination against women in many countries (WHO, 2010b). For Peter Hotez, 'interventions focused on NTD control and elimination could offer an opportunity for improving the health and rights of girls and women in the poorest countries of Africa, Asia, and Latin America and the Caribbean' (2009: e559). This is partly due to anaemia, the condition in which the body does not have enough healthy red blood cells. Hotez explains:

> 20 per cent of maternal deaths in Africa are attributed to anemia, while simultaneously anemia represents a key risk factor for poor pregnancy

outcome and low birth weight. It now appears that human hookworm infection, one of the most common NTDs affecting 576–740 million people in developing countries, considerably adds to the iron loss and anemia that occurs during pregnancy. An estimated 44 million pregnant women are infected with hookworm at any one time, including up to one-third of all pregnant women in sub-Saharan Africa. (2009: e559)

NTD control and elimination, in other words, would go a long way towards achieving the MDGs' target of reducing maternal mortality. But NTDs have been largely side-lined in the MDG literature, and they have seldom appeared in the work on gender inequality and human rights. And, despite their devastating effects, NTDs have not been seen as a priority for research. For-profit pharmaceutical companies have seen little market potential in these conditions (Abad-Franch *et al.*, 2010; Crager and Price, 2009; Trouiller *et al.*, 2002), as the victims of NTDs are entirely too poor to ever serve as a fee-paying market for specialized new pharmaceutical products. In her analysis of access to essential medicines, Judy Rein observes: 'diseases suffered by populations with no purchasing power are not going to be addressed by commercial producers' (2001: 404). Along these lines, Bryanna Mantilla observes that 'scientists have a great deal of knowledge about organisms that cause sleeping sickness, Chagas disease, and leishmaniasis, but because the populations affected by neglected diseases have no purchasing power, there is no financial incentive for drug companies to develop the drugs' (2011: 124). Social science research has also neglected NTDs (Allotey *et al.*, 2010), mirroring, perhaps, sociology's lack of engagement with global health in general.[4]

Despite all this, there are some promising signs: OneWorld Health, a United States-based not-for-profit pharmaceutical company seeks to develop new medicines for NTDs. Launched in 2000, it has already been successful in developing new treatment for visceral leishmaniasis, a parasitic disease estimated to cause more than 50,000 deaths every year (WHO, 2007a). The Sabin Vaccine Institute, under the direction of Peter Hotez, is also working on a range of new treatments for NTDs, including Chagas, schistosomiasis, and hookworm.[5] The Drugs for Neglected Diseases Initiative (DNDi), a not-for-profit partnership lead by MSF, has brought together the capacities and resources of a wide range of global partners, including Brazil's Oswaldo Cruz Foundation, the Indian Council for Medical Research, and the Kenyan Medical Research Institute, as well as academic and drug industry partners. They are slated to deliver new treatments for some of the most prevalent NTDs by 2014. Also, the WHO has taken on a greater leadership position, publishing a landmark report on neglected diseases in 2010 and an updated 'roadmap for implementation' in 2012 – though as we shall see, both documents can be criticized for failing to see the underlying structural violence that shapes people's exposures to NTDs.

Descriptive epidemiology

The burden of NTDs falls primarily in sub-Saharan Africa and some parts of Latin America, but is also felt in the Eastern Mediterranean, South-East Asian, and Western Pacific regions of the WHO. The most common approach to measuring the burden of disease has been the disability-adjusted life year (DALY), which is defined as the number of years of life lost due to disease, taking into account not only premature mortality, but also discounting for life 'lost' due to morbidity and disability (Asada, 2007; Barker and Green, 1996). The DALY is a controversial measure, and was originally used in the World Bank's 1993 *World Development Report*.[6] Its calculation requires a host of assumptions, most of which remain obscured in technical reports. For example, the DALY framework not only assumes that men will live to 80 years and women to 82.5 years, but it also assumes that disease at *different ages* carries varying levels of burden. Early adulthood is most heavily weighted, and the extremes of age are *discounted*. An infant death, for example, is calculated as 33 DALYs. The DALY framework also incorporates a weighting for disability, taking into account the duration of the disability as well as its own relative 'weight'. Michael Seear explains: 'Disability score varies from zero (perfect health) to one (dead); blindness is scored at 0.6 and the loss of a limb is 0.3' (2007: 111). These assumptions are highly controversial; for as Howard Waitzkin argues: 'A measure that attaches more value to life without disability, many have argued, implicitly devalues the lives of disabled people' (2003: 526). These assumptions – generally hidden in technical reports – greatly influence the final data, and debates continue in the literature surrounding the statistic's computation.

Additionally, the calculation of DALYS requires detailed data on disease prevalence and incidence; data that are often not available in countries of the global south. Nevertheless, DALYS remain the most often cited statistic on the global burden of disease. Richard Skolnik presents the case for their usefulness: 'A society that has more premature death, illness, and disability has more DALYS than a society that is healthier and has less illness, disability, and premature death. One of the goals of health policy is to avert these DALYS' (Skolnik, 2008: 26). Table 5.1 presents estimates of the number of DALYS by NTD.

Lymphatic filariasis

The highest worldwide burden is associated with lymphatic filariasis, a condition brought on from infection with mosquito-borne filarial worms (*Wuchereria bancrofti, Brugia malayi* and *Brugia timori*). These worms lodge in the lymphatic system, disrupting its capacity to function. It is a painful and disfiguring disease, associated with social stigma and discrimination. It can cause limbs to swell and produces painful acute attacks. It is thought to generate almost 6 million DALYs every year, with significant effects in South-East

Table 5.1 Estimated number of disability-adjusted life years (000s) by neglected tropical diseases, by region

Neglected disease	World	Region				
		Africa	Americas	Eastern Mediterranean	South-East Asia	Western Pacific
Human African trypanosomiasis	1,673	1,609	0	62	0	0
Chagas' disease	430	0	426	0	0	0
Schistosomiasis	1,707	1,502	46	145	0	13
Leishmaniasis	1,974	328	45	281	1,264	51
Lymphatic filariasis	5,941	2,263	10	75	3,525	65
Onchocerciasis	389	375	1	11	0	0
Leprosy	194	25	16	22	118	13
Dengue	670	9	73	28	391	169
Trachoma	1,334	601	15	208	88	419
Ascariasis	1,851	915	60	162	404	308
Trichuriasis (soil-transmitted helminthiases)	1,012	236	73	61	372	269
Hookworm disease	1,092	377	20	43	286	364

Note: Numbers for the regions do not always add up to the world's total, as estimates from the European region were not included by the WHO.
Source: WHO (2010b) (used with permission).

Asia and Africa, where more than 120 million people are thought to be infected and more than 1.2 billion are at risk of becoming infected (Ottesen *et al.*, 2008). Infection is usually acquired in childhood, but the most visible manifestations of the infection – elephantiasis of limbs – occur in adulthood.

Lymphatic filariasis has been the subject of a worldwide campaign: the *Global Programme to Eliminate Lymphatic Filariasis*. Launched by the WHO in 2000, the programme has delivered 2.45 billion treatments of anti-filarial drugs to more than 570 million people around the world, in an attempt to interrupt transmission of the disease and control its effects among those already infected (Addiss, 2010b). The programme is an example of MDA – the large-scale distribution of pharmaceuticals for both therapeutic and preventive benefits. Eric Ottesen *et al.* point out, for example, that 'not only do the GPELF [Global Programme to Eliminate Lymphatic Filariasis] drugs prevent the spread of LF [lymphatic filariasis], but they also stop the progression of disease in those already infected. In addition, since two of the three drugs used for LF elimination have broad anti-parasite properties, treated populations are freed from both intestinal worms and from skin infections' (2008). Most recently, efforts have been launched to combine MDA for lymphatic filariasis with treatments for other NTDs (Addiss, 2010a; Baker *et al.*, 2010). Some analysts, however, have raised concern about the feasibility of 'scaling' up this approach to include other NTDs, particularly if new sources of funding are not readily forthcoming (Zhang *et al.*, 2010).

Global health researchers have praised two major pharmaceutical companies, GlaxoSmithKline and Merck & Co., Inc., for their extraordinary pledges to provide anti-filarial medicines free for the long-term. Indeed, without the participation of those companies, it is unclear that this programme could have been started at all. By most accounts, it has been a remarkable success; of 81 endemic countries, 52 (64.2 per cent) have active MDA programmes, and the majority have now completed the recommended ≥ 5 rounds of MDA in at least some of their most burdened areas (Addiss, 2010a). More than 8 million children under the age of 9 are estimated to have been saved from infection (WHO, 2010b). China and the Republic of Korea have eliminated the disease as a public health problem, and nine other countries, including Sri Lanka, have lowered their prevalence rates to the point where further MDA may not be warranted. Parts of Egypt, Ghana, India and the Philippines have also achieved significant reductions in the prevalence of lymphatic filariasis in recent years (WHO, 2010b). These gains are dependent, however, on the charity of for-profit companies – raising serious questions about the long-term sustainability of treatment efforts.

Leishmaniasis

The second-highest burden of disease is associated with leishmaniasis, an infection caused by more than 20 species of the protozoan parasite *Leishmania*. It can be transmitted to humans by more than 30 species of sandflies. Infection is characterized by fever, enlarged spleen and liver, weight loss, anaemia, and an assortment of other clinical symptoms (with different manifestations arising from infection with different species of *Leishmania*). Symptoms progress in severity over weeks or months. Symptomatic patients can die within two years if the infection is not treated (WHO, 2010b), and the disease threatens more than 350 million people in 88 countries worldwide. Visceral leishmaniasis is the most severe form of the disease, where it attacks internal organs. Cutaneous leishmaniasis is the most common form of the disease, and usually results in ulcers on the face, arms, and legs of the infected person. The WHO emphasizes that these ulcers 'cause serious disability and leave severe and permanently disfiguring scars' (WHO, 2010b: 91).

Treatment options for leishmaniasis reveal the underlying structural violence. The WHO points out that for more than 70 years, first-line treatment in most countries has consisted of injections of a group of medicines called 'pentavalent antimonials', but:

> the treatment is lengthy, potentially toxic, and painful; it has become ineffective in parts of India and Nepal as resistance has developed. In the case of relapse, patients need treatment with a more toxic, second-line

medicine, such as amphotericin B or pentamidine. Newly developed ... amphotericin B is highly effective, has almost no side-effects and is now the preferred first-line treatment ... [however] *this medicine is too expensive to be widely used by most developing countries.* (WHO, 2010b: 95; emphasis added)

The fact that the new treatment is *accepted* by the WHO as being too expensive to be used where it is needed most is a testament to the notion that biomedical advances cannot be expected to diminish the burden of NTDs in the global south by themselves.[7] Deeming a treatment to be 'too expensive' is an explicit judgement on human value, and belies a neoliberal paradigm where the worth of individuals can be calculated and compared with budget constraints. The question of *why* these medicines are so expensive is rarely asked in this literature. And campaigns to expand access to medicines continue to rely on charity as underlying philosophy – the frame of social justice, where we might assert that populations at risk of leishmaniasis have a *right* to treatment is subsequently dismissed as utopian.

Schistosomiasis

Schistosomiasis is another of the top-ranked NTDs by burden of disease estimates, thought to generate more than 1.7 million DALYS, almost all in sub-Saharan Africa (Chitsulo *et al.*, 2000; King and Dangerfield-Cha, 2008). It is a disease caused by infestation with parasitic worms (*Schistosoma*). More than 200 million people are thought to be infected worldwide (WHO, 2010b), and a total of 600–800 million people are at risk of infection (Muhumuza *et al.*, 2009; Steinmann *et al.*, 2006). The disease is thought to be the most important human parasitic worm infection in terms of global death toll (Bethony *et al.*, 2008). As with other NTDs, schistosomiasis afflicts mostly those living in poor communities without access to safe drinking water and sanitation.

One becomes infected with schistosomiasis when larval forms of the parasite, released by freshwater snails, penetrate the skin during contact with infested water. In the body, the larvae develop and grow; adult worms live in the blood vessels where the females release eggs. Some of the eggs are passed out of the body in the faeces or urine; others become trapped in body tissues, causing an immune reaction and progressive damage to internal organs (WHO, 2010b). Schistosomiasis is also linked to anaemia, growth-stunting, under-nutrition, and impairment of cognitive development in those infected (King and Dangerfield-Cha, 2008). Schistosomiasis has significant effects on the reproductive health of women, producing cervical lesions that are thought to increase the likelihood of HIV infection and that may also lead to infertility (Swai *et al.*, 2006).

During the 1990s, global efforts against schistosomiasis focused on periodic treatment with praziquantel, a medicine that works by killing worms in the human body. Jeffrey Bethony *et al.* raise an important critique of this approach, noting the 'high rates of post-treatment re-infection and the possible development of drug resistance' (Bethony *et al.*, 2008: 3373). They conclude that effective control of schistosomiasis 'is unlikely in the absence of improved sanitation and a vaccine' (Bethony *et al.*, 2008: 3373). Along these lines, Patrick Lammie *et al.* argue that 'an elimination strategy based exclusively on drug treatment will not be successful. On the other hand, provision of safe water and sanitary improvements ... is a valid public health goal that will yield important dividends beyond schistosomiasis control' (2007). Most recently, praziquantel has been added to the WHO-led efforts focused on MDA, thereby nurturing synergy with the distribution of medicines for other NTDs (Hotez *et al.*, 2008a). But, overall, the global effort against NTDs has been almost entirely focused on the potential of biomedical/pharmaceutical solutions. The warnings from Bethony *et al.* and Lammie *et al.* have not altered the dominant approach to NTD control worldwide, with the social and economic arrangements that engender a population's risk of NTDs being ignored. A similar situation is occurring with Chagas disease, where prevention and control efforts have focused almost exclusively on the large-scale spraying of insecticide.

Chagas disease

Among the NTDs in Table 5.1 is Chagas disease. Unique to the Americas, Chagas generates an estimated burden of 426,000 DALYs every year. Its history demonstrates how international cooperation based on public health principles can lead to the control of a so-called disease of poverty, as some countries have been successful in largely eradicating the disease, while others have not (WHO, 2010b). It is a primarily a vector-borne parasitic disease (though as will be discussed, can also be spread through blood transfusion, as well as from infected mother to foetus through the placenta). It is also almost entirely associated with poor quality housing in rural settings. Little attention has been given to Chagas by the pharmaceutical industry, reflecting a true 'market failure' whereby the lives of the poor are deemed to be of little value; the development of new vaccines or treatments deemed to fail contemporary judgements of 'cost-effectiveness' (Trouiller *et al.*, 2002).

To understand Chagas, first, we need to return to the notion of DALYS, and how they are used in the global health discourse. Indeed, while DALYS are taken by many researchers to be a valid measure of the burden of disease, there are strong reasons for considering that DALYS actually underestimate the true burden of NTDs. In particular, DALYS are known to be primarily driven by mortality – and to the extent that NTDs are not associated with high mortality rates but, rather, with lengthy periods of suffering and disability, along with stigma and reduced social capacities, the DALY count associated with NTDs may actually be too low (Engels and Savioli, 2006). According to Lesong Conteh *et al.*, 'DALYS might not adequately indicate the severity of many neglected tropical diseases and the effects on an individual's quality of life' (2010:

239). The implication of this is that any assessment of the 'cost effectiveness' of interventions for NTDs are bound to be biased. Conteh *et al.* explain: 'If the DALY used for schistosomiasis is underestimated, the incremental cost-effectiveness ratio will seem less cost effective because the costs (the numerator) would be divided by a smaller benefit in the form of an underestimated DALY (the denominator)' (2010: 239). In other words, to the extent to which global health relies on the notion of 'cost-effectiveness' to guide decision-making (and there is much to be said against the research community's overreliance on cost-effectiveness), we may be making systematic errors in underestimating the potential benefits of treatments for NTDs. At the same time, DALYS are used not only to gauge the cost-effectiveness of treatment, but also to measure – with varying levels of precision – the economic costs of disease in particular settings.

Despite the very real concerns about the economic quantification of disease one might have, such evidence is often cited in health research, and what has been published is worth considering. Conteh *et al.* argue that 'understanding the effect of neglected tropical diseases on the economy is crucial if we want to better estimate the benefit of their control' (2010: 240). To calculate the costs of NTDs, they add the direct costs of expenditure on prevention and treatment with the indirect cost of lost labour lost due to illness and premature death. However, just like as calculation of DALYS requires researchers to make a host of assumptions, so does the calculation of cost of illness. Table 5.2 presents the reported 'productivity' costs associated with Chagas, lymphatic filariasis, and schistosomiasis.

Chagas alone is thought to generate a loss of US$1.2 billion in annual productivity for Latin American economies, and lymphatic filariasis is estimated to produce a similar amount in loss productivity in sub-Saharan Africa. Along with these economic costs, we must bear in mind that NTDs exert a toll that is not easily subjected to economic analysis. Their presence is an indictment of the global community's neglect of the right to health in poor places, and a reflection of the moral failures associated with 'cost-effectiveness' analysis.

Table 5.2 Economic costs of Chagas disease, lymphatic filariasis and schistosomiasis

	Setting	Reported productivity loss
Chagas disease	Latin America	Estimated 752,000 working days per year lost because of premature deaths. US$1.2 billion per year in lost productivity in seven countries.
Lymphatic filiarisis	Various countries	Estimated $1.3 billion per year in lost productivity.
Schistosomiasis	Phillipines	Estimated loss of 45.4 working days per year per infected person.

Source: Adapted from Conteh *et al.* (2010) (reprinted by permission of Elsevier).

NTDs are the product of structural violence. They are the direct effects of populations being exposed to unsafe water, to a lack of adequate nutrition, and to sub-standard living conditions. Their epidemiology is actually quite well-known – we know where endemic areas exist, and we know that overall improvements in living standards are associated with the eradication of NTDs (there is no advanced industrialized area in the world that is endemic for NTDs). Yet, as I shall discuss, the global health community's efforts have largely ignored the structural dimensions of NTDs, preferring instead to target the poor with MDA of preventive chemotherapy and/or repeated large-scale spraying of insecticides, without a concerted effort to improve the living conditions that nurture vectors of NTDs. An equity-based analysis has not featured, despite the fact that NTDs overwhelmingly affect the poor. Globalization – as a force that influences patterns of migration and opportunities for employment, and shifts the distribution of resources – has been at the margins of the NTD literature.

At the same time, there are signs that something of a shift in the NTD literature is occurring, and certainly there is newfound public and research attention devoted to these diseases, particularly as a result of the successful outreach and dissemination strategies used by the new Global Network for Neglected Tropical Diseases. Lead by Peter Hotez, they are highlighting the fact that NTDs are the 'forgotten diseases of forgotten people,' and must be incorporated into global health advocacy and research. Along these lines, Conteh *et al.*, in an important review of the burden of NTDs, proclaim: 'Equity analysis must ensure that interventions are reaching the most vulnerable groups and target those with the greatest need' (2010: 244). In the following section, I examine how sociological analysis might be used in relation to Chagas, in an effort to strengthen a true equity-based analysis that takes structural violence into account as an integral analytical tool.

Chagas and globalization

Chagas ranks high among NTDs in the Americas (Hotez, 2007), and it is the region's most important parasitic disease (Reithinger *et al.*, 2009). In 1990, the burden associated with Chagas was higher than that of tuberculosis, though since that time the burden of tuberculosis has increased and the indicators for Chagas have improved (Schmunis, 2007). It is caused by the protozoan parasite *Trypanosoma cruzi* (*T. cruzi*). The parasite is most commonly transmitted to humans through contact with the faeces or urine of a triatomine bug who acts as a vector, carrying *T. cruzi* in its digestive system. Several triatomine bugs are known to carry *T. cruzi*, including *Triatoma infestans* (commonly referred to as *vinchuca* in Argentina and Boliva, or *barberio* in Brazil) and *Rhodnius prolixus* (the principal vector in Venezuela and Colombia). These blood-sucking bugs often strike at night, usually near the mouth or eyes and, while feeding, defecate on their victim (they are often called 'kissing bugs' for their tendency to bite near the mouth). When the person scratches the bite site, material enters the body (or enters through the mucus membranes). *Vinchucas* live in the cracks and crevices found in homes constructed of thatch, grass, sticks, unplastered cement, and other materials that are characteristic of construction in poor rural settings. *Vinchucas* are a particular concern in rural areas characterized by close contact between humans and animals, as they can also feed on dogs, chickens, and other farm animals. *T. cruzi* can also be transmitted in blood and organs from infected donors and may also pass from an infected mother to the foetus through the placenta (Senior, 2007). Vectoral transmission is the most common (Prata, 2001).

Infection is followed by two phases: acute and chronic. The acute phase can last between 4 and 8 weeks, and is characterized by fever, swollen lymph glands and, often, inflammation at the biting site. Anywhere from 2 per cent to 8 per cent of infected children die in this phase of the disease (Ribeiro *et al.*, 2009). Up to 40 per cent of infected people are thought to develop chronic Chagas disease (Reithinger *et al.*, 2009), which is characterized by cardiac and gastrointestinal complications. If left untreated, these can be fatal. In disease endemic areas like Bolivia and northern Argentina, Chagas is the leading factor in cardiovascular deaths (Reithinger *et al.*, 2009). Almost one third of patients are thought to develop Chagas-related heart damage, and 10 per cent develop damage to the oesophagus, colon, or nervous system (or a combination of these), typically in the late chronic phase of the disease (WHO, 2010b).

An estimated 7–8 million people are thought to be infected in the region of the Americas (with some estimates more in the 10–20 million range – there is considerable imprecision in these estimates), with most of these cases being asymptomatic and undiagnosed. Endemic areas exist in 21 countries of Latin America, as shown in Figure 5.1.

Argentina, Brazil, and Mexico are thought to have the largest number of cases of *T. cruzi* infection, at more than 1 million cases in each country. But Bolivia has the highest rate of *T. cruzi* infection in the world, with an estimated 6 per cent of the overall population infected. Some surveys of pregnant women and blood donors in hyper-endemic communities reach prevalence rates of 30–40 per cent in that country (Brenière *et al.*, 2002; Pirard *et al.*, 2005).

Chagas disease has also been detected in non-endemic countries where vector transmission does not exist (due either to climate and/or housing infrastructure which is unsuitable for triatomine insects). There, migrants have brought *T. cruzi* infection with them and pose a danger of transmitting the parasite into the blood supply, and congenital transmission remains a possibility with infected immigrant women.

There are two drugs currently available to treat Chagas – benzazole and nifurtimox – but they are effective only among young children (younger than 13 years of age) and in the early stages of the disease. Both have 30–60 treatment regimens with challenging compliance issues and toxic side effects (Senior, 2007). Neither drug can be used by pregnant women. Reflecting the lack of pharmacological innovation in this area, both drugs have been around for more than 25 years.

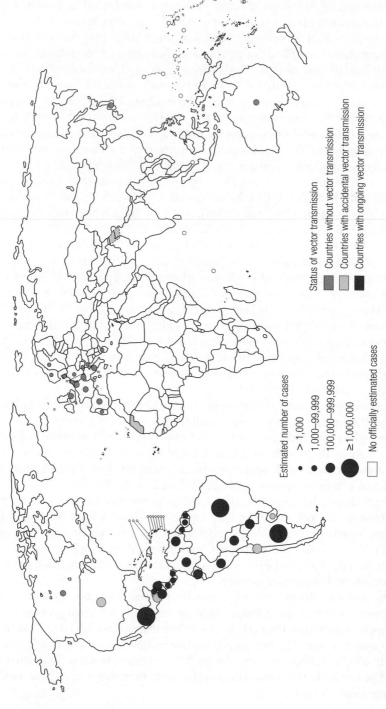

Figure 5.1 Distribution of cases of *T. cruzi* infection, official estimates, 2006–09

Source: WHO (2010b) (used with permission).

Despite limited pharmacological treatments, the consensus seems to be that epidemiological parameters are improving significantly. Dias *et al.* (2008) report that the size of the overall population thought to be at risk has declined substantially, reflecting both improvements in living conditions and an increasing rate of urbanization in the region, as vector transmission of Chagas is primarily a rural phenomenon. The number of deaths attributable to Chagas infection is estimated to have decreased from over 45,000 per year in 1990, to 21,000 in 2000, to 12,500 in 2006. DALYs have also seen a stark decline over that period, from 2.7 million in 1990 to 867,000 in 2006 (and to almost half that in the latest WHO estimates; see Table 5.1), leading the Pan American Health Organization's Dr Gabriel Schmunis – a world-leader in Chagas research – to claim that 'Chagas disease is in retreat in Latin America' (2007: 76).

The greatest improvements have been made in parts of Latin America's Southern Cone countries (Argentina, Brazil, Chile, Uruguay, and Paraguay), where large regional vector control programmes have reduced the incidence of Chagas considerably. Vector borne transmission (the main mechanism behind human Chagas infections) has been greatly inhibited or halted, primarily as a result of programmes which have sprayed pyrethroid insecticide in domestic and peridomestic household structures. Uruguay reported to have interrupted vector transmission of *T. cruzi* by *Triatomine infestans* in 1997, followed by Chile in 1999 and, most recently, Brazil in 2006. Successful programmes have also been reported in El Salvador and Guatemala (Schmunis, 2007).

Yet, these successes need to be interpreted cautiously. Vector control through insecticide spraying – while effective in the short term – does raise long-term questions, beginning with the long-term health effects of exposing populations and the environment to toxins, as well as the very real threat of vectors developing insecticide resistance, signs of which have already been documented (Dias *et al.*, 2008). Instead of relying on vector control through the spraying of insecticides, a structural approach to reducing the burden of Chagas disease in the Americas would focus on improving the housing stock of poor populations, recognizing that the bug vectors thrive in the building materials use by rural peasants throughout the region. The WHO admits: 'for most NTDs, sustained elimination is possible only with full access to safe water, waste disposal and treatment, basic sanitation and improved living conditions' (WHO, 2012a: 1). Yet in that very same paragraph, the WHO states: 'However, *since this area of work is related to development and not directly to the work of WHO's Department of Control of Neglected Tropical Diseases, it is not discussed in the roadmap*' (WHO, 2012a: 1–2; emphasis added). The statement, in effect, moves discussion of poverty, of inequality, of structural violence off the table – and leaves room only for technical cures such as insecticides and the distribution of mass quantities of pharmaceuticals in the global south as a way of preventing and controlling NTDs.

The quality of housing has been shown to be an important predictor of vector presence and disease transmission (Cedillos, 1988; Feliciangeli *et al.*, 2007;

Prothero and Davenport, 1986). According to the University of Buenos Aires' Ricardo Gürtler *et al.*, 'housing improvement should largely reduce infestations, but it has had a marginal role in vector control programmes except in Venezuela' (2007: 16194). The modus operandi of vector control programmes has been the spraying of insecticides, leaving living conditions in poor states and ignoring the root causes sustaining Chagas disease in poor communities. The structural violence of inequitable access to clean water and safe housing materials is thereby ignored.

As mentioned, vector transmission is the most important way of spreading Chagas disease – but it can also be spread through transfusions with infected blood and can also be passed from mother to foetus through the placenta.[8] Improved blood donation screening mechanisms in Latin America have diminished disease transmission as a result of transfusion (WHO, 2010b). Whereas in 1990 only Argentina, Honduras, Uruguay, and Venezuela performed serological screening of all blood donors for *T. cruzi*, the list of countries that screen all donors now totals 8, including Brazil, the most populous country in the region. Four other countries now screen 99 per cent of blood donors (see Table 5.3).

However, that is not to say that this has resulted in diminished attention to the prospect of *T. cruzi* transmission through blood transfusion and/or organ transplantation. A new wave of articles and WHO reports raise the spectre of a 'globalized Chagas' which will affect non-endemic countries in Europe (Spain, France, UK), as well as Canada and the United States (Basile *et al.*, 2011; Senior, 2007) and, while the risk of vector-transmission is minimal (due to climate, geography, and living conditions), the risk of 'migrating' Chagas is being described with more frequency in the literature. This fits well with Davies' (2010) description of the statist position on global health, wherein a disease is prioritized if it threatens, above all, populations in the advanced industrialized countries. It is a rare time when an NTD overcomes its neglect by virtue of becoming a threat to non-endemic countries as, generally, agents and vectors that transmit NTDs are bound by biology, ecology, and climate to the tropical and sub-tropical zones of the world (Mantilla, 2011).

Schmunis' (2007) analysis of Chagas spreading along immigration routes is an important article in this area. He plotted legal and undocumented migration flows from Latin America to the global north to estimate the global epidemiology of Chagas in non-endemic countries. The result, shown in Figure 5.2, is in stark contrast to the map illustrating the actual distribution of *T. cruzi* infection in the world shown in Figure 5.1.

Schmunis gathered information on the number of immigrants, both documented and undocumented (estimated), from national statistical agencies in receiving countries; he then took into account the prevalence of infection in the country of origin, and estimated the size of the population in each country that may be expected to have *T. cruzi* in their blood. He estimates that the number of infected migrants is in the thousands for Australia, Canada, and Spain, and in the tens or even hundreds of thousands in the United States.

Table 5.3 Countries that screen blood donors for *T. cruzi*, over time

Percentage of donors screened[a]

1993/1995

100	≥ 80 ≤ 90	≥ 70	≥ 50/ ≤ 70	≥ 50
ARG	PAR	CHI	NIC	BOL
HON		GUT	ECU	COL[b]
URU				COR[c]
VEN				ELS
				PAN

1997

100	≥ 99	≥ 70 ≤ 80	≥ 50/ ≤ 70	>50
ARG	HON	CHI	NIC	BOL
ELS	COL	ECU	PER	COR
PAR				PAN[d]
URU				
VEN				

2001/2002

100	≥ 99	≥ 90 ≤ 98	≥ 70 <90	<50
ARG	COL	GUT	BOL	PAN
BRA	PAR	NIC	CHI	COR
ECU	PER			MEX
ELS				
HON				
URU				
VEN				

2004

100	≥ 99	≥ 75 <90	<50
ARG	COL	BOL	MEX
BRA	GUT	CHI	PAN
COR	HON	PER	
ECU	PAR		
ELS			
NIC			
URU			
VEN			

a. Brazil and Mexico reported screening coverage for the first time in 1999; b.: screening coverage, 1.42%; c.: screening coverage, 0%; d.: screening coverage, 0.7%; ARG: Argentina; BOL: Bolivia; BRA: Brazil; CHI: Chile; COL: Colombia; ECU: Ecuador; ELS: El Salvador; GUT: Guatemala; HON: Honduras; MEX: Mexico; NIC: Nicaragua; PAN: Panama; PER: Peru; URU: Uruguay; VEN: Venezuela.

Source: Schmunis (2007) (used with permission).

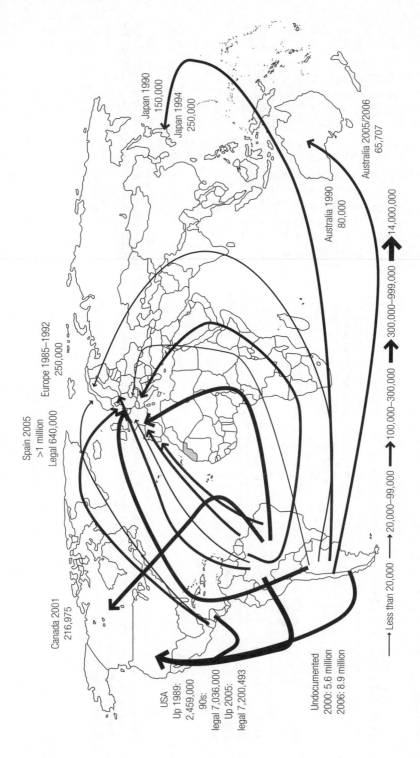

Figure 5.2 Migration flows and Chagas disease in non-endemic countries

Source: Schmunis (2007) (used with permission).

Some work now cites that up to 1 million people may carry Chagas in the United States (Hotez *et al.*, 2012). Schmunis affirms: 'there is ample evidence that non endemic countries harbor a population of individuals infected with *T. cruzi*, and that, sooner or later, nations should have to confront the prevention of transfusion or organ-acquired infection, as well as secondary prevention of congenital infection' (2007: 79). At the same time, Schmunis thoughtfully raises a warning of a possible unintended consequence of this line of analysis, urging that legislation be developed to protect immigrants from discrimination over their *potential* infection.

The spectre of a globalized Chagas has also been raised in other studies. For example, Ana Pérez de Ayala *et al.* (2009) document cases of chagasic cardiomyopathy in immigrants from Latin America in Spain, and Yves Jackson *et al.* (2009) describe congenital transmission of Chagas among Latin American immigrants in Switzerland. Studies such as this perhaps appropriately signal the need for public health efforts against Chagas disease in non-endemic countries; this could be aimed at raising awareness among physicians about the disease, for example. And new procedures could be implemented to ensure that *T. cruzi*-infected blood is not accepted by blood banks. Indeed, the US Food and Drug Administration (FDA) recently issued guidance to blood banks in the United States for screening of Chagas (Ribeiro *et al.*, 2009).

Yet, studies like these can have adverse implications; they take our attention away from the more important picture – from the poor of the global south to the 'worried well' of the global north. Chagas disease in non-endemic countries is part of 'global health', certainly; however, the shift in emphasis and gaze distracts us from the real victims of NTDs, the poorest of the poor, and harkens back to images of the 'sick immigrant' paradigm,[9] where immigrants are to be feared and immigration to be controlled if disease is not to run rampant in otherwise 'clean' places. If this remains the focus, we may end up in a situation where more research funds are spent on Chagas in non-endemic countries than in the places where it really is needed most.

The recent history of Chagas demonstrates how formidable a challenge it presents, and suggests that recent victories need to be considered in context (Briceño-León, 2009). In 1991, the 'Southern Cone Initiative', a regional intergovernmental programme, was launched with the objective of eliminating all domestic and peridomestic populations of *vinchucas* by 2000. Insecticide spraying in that decade showed remarkable effects – particularly in Uruguay, Chile, and Brazil. However, parts of Bolivia, Paraguay, and Argentina showed far more mixed results – suggesting that vector control was not an easy technical enterprise, but that its success depends a great deal on the participation, will, and capacity of local communities, as well as the political force and economic power of regional and national governments. The success of insecticide-based vector control also varies by region, and experts warn that the Southern Cone's success cannot be readily transferred to Central America, where the ecology of the infection and the vector differ in important ways (Hotez, 2008a).[10]

In 1998, the World Health Assembly set a 2005 target date for the interruption of transmission of Chagas disease; a target that was not met. More recently, the WHO Global Network for Chagas Elimination was launched in July 2007. It aims to coordinate global efforts. At its launch, its stated goal was to eliminate the disease by 2010, which unfortunately proved to be an overly optimistic projection (Senior, 2007). Most recently, a 2012 'roadmap' published by the WHO seeks to 'interrupt transmission via intra-domiciliary vectors in Latin America and transmission via blood transfusion in Latin America, Europe and the Western Pacific by 2015' (WHO, 2012: 11), with efforts focused on the large-scale spraying of insecticide.[11]

Notable challenges remain, and the goal of interrupting vectoral transmission remains difficult to achieve (Biolo *et al.*, 2010). Areas treated with insecticide may become reinfested with *vinchucas*, particularly if surveillance systems are not developed with the active participation of the communities involved. Insecticide resistance of bugs is reducing the effectiveness of vector control in some Argentine and Bolivian regions (Dias *et al.*, 2008), and this raises the significant possibility that recent gains will be lost in the near to medium-term future.

Angela Bayer *et al.* (2009) note that Chagas disease in poor *urban* areas is also a very real possibility – with an increase in cases in Peruvian shantytowns. Similarly, Alicia Hidron *et al.* (2010a) have studied *T. cruzi* infection in a large urban public hospital in Bolivia, where they found that 59 per cent of cases of congestive heart failure were attributable to Chagas, and fully 79 per cent of deaths among patients with advanced congestive heart failure occurred among patients infected with *T. cruzi*. Consideration of Chagas in urban settings adds considerable complexity to public health prevention and control strategies, which have until now been focused on rural populations. These are therefore significant warning signs that Chagas will remain very much a threat to the lives of the poor in Latin America. Millions of people with Chagas disease in Latin America will go on to develop chagasic cardiomyopathy and other chronic complications. Only a small percentage will be helped by advanced biomedicine; Isabela Ribeiro *et al.* note 'still to this day, millions of patients remain without adequate treatment for this silently debilitating and potentially fatal disease. Although no official global figures exist, it is estimated that no more than 1 per cent of those infected are believed to receive any treatment at all' (2009: e484). And to be clear: this is a disease spread by a vector that thrives amidst poverty, living and reproducing in the crevices in walls, roofs, and floors of peasant homes.

Overall, the warnings are clear: 'without proper planning or emphasis on consolidation and sustainability, successes may be short lived' (Reithinger *et al.*, 2009: 338). For João Dias *et al.*, 'this is still unfinished business and much remains to be done. The greatest danger ... [is] undue triumphalism' (2008: 195). Eradicating Chagas disease is very much a possibility. But doing so will not require a biomedical vaccine or extraordinary health-producing technologies; instead, something much more basic is required: the large-scale improvement of the living conditions of the poor in Latin America.

A sociology of neglected tropical diseases

In terms of epidemiological indictors, research activity, and policy attention, notable progress has been made against NTDs, but much remains to be done. In particular, much remains to be done from the perspective of social science. For example, sociological or anthropological accounts of NTDs have been scarce – aside from Roberto Briceño-León's (1990) classic book *La Casa Enferma: Sociología de la Enfermedad de Chagas* [*The Sick House: Sociology of Chagas Disease*] and Joseph Bastien's (1998) *The Kiss of Death: Chagas' Disease in the Americas*, no more major sociological or anthropological works on Chagas disease have been published. Moreover, scholarly discussion surrounding NTDs in *The Lancet Infectious Diseases*, the *British Medical Journal*, and the *Pan American Journal of Public Health* has seen limited, if any, engagement by sociologists. NTDs have not featured in discussions in mainstream sociological journals. As a result, the framing of NTDs has been overly narrow, and a situation that is perhaps best understood as a manifestation of structural violence has instead been seen through a technical, rather than socio-political, lens. Solutions proposed for fighting NTDs have been primarily framed as medical interventions (Spiegel *et al.*, 2010) and have taken the form of the MDA of preventive chemotherapy, as well as large-scale spraying of insecticides. As noted earlier in this chapter, the latest WHO 'roadmap' report rules out solutions touching upon development. It does not venture at all into analysis of the issue as one of *social justice*; while the WHO acknowledges that 'for most NTDs, sustained elimination is possible only with full access to safe water, waste disposal and treatment, basic sanitation and improved living conditions' (WHO, 2012: 1) – the WHO pushes those solutions off the agenda by insisting that 'development' is not part of the Organization's mandate.

It is here where the need for sociological engagement is clearest. Sociology – perhaps more than any other discipline – has developed analytical tools for connecting our most personal troubles with the grand public issues in which our lives are enmeshed. A sociological perspective may be particularly helpful in *contextualizing* the role of large-scale insecticide use to control Chagas vectors, and the use of MDA to treat and prevent other NTDs such as schistosomiasis. Such a perspective would highlight, for example, that these approaches for fighting against NTDs need to be understood from a wider perspective, a structural perspective that would incorporate insight from political economy as well as epidemiology.

And while sociology has been slow to enter the field of global health, that is not to say that a 'sociology of NTDs' could not have value for both affected populations and for the discipline itself. A sociological lens may very well be useful in balancing the overly technical/medical perspective that has dominated discussions of MDA and 'anti-poverty vaccines'. Much like the WHO Commission on the Social Determinants of Health (featured in Chapter 7), a sociology of NTDs could emphasize the structural role of the social determinants of health, most of which are now global in nature. The 'promise', to use a term favoured by Mills (1959) in *The Sociological Imagination*, of this line of research would be fundamental improvements in the lives of millions of poor people.

The foundational elements of such a framework have already been offered by Paul Farmer, the noted infectious disease specialist and medical anthropologist. In particular, he urges us to examine four inter-related dimensions of disease:

- social inequalities
- transnational forces
- the dynamics of change
- critical epistemology.

All four dimensions are critical if we are to expand the frame of analysis used in NTD research.

Social inequalities

The questions here are essentially: 'What are the precise mechanisms by which these diseases come to have their effects in some bodies but not in others? What propagative effects might inequality per se contribute?' (Farmer, 1999: 53). Farmer rightfully points out that these kinds of queries were once major research questions for epidemiology and medicine, but that they 'have fallen out of favor, leaving a vacuum' (1996: 265). In terms of NTDs in general, and Chagas in particular, the framing of social inequalities is largely absent in key reports – the WHO report '*Working to Overcome the Global Impact of Neglected Tropical Diseases*' describes how *vinchucas* reside 'in crevices in the walls and roofs of poorly constructed houses' (2010b: 75) – notice the use of 'poorly constructed' *instead* of poor. The issue is not one of housing materials but of poverty, of economic and political marginalization and the inequitable distribution of goods, including construction materials. And while WHO Director-General Margaret Chan's introduction to the report hails its new 'pro-poor' strategy, the phrase 'pro-poor' does not appear in the report itself, other than in her introduction. Chan writes:

> Efforts to control neglected tropical diseases constitute a pro-poor strategy on a grand scale. The logic has changed: instead of waiting for these diseases to gradually disappear as countries develop and living conditions improve, a deliberate effort to make them disappear is now viewed as a route to poverty alleviation that can itself spur socioeconomic development. (WHO, 2010b: v)

Poverty alleviation is still not the starting point in the causal chain and, subsequently, the role of social inequalities as fundamental causes of disease goes unaddressed. Indeed, in this observation, the endpoint is economic development, rather than social justice where no child dies or is disfigured from a disease of poverty.

The global effort against NTDs has been dominated by the goal of nurturing new drug development. And there certainly is a need for this. Yet, as the University of British Columbia's Jerry Spiegel et al. observe, this approach ignores the social roots, the structural foundations, of NTDs: 'these initiatives have largely ignored other manifestations of neglect, such as the weak health systems and poor socio-environmental conditions that cause and/or perpetuate NTDs (Spiegel et al., 2010). There certainly is a great deal to be said for the pharmaceutical industry's neglect of NTDs, despite some welcome developments such as extraordinary donations of medicines for lymphatic filariasis from GlaxoSmithKline and Merck, and the very important new therapies being developed by companies based in the global south (Frew et al., 2009). There is a grave danger, however, that the global fight against NTDs will focus entirely too much on pharmaceutical solutions to structural problems – ignoring the very root causes of infection, and disregarding the historical evidence from the industrialized countries, which shows that the large-scale declines of death rates from infectious diseases, in the long run, are not attributable to biomedical interventions but, rather, to improvements in living conditions (McKinlay and McKinlay, 1977).

Transnational forces

The notion here is that 'A useful means of delimiting a sphere of action – a district, a county, a country – is erroneously elevated to the status of explanatory principle whenever the geographic unit of analysis is other than that defined by the disease itself' (Farmer, 1999: 54). Farmer urges us to go *beyond* geopolitical boundaries in our analyses, noting that 'political borders serve as semipermeable membranes, often quite open to diseases and yet closed to the free movement of cures' (Farmer, 1999: 55). And this turns out to be an incredibly difficult thing to accomplish in health inequality research, for many of our data sources are derived from national governments and agencies. Much of the best data in global health is produced by national ministries of health, and, of course, they only collect data on their own populations.

It is here that the concept of globalization – though contested and defined in different ways by different scholars – offers us a way of overcoming Farmer's challenge. The concept of globalization – encompassing, primarily, economic, but also cultural and political dimensions – allows us to link our biology with global political economy. Above all, it allows us to see how structural violence – social, economic, and political arrangements that harm populations – is the fundamental cause of preventable morbidity and premature mortality around the world.

Perhaps most importantly, the concept of globalization allows us to move *beyond* outdated modernization ideas embedded in Omran's model of epidemiological transition. For it is not enough to posit that the burden of communica-

ble diseases will decrease with further economic development, as if development is a naturally occurring process that will unfold in all places. Dependency
and world-systems theories have suggested that this is not the case, and NTDs
show that this is not the case. NTDs are a pathological manifestation of
inequality; they are the embodiment of living in marginalized and peripheral
conditions. This was perhaps most clearly stated by Mansell Prothero and
Jeffrey Davenport, in their analysis of Chagas disease in Mexico, when they
observed that Chagas is 'closely related to the concept of the periphery', the
disease is directly related to 'the existence of groups of people which are
peripheral in spatial, social, cultural, economic and political terms' (1986:
1322). Only by examining transnational (global) forces can we come to understand the processes that lead to marginalization and, for millions, to lives with
parasitic and bacterial infections.

This calls for work that acknowledges that the lives of the poor are not
divorced from the lives of the wealthy. From this perspective, we see that the
productive capacity of farmers in the global south is significantly constrained
by global trade rules which allow the 'dumping' of foodstuffs in their countries while simultaneously subsidizing producers in the north. And following
Amartya Sen (1981), we see that markets invariably ignore social need – with
hard-hit famine areas continuing to export food, for example, as long as purchasing power is tilted against those in need. The poverty that keeps populations at risk of NTDs is not self-made; it does not exist in a vacuum but,
rather, exists as a social relation with the global economy. Understanding marginalization is not possible without questioning the structural violence that
generates and perpetuates that marginalization; we cannot understand the
periphery without analyzing its ties to the core.

The dynamics of change

Third, Farmer urges: 'As we elaborate lists of the factors that influence the
careers of infectious diseases, we need conceptual tools that will perforce be
historically deep, geographically broad, and at the same time *processual*,
incorporating concepts of change' (Farmer, 1999: 55–6). And it is here where
empirical sociology, combined with efforts from related fields of social epidemiology and medical anthropology, may make the greatest contribution.
What Farmer's notion of the 'dynamics of change' calls for, above all, are rig-
orous empirical and theoretical accounts of how social structure affects vector
transmission and infection with NTDs.

Along these lines, colleagues in Argentina and I have analyzed the social
patterning of Chagas disease using survey data from Santiago del Estero, an
economically marginalized province in northern Argentina (Llovet *et al.*,
2011). We compared households in two communities: Avellaneda and Silípica,
the former area known for 'horizontal' strategies that nurtured community
participation in vector surveillance and control, and the latter an area that,
since 1990, relied on a 'vertical' strategy focused on the spraying of insecticide.

We found that households in Avellaneda – the community with a stronger tradition of community participation in vector surveillance and control activities – had the lowest odds of having *vinchucas* in their home. Additionally, we found greater social inequality in Chagas exposure in Silípica. Our results reinforced the notion that community participation, or perhaps something better seen described as community *empowerment*, could have an important role to play in reducing the burden of NTDs. The *dynamics of change* will be affected, therefore, not just by the behaviours of individuals, but also by the particular histories of communities. Sociological research may yet prove most useful in responding to this challenge.

Critical epistemology

Lastly, Farmer urges us to consider: 'What qualifies as an emerging infectious disease? ... Why do some persons constitute 'risk groups', while others are 'individuals at risk'? ... Why are some epidemics visible to those who fund research and services, while others are invisible?' (Farmer, 1999: 56). The task here is one of identification and framing. Farmer's poignant questions help us to understand why NTDs are not readily known outside specialized research communities, and why they emerge in the mass media of the industrialized nations only if they are seen as a sensationalist *threat*.

The remarkable attention given in the popular press to an editorial calling Chagas 'The New HIV/AIDS of the Americas' in the specialist journal *PLoS Neglected Tropical Diseases* is a case in point. Hotez *et al.*'s provocative essay centred on some features that Chagas and HIV/AIDS have in common, concluding that 'a patient living with Chagas disease faces formidable challenges that resemble those faced by someone living with HIV/AIDS, especially the challenges that occurred in the early years of the HIV/AIDS epidemic' (Hotez *et al.*, 2012). They based their conclusion on the fact that both diseases can be defined as inequities, 'disproportionately affecting people living in poverty'. Hotez *et al.* point out that both diseases are chronic conditions, calling for prolonged and expensive regimens, and that access to treatment for both conditions is highly structured by socioeconomic status and political will. Moreover, both diseases can be 'vertically transmitted' during pregnancy and can also be spread through contaminated blood transfusions. Lastly, they argue that both diseases are highly stigmatizing, raising further barriers to effective diagnosis and treatment.

The Hotez editorial received a very mixed response in the academic literature, with many analysts decrying the comparison as inappropriate, alarmist, and unhelpful (Pays, 2012; Tarleton and Curran, 2012). However, commentators in the mass media seized on the editorial, framing Latin American immigrants as a 'risk group' rather than as 'individuals *at* risk', suggesting that the story was really about the spread of a Third-World disease to the developed world, rather than the continued burden of that disease for millions of people in the global south (for example, see Jauregui, 2012; McNeil, 2012).

If the attention of the global health community is adverted to the 'global Chagas' of infection in non-endemic countries at the expense of the persistent and far higher burdens experienced by the poor in Latin America, much avoidable morbidity will be left unaddressed. The root of the issue will be hidden and, instead of addressing health inequities among populations at risk, the focus may generate a renewed 'sick immigrant' paradigm that sees immigrants as 'risk groups', carriers of disease, and burdens on North American and European health care systems. Moreover, the role of global economic forces in shaping living conditions where NTDs thrive will remain obscured.

A critical epistemology of NTDs is guided by the health of the poor. Such an approach recognizes the considerable improvements that have been made in the past fifteen years, yet refuses to claim victory just yet. Instead, a critical epistemology of NTDs raises alarm about what remains to be done, recognizing that victories to date could easily be overturned by the neglect of the social conditions in which NTDs thrive.

Conclusion

Omran's model of epidemiological transition holds diseases such as Chagas as characteristic of the age of pestilence and famine; it – and the other NTDs – are not supposed to exist in 'post-transition' countries such as Argentina. Yet, diseases like Chagas do continue to afflict the most marginalized segments of society, even in 'middle-income' countries. This shows, once again, the very deep social divides that generate different 'epidemiological worlds,' even within the same nation state. Along these lines, the growing economic powers of India and Brazil continue to be burdened by the presence of NTDs among the poorest of their citizens, and in low-income countries such as Bolivia, NTDs like Chagas produce seemingly 'post-transition' deaths from heart failure.

NTDs are clearly a product of structural violence. They thrive on poverty, on political marginalization and neglect, on unmet basic needs. Global health researchers have mapped the distribution of NTDs, and we now know more than ever before about their prevalence and incidence. Long-hindered by a lack of interest from the brand-name pharmaceutical industry, there are promising signs that new medications may soon be available to treat NTDs – and some of these medications being developed by innovative partnerships including organizations in the global south. At the same time, an excessive focus on biomedical solutions may mean that we will miss a very real opportunity to address the fundamental causes of NTDs – the dire poverty that continues to afflict the poorest billion people of the world in the twenty-first century. Finding the correct balance between biomedical and structural solutions is clearly a pressing challenge. In Chapter 6, I take a closer look at the world's access to medicines and, in particular, I examine the dramatic developments that have unfolded in the past fifteen years in relation to access to antiretroviral medicines for HIV/AIDS.

Treating the Sick

We have seen that structural violence shapes what sociologists call the social determinants of health. These determinants – often global in scope – influence the social gradient in diabetes, obesity, and other risk factors for chronic diseases, as well as one's exposure to neglected tropical diseases that are nurtured by poverty. It is the conditions in which we live and work that shape our life expectancies, that define what Amartya Sen (1999), in *Development as Freedom*, describes as our *capabilities*. Yet, a focus on the social determinants of health should not lead us to ignore medical services; we can appreciate the powerful effects our living conditions have on our health while, at the same time, recognizing that both social determinants and medical services interact, often in ways that multiply the effect of unjust policies. Structural violence is not only the key culprit behind poverty and inequality, it also influences a population's access to medicine and health care services. It affects whether a sick person sees a doctor, whether a woman experiencing life-threatening complications in labour receives medical attention, and whether a person living with HIV can benefit from the remarkable advances of antiretroviral therapy.

Political and economic arrangements *define* a health care system, and to varying extents, political and economic arrangements can serve to exclude people from accessing required health services, be they 'curative' or 'preventive' in nature.[1] In this chapter, I discuss the global epidemiology of the HIV/AIDS pandemic and consider access to highly active antiretroviral medicines. Access to HIV/AIDS drugs has been, as might be expected, a hotly contested area, pitting for-profit pharmaceutical companies against sovereign governments, social movement organizations and non-governmental organizations, as well as global governance institutions such as the WTO.

Advances in HIV therapy have turned the disease, at least for those able to access treatment, into a manageable chronic disease. But HIV therapy remains one of the most challenging tasks in medical care ('t Hoen *et al.*, 2011; Gold, 2002), particularly when the patient is co-infected with tuberculosis, calling for long-term patient–doctor consultation, expensive testing of the patient's CD4 cell count, viral load, and modification of the drug cocktail mix to deal with side-effects and the mutability of the virus.[2] The 'scaling up' of HIV treatment in the global south has been one of the most important challenges in global health in the past fifteen years (Kovsted, 2005; WHO, 2008). Global efforts have resulted in more than 5 million people living with

HIV now benefiting from antiretroviral therapy; yet this amounts to only one third of people thought to be in need of treatment actually receiving it (WHO, 2010a).[3]

After reviewing the global epidemiology of the HIV/AIDS epidemic, I examine access to medicines through the lens of structural violence. In this way, we come to see access to life-saving medicines as dependent on political and economic structures. Some of these structures hinder the widespread distribution of medicines; policies and regulations focused on patent protection for pharmaceutical products and profits for pharmaceutical companies being the most important of these. Yet, some political and economic arrangements have been devised in countries such as Brazil, India, and South Africa with the goal of *increasing* access to life-saving medications. Their experiences show that the key to arresting the epidemic is thus partly within the power of countries in the global south. And as we shall see, countries such as Brazil have not only lead the way by showing that universal access to antiretroviral medicines is feasible, but have also demonstrated remarkable success via multisectoral efforts aimed at prevention (Okie, 2006). Much *can be*, and *has been*, done by applying the principles of social solidarity to the fight against HIV/AIDS.

A country's capacity to enact such policies is partly dependent on their internal resources (with Brazil and India benefiting from a high level of domestic capacity to manufacture generic medicines). However, it is also dependent on external regulations – and, here, the strong influence of global policy enacted at the WTO and operationalized through the agreement on Trade-Related Aspects of Intellectual Property Rights (TRIPS) is of paramount importance ('t Hoen, 2002; Smith *et al.*, 2009). Low- and middle-income countries have overcome tremendous challenges in 'scaling' up access to HIV/AIDS medications for their populations (Bartlett and Shao, 2009); analysis of their successes and the challenges they have overcome offers us a sense of optimism that we can overcome the burden of unnecessary morbidity and premature mortality. The experience of expanding access to HIV drugs since 2001 is, indeed, a good news story of global health, though important challenges loom on the horizon.

Descriptive epidemiology of HIV/AIDS

UNAIDS' latest estimates of the global burden of the AIDS epidemic are truly striking (UNAIDS, 2009). An estimated 33.4 million people were thought to be living with HIV in 2008, as shown in Table 6.1.

The total number of people with HIV reflects two contradictory forces – it rises with increasing rates of infection, but it also rises with increasing effectiveness of treatment; there is therefore bad and good news in the data. Along with the overall number of people that are infected, researchers and policymakers are often even more interested in the incidence of infection; that is, the number of new cases. It is incidence that allows us to determine if the 'tide is

Table 6.1 UNAIDS estimates of the global AIDS epidemic, 2008

Number of people living with HIV	Total	33.4 million
	Adults	31.3 million
	Women	15.7 million
	Children under 15 years	2.1 million
People newly-infected with HIV	Total	2.7 million
	Adults	2.3 million
	Children under 15 years	430,000
AIDS-related deaths	Total	2.0 million
	Adults	1.7 million
	Children under 15 years	280,000

Source: Adapted from UNAIDS (2009) (used with permission).

turning,' so to speak. In 2008, an estimated 2.7 million new infections occurred, with almost half a million new infections among children aged under 15 years. Renewed efforts centred around the MDGs have been launched in recent years to further decrease the number of new cases (WHO, 2010a).

The geographical patterning of the AIDS pandemic is well-known. Of the estimated 33.4 million cases in 2008, 22.4 million were thought to occur in sub-Saharan Africa. South and South-East Asia was estimated to host 3.8 million cases, and Latin America 2.0 million. In contrast, Western and Central Europe were estimated to have 850,000 cases of adults or children with HIV in 2008 and North America 1.4 million (see Table 6.2).

Table 6.2 Geographical distribution of HIV/AIDS, 2008

	Adults and children estimated to be living with HIV	*Estimated number of adults and children newly infected with HIV*	*Estimated adult and child deaths due to AIDS*
North America	1.4 million	55,000	25,000
Caribbean	240,000	20,000	12,000
Latin America	2.0 million	170,000	77,000
Western and Central Europe	850,000	30,000	13,000
Eastern Europe and Central Asia	1.5 million	110,000	87,000
East Asia	850,000	75,000	59,000
South and South-East Asia	3.8 million	280,000	270,000
Oceana	59,000	3,900	2,000
Middle East and North Africa	310,000	35,000	20,000
Sub-Saharan Africa	22.4 million	1.9 million	1.4 million
Total	33.4 million	2.7 million	2.0 million

Source: Adapted from UNAIDS (2009) (used with permission).

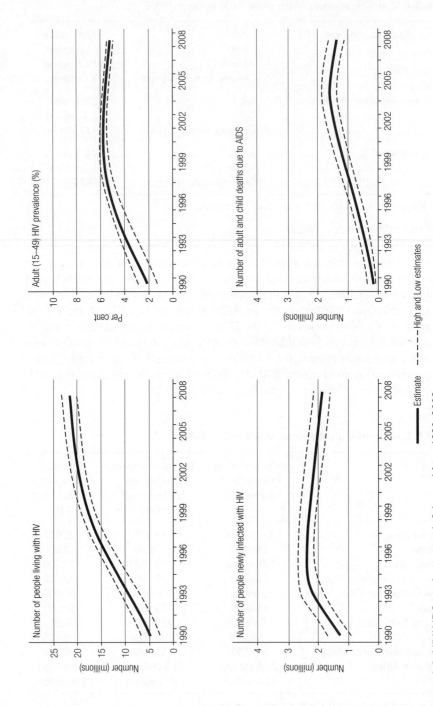

Figure 6.1 HIV/AIDS pandemic in sub-Saharan Africa, 1990–2008
Source: UNAIDS (2009) (used with permission).

The 2008 estimates reveal a striking pattern of geographic concentration. But, being cross-sectional, they do not give us a sense of the dynamics of the HIV/AIDS pandemic. In all areas of the world, the number of people living with HIV has increased since 2001 – again, reflecting continued transmission/infection, as well as improved treatment (and thereby longer life) of people with HIV/AIDS. UNAIDS estimates of the HIV/AIDS pandemic in sub-Saharan Africa for the period 1990–2008 is worth examining in close detail (see Figure 6.1).

Notice that adult HIV prevalence has actually decreased slightly since the late 1990s, as has the number of new people infected (incidence), reflecting the success of prevention, as well as 'treatment as prevention' programmes.[4] The high number of adult and child deaths due to AIDS stands as rebuke against any premature triumphalism, however, as it has only recently started a downward trend.[5]

The effect of antiretroviral therapy

The development of highly active antiretroviral medicines has revolutionized the epidemiology of HIV/AIDS. First available in 1996, these medicines attack the HIV virus at various points, effectively shutting down the virus' capacity to replicate. Antiretroviral treatment can comprise several different drugs (hence the name 'drug cocktail'), and new antiretrovirals continue to be developed – as such, the term 'antiretroviral' applies to a class of drugs, rather than to any one drug in particular. Since its launch, antiretroviral therapy has been highly successful. Consider, for example, Figure 6.2, which illustrates the effect

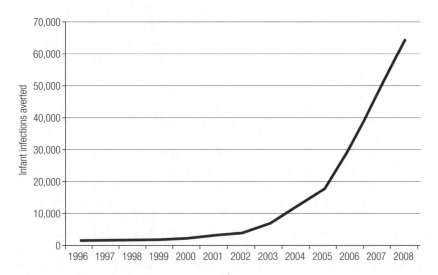

Figure 6.2 Estimated effect of anti-retroviral therapy on infant infections (global figures), 1996–2008

Source: UNAIDS (2009) (used with permission).

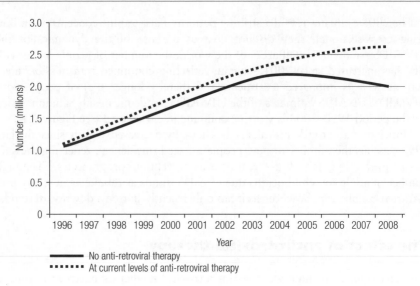

Figure 6.3 Estimated number of AIDS-related deaths with and without anti-retroviral therapy, 1996–2008
Source: UNAIDS (2009) (used with permission).

of antiretroviral medications given to pregnant women. An exponential curve reflects the tremendous worldwide efforts to scale up access to medicines, with more and more lives being saved.

But if we consider this improvement in the wider context of the pandemic, a different picture emerges, as shown in Figure 6.3. The line plotting deaths at current levels of antiretroviral therapy is certainly an improvement over the line plotting deaths with no antiretroviral therapy. But the area *under* the line plotting current levels of antiretroviral therapy is what perhaps matters most – as these are deaths that occurred *as if* medicines were not available.

If analyzed according to the number of life-years added because of antiretroviral medicines, a regional bias is clear: 7.2 million years of life have been added because of these medications in Western Europe and North America, while only 2.3 million and 1.4 million have been added in sub-Saharan Africa and Latin America, respectively – despite their far higher prevalence rates (UNAIDS, 2009). In other words, disease prevalence and therapeutic benefit do not align, and the hardest-hit areas have accrued the lowest level of benefit.

In Chapter 1, I noted that philosophical differences underpin the distinction between a health inequality and a health inequity. The former describes a *difference*, while the latter describes a difference that is deemed to be unnecessary, avoidable, and unfair (Whitehead, 1992). I would argue that the global epidemiology of the HIV/AIDS pandemic is clearly an inequity, and, indeed, one of the most significant of our time. As Judy Rein observes, 'the human tragedy of the global AIDS epidemic often has been compared to the 14th century plague in Europe' (Rein, 2001: 400). And in scope, in level of epidemiological burden, it certainly is comparable. However, the level of inequity is actually *greater* – for, unlike with the fourteenth century plague, we now have the technological and scientific capacity, as well as the human resources, to control the spread of the disease and to treat those infected. But, as a society, we have not done so, and millions have perished – millions perish every year – in large part because of structural barriers enacted to curtail distribution of medicine.

Access to medicines

Access to antiretrovirals has been a fundamental issue in this field, and there have been some notable improvements recent years (UNAIDS, 2009; WHO, 2008c). Yet, the fundamental picture is bleak: the WHO estimates that only one third of people thought to be in need of antiretroviral medicine actually receives it (WHO, 2010a). While it represents a remarkable improvement over the situation in 2001, when only 1 in 1,000 people living with HIV in Africa had access to antiretrovirals ('t Hoen *et al.*, 2011), it nevertheless represents one of the greatest inequities in the era of globalization. Medical science has developed efficacious treatments that render HIV a chronic disease, one that need not cause premature mortality. But the benefit of that medical advance has not been shared across the world. Ambitious targets such as the '3 by 5' programme, which aimed to have 3 million people on antiretroviral therapy by 2005, have increased the reach of these medicines. The latest global target agreed to by world leaders at a special meeting of the United Nations in 2010 calls for universal access to be achieved around the world by 2015 (United Nations, 2011b). And while a decade ago treatment had a price tag of US$10,000–15,000 per patient per year, the ramping up of production of generic medications in places such as India has seen prices for first-line HIV treatment decrease to less than US$1 per day ('t Hoen *et al.*, 2011).

A fundamental issue in the pricing, distribution, and eventual availability of HIV medicines revolves around patent protection. A patent is a legal instrument that places restrictions on the use of intellectual property; in the case of pharmaceuticals, a patent awards the patent-holder (usually the firm that developed the drug) exclusive rights to produce and sell the medication. A patent works by 'creating artificial scarcity and sustaining a higher price than the market would bear under normal, competitive circumstances' (Zacher and Keefe, 2008: 113). According to the London School of Hygiene and Tropical Medicine's Richard Smith *et al.*, 'patents have been the mainstay of policy to ensure investments in pharmaceutical research and development, acting as guarantor of monopoly rents' (2009: 685). Supporters of the patent system argue that a patent, and hence the short-term monopoly it provides, are required for the pharmaceutical industry to make up the costs of research and development. According to that perspective, the excessive short-term profits a company may make while their medicine is patented pay back their expenditure in research and development.

Critics, on the other hand, emphasize the need for radical expansion of access to medicines, and show that generic production of medicines reduces costs of pharmaceuticals by significant amounts. For example, the HIV drug *fluconaloze* can cost US$55/150 mg from a generic manufacturer in India, as opposed to US$697 in Malaysia, US$703 in Indonesia, and US$817 in the Philippines, where it is manufactured under patent protection (Sykes, 2002; Zacher and Keefe, 2008). At the same time, critics of patent protection for medicines point out that much of the basic science underlying drug development is publicly funded in the United States through the National Institutes of Health, rejecting the pharmaceutical industry's claim that short-term monopoly profits are needed to recover research and development costs. Critics have also pointed out that brand-name pharmaceuticals spend more on marketing than they do on research and development of new products (Moynihan and Cassels, 2005). Lastly, critics of patent protection for pharmaceutical products argue that this is a market where the standard assumptions of economic markets are not viable; there is no 'choice' in the decision to purchase a drug, for example, as there is in the choice of purchasing a consumer good (Stiglitz, 2008). And relying on demand to generate supply is problematic, in the sense that poor populations in the global south will never be able to amass the 'market power' needed to entice production of medicines for diseases that afflict only them: the very definition of a 'market failure'. The result is the '10/90' gap, where approximately only 10 per cent of the global drug research and development expenditure is devoted to diseases that generate 90 per cent of the global burden of disease (Zacher and Keefe, 2008).

Prior to the establishment of the WTO, most countries in the global south had a very lax regulatory structure with respect to patents for pharmaceuticals. According to Jillian Cohen and Patricia Illingworth, 'prior to TRIPS, many governments in developing countries had adopted an explicit policy preference not to honour intellectual property protection for pharmaceuticals in an effort to promote self-sufficiency in the production of basic medicines and as in the case of India, develop a competitive local industry' (2003: 33). Indeed, prior to the TRIPS agreement, India's legislation allowed for patents on pharmaceutical processes but not products, meaning that generic manufacturers could produce pharmacologically similar substances but through a different manufacturing process. Brazil, in contrast, did not allow patents to be established for pharmaceutical products at all (Rein, 2001). Both countries developed substantial domestic industries capable of producing world-class pharmaceutical products. In other words, a protectionist perspective held sway, and what in other industries is called 'import substitution' was prioritized. Local access to locally produced medicines was central to this strategy.

With the formation of the WTO in 1995, a renewed effort to strengthen worldwide intellectual property rights took hold. The WTO developed out of the 1947 General Agreement on Tariffs and Trade (GATT), the post-World War II multilateral body charged with developing international trade regulations. As part of the formation of the WTO during the global negotiations known as the 'Uruguay Round', four major agreements were signed that affected global public health:

- the Agreement on Sanitary and Phytosanitary Measures (SPS)
- the General Agreement on Trade in Services (GATS)
- the revised Agreement on Technical Barriers to Trade (TBT)
- the Agreement on Trade-Related Aspects of Intellectual Property (TRIPS).

In principle, all of the agreements sought to balance the desire to lower barriers to trade with a country's power to protect in citizenry (for example, by rejecting imports of contaminated beef or other foodstuffs). And while all of these agreements have public health implications, it is the TRIPS agreement that has generated the most important disagreements between countries of the south and the north. Through its regulations on intellectual property rights, TRIPS affects the health of millions of people around the world.

The University of British Columbia's Mark Zacher and Tania Keefe (2008) show that TRIPS emerged as the policy objective of a powerful intellectual property lobby that sought to strengthen protection against the appropriation of intellectual property around the globe. The lobby reflected the concern that technological advancement had made intellectual property more difficult to protect (in the case of medicines, this amounts to a growing industrial capacity among generic manufacturers in the global south). According to Zacher and Keefe (2008), the intellectual property lobby was particularly strong in the United States, where they succeeded in getting legislation passed that enabled the United States to act unilaterally against countries that failed to protect US-held intellectual property rights. Their analysis is supported by Joseph Stiglitz's assessment: 'I believe one of the main reasons the pharmaceutical industry was pushing for TRIPS was that they wanted to reduce access to generic medicines' (Stiglitz, 2008: 1701). Overall, the US-based lobby succeeded in framing the discussion as one of intellectual property rights at the WTO, where they formed a formidable bloc with representatives from the European Union and Japan.

The TRIPS agreement required WTO member countries to align their national policies with respect to intellectual property, including patents, by 2005 for developed countries and by 2016 for developing countries (Morris, 2009).[6] It established global minimum standards for the protection of intellectual property, and called for a minimum of twenty years' patent protection on pharmaceutical products (Smith et al., 2009). If a country did not align with TRIPS regulations, they could face crippling trade sanctions. The agreement generated immediate backlash, as low- and middle-income countries would face new and more stringent barriers on their capacity to protect public health in their territories. For example, complying with TRIPS norms would significantly curtail India's capacity to manufacture generic medicines and sell them (or even donate them) abroad. It is with respect to access to HIV medicines where this conflict came to a head; as 't Hoen et al. note, 'The AIDS crisis has radically changed conceptions of and policy approaches to patents on medicines' (2011). The scope of the AIDS pandemic, combined with a strong global social movement organized around issues of health equity and effective antiretroviral therapy, created politically charged battles over intellectual property rights, patents, national sovereignty, and human suffering.

Perhaps most important in coming to understand the structural barriers posed by the TRIPS agreement are the so-called 'flexibilities' in the agreement itself.[7] These aspects of the agreement give countries significant political leeway, though the extent to which countries can enact some of the flexibilities has been called into question, as I shall show when considering the experiences of Brazil and South Africa.

Consider that TRIPS contains the following clauses:

- Article 8(1), *Principles*: 'Members may, in formulating or amending their laws and regulations, adopt measures necessary to protect public health and nutrition, and to promote the public interest in sectors of vital importance to their socio-economic and technological development.'
- Article 30 *Exceptions to Rights Conferred* 'Members may provide limited exceptions to the exclusive rights conferred by a patent, provided that such exceptions do not unreasonably conflict with a normal exploitation of the patent and do not unreasonably prejudice the legitimate interests of the patent owner, taking account of the legitimate interests of third parties.'
- Article 31 *Other Use Without Authorization of the Right Holder* 'Where the law of a Member allows for other use of the subject matter of a patent without the authorization of the right holder, including use by the government or third parties authorized by the government ... any such use shall be authorized predominately for the supply of the domestic market of the member authorizing such use.' (WTO, 2012)

Together, these clauses have come to be understood as granting countries that are members of the WTO two very important capacities:

- the power to grant *compulsory licenses*
- the ability to use *parallel imports*.

A compulsory licence is 'granted by a WTO member to another producer, giving them the right to produce the patented product without the consent of the patent holder' (Cockerham and Cockerham, 2010: 135). In other words, a country – despite signing up to TRIPS – can, in theory, grant a compulsory licence to a company that is not the patent-holder and that company can go on to produce the patented product. It is important to note, however, that compulsory licences come with export restrictions; a country is given a compulsory licence to produce for its own population, and *only* under public health emergencies. They are not supposed to sell or donate it to other countries. This has been an incredibly powerful provision in the agreement; the *threat* of compulsory licences has helped Brazil to negotiate lower prices for antiretrovirals from brand-name pharmaceuticals, as we shall see.

Parallel imports have proved to be equally important – and controversial – with respect to HIV treatments. The term refers to a country importing goods that were lawfully made in another country but were not intended for distribution in the country importing the goods. Rein observes that 'this loophole/ambiguity is especially relevant to the parallel importation of pharmaceuticals, as there are significant price differentials on the same medicines legally produced in, or exported to, different countries' (2001: 385). Compulsory licences and parallel imports were both sources of conflict in the recent experiences of Brazil and South Africa, as will be shown.

The contested production of pharmaceuticals

Countries such as Brazil and India have well-developed industrial capacities for manufacturing pharmaceuticals, particularly generics. And they have leveraged that capacity to improve the health of their populations. Their experience offers important lessons on access to medicines and the feasibility of universalizing access to antiretroviral therapy.

Brazil is often hailed in the global health literature as a success story for its innovative approach to HIV/AIDS prevention and care (Murray *et al.*, 2011; Nunn *et al.*, 2007; Okie, 2006). Part of its success is derived from a very persistent and aggressive effort to prevent new HIV infections. According to Susan Okie:

> At the beginning of the 1990s, the epidemics in Brazil and South Africa, both ranked as middle-income countries, were at a similar stage, with a prevalence of HIV infection of about 1.5 percent among adults of reproductive age. But by 1995, the year before Brazil's treatment program was established, the HIV epidemic in South Africa had begun to explode, with a prevalence already greater than 10 percent, whereas the infection rate in Brazil had declined by half. (2006: 1977)

Brazil captured the global health research community's attention with its prevention efforts, which include targeting high-risk groups, including injection-drug users (through needle- and syringe-exchange programmes) and commercial sex workers (Malta *et al.*, 2010).[8] Brazil has also emphasized HIV prevention in prisons, 'a setting for viral transmission that can greatly influence a country's epidemic, but an environment that has been neglected in the United States and most other countries' (Okie, 2006: 1979). Its programme has been described as 'multilevel' (Murray *et al.*, 2011), as it incorporates responses implemented through national, state, and municipal governments, the Catholic church, as well as civil society groups representing a range of vulnerable populations (Berkman *et al.*, 2005; Le Loup *et al.*, 2009).

Brazil's globally recognized National AIDS programme 'has arguably produced the largest and broadest response to HIV/AIDS of any country in the developing world through a rights-based, solidarity approach to HIV prevention and care' (Murray *et al.*, 2011: 946). Building strategic alliances with a range of sectors – from the Church to the pornographic film industry – Brazil's strategy has emphasized *solidarity over ideology* for the sake of reaching as many people as possible (Garcia and Parker, 2011; Grangeiro *et al.*, 2009).

Along with establishing aggressive programmes for preventing the spread of HIV, Brazil caught the world's attention when its Congress enacted legislation in 1997 providing free treatment with new antiretroviral medicines (Galvão, 2002). From 1997 to 2005, the Brazilian government spent US$3.5 billion in its response to HIV/AIDS, and more than half of that was allocated to antiretroviral pharmaceuticals (Okie, 2006). Much of that money was spent producing generic versions of antiretroviral medicines that were patented before 1996, and therefore were not covered by TRIPS regulations. According to Okie:

> Of 16 antiretroviral drugs currently purchased by the government, Brazil manufactures 8 [as of 2006]. Relying chiefly on domestic generic AIDS drugs and negotiating discounts for drugs that were to be imported have helped the government to steadily reduce its average annual cost for antiretroviral therapy, from $6,240 per patient in 1997 to $1,336 in 2004. (2006: 1980)

One approach used by Brazil to lower the price of HIV medicines was to invoke the 'compulsory licence' clause of TRIPS. Indeed, it is in Brazil where the TRIPS regulations came to the foreground of international attention. Brazil was able to use its capacity to issue compulsory licences in negotiations with drug companies, saving what experts estimate to be US$1 billion between 2001 and 2005 in the process (Day, 2007). Brazil also used its capacity to import (via the process of parallel importing) generic medicines from India, further pressuring the pharmaceutical industry to lower its prices in Brazil (Ahmad, 2001).

Not only did Brazil challenge the holders of existing patents, it also rejected new patent claims based on existing medications. Indeed, new patents for antiretrovirals that already comprise part of the first-line WHO-recommended treatment have been rejected by Brazil (for tenofovir disoproxil fumarate) and also by India (for tenofovir disoproxil and darunavir) (Morris, 2009). Both Brazil and India have patent laws prohibiting 'evergreening' – the pharmaceutical industry strategy of patenting molecules with small chemical changes to an existing parent molecule – and both countries consider opposition to patent applications (which is ignored in most other countries). In both countries, MSF filed opposition statements to the patent applications.

Brazil's lesson to the world is incredibly important: 'Brazil was the first developing country to provide widespread access to HIV/AIDS treatment through its national programme; the Brazilian programme demonstrated to the world that ARVs could be provided safely even with limited toxicity and efficacy monitoring' ('t Hoen *et al.*, 2011). Brazil's success started with its capacity to produce low-cost generic versions of patented medications. However, with the development of TRIPS, Brazil experienced the same pressure as other developing countries to respect intellectual property rights and patent protections of brand-name pharmaceutical companies. Indeed, Brazil even advanced the implementation of TRIPS regulations, bringing national laws in line with the new WTO framework far in advance of the 2016 date set in the TRIPS agreement. And while TRIPS has certainly constrained the Brazilian generic pharmaceutical industry's capacity to circumvent patents, the sheer size of the economy has meant that Brazil – more than any other country in the global south – has been able to use the flexibilities in the TRIPS agreement to its advantage (Nunn *et al.*, 2007). However, the same cannot be said for other global south countries. Thailand – which also tried to use domestic compulsory licensing flexibilities to improve its population's access to antiretroviral treatment – was not as successful, and backed away from issuing licences in response to strong trade pressure from the United States (Cawthorne *et al.*, 2007; Ford *et al.*, 2007; Kuek *et al.*, 2011; Rein, 2001).

South Africa's experience with antiretroviral medicines in the 1990s also represents a watershed moment in global health. At the end of the 1990s, the country faced one of the world's fastest-growing rates of HIV infection. The situation was particularly dire. Life expectancy at birth – one of the crudest, but most important of all epidemiological indicators – stood at 61.5 years in 1990, having risen from a 1980s value of 56.9, despite the pathogenic effects of the discriminatory apartheid regime. But South Africa's life expectancy data reveal the devastating impact of the HIV/AIDS crisis: by 1995, life expectancy had decreased to 59.98, by 2000 life expectancy had decreased to 54.8 (lower than the figure in 1980), and by 2005, life expectancy had decreased to only 51.1 years (UNDP, 2012). As the University of Witwatersrand's Patrick Bond points out:

> at least 16 percent of the population, 20 percent of pregnant women, and 45 percent of the armed forces tests HIV-positive; and black people are predominantly at risk of dying early from AIDS ... paying for expensive pharmaceutical products licensed to extremely profitable international companies (one of which paid its chief executive officer a salary of $146 million in 1998) intensifies the problems South Africa faces. (1999: 765–6)

South Africa realized that savings of 50 per cent to 90 per cent could be made if it could switch from purchasing brand-name antiretrovirals from international pharmaceutical companies and, instead, rely on generics. To this effect, the country passed the 'Medicines Act' of 1997; it was signed by President Nelson Mandela and promised a revolutionary expansion of treatment capacity. In particular, the South African legislation gave the Minister of Health explicit power to issue compulsory licences and simultaneously increased the country's capacity to import drugs from any other country (via the process of parallel importing). Rein notes that 'these provisions prompted a political storm initiated by the multinational research pharmaceutical industry concerned about the global effect that South Africa's actions would have on securing patent rights to pharmaceuticals' (Rein, 2001: 401). Indeed, the pharmaceutical industry challenged the law in court with significant backing from the United States.

South Africa's 1997 Medicines Act enabled 'parallel importing' and offered to impose compulsory licensing, wherein the country's generic drug industry could make patented medications without permission of the patent holder. While controversial, both of these stipulations are permissible under international law in the case of health emergencies. But the pharmaceutical industry took it as a direct challenge. Bond cites a spokesperson for the Pharmaceutical Research and Manufacturers of America (PhRMA) as stating: 'There are ways to make drugs available to the poor in a country like South Africa. We need to look for economic answers to economic questions ... and not say the answer to this economic question is we'll just steal' (1999: 768). A total of 40 South African and international pharmaceutical companies joined the fight against the Medicines Act, claiming violation of intellectual property rights. They were supported by the US government, which in retaliation withheld 'preferential tariff treatment' from certain South African exports in 1998.

The result was a public relations disaster for the pharmaceutical industry. As a result, the industry responded to the global outcry and withdrew their case a few days after the start of the trial ('t Hoen *et al.*, 2011; Singh *et al.*, 2007).[9] The controversy was also a public relations concern for then-US Vice-President Al Gore, whose role in the affair received scathing critique from AIDS activists in the 2000 Presidential election; he was seen as siding with the pharmaceutical industry. Signs proclaiming 'No Medical Apartheid!', 'Gore's Greed Kills', and 'AIDS Drugs for Africa Now!' were fixtures of protests in his election campaign (Bond, 1999). One of Al Gore's opponents in the 2000 US election, Ralph Nader, commented: 'the US government is officially punishing South Africa for permitting its public health officials to speak out on trade and intellectual property issues in the World Health Organization ... In fact, everything South Africa is seeking to do is legal under the WTO/TRIPS agreement' (quoted in Bond, 1999: 776).

The South African crisis galvanized global attention towards the question of patent protection for live-saving HIV treatments. Building on that momentum, the developing countries pressured the WTO Ministerial Conference in November 2001 to adopt the 'Doha Declaration' on TRIPS and Public Health. The Doha Declaration affirmed that the TRIPS agreement 'can and should be interpreted and implemented in a manner supportive of WTO Members' right to protect public health and, in particular, to promote access to medicines for all' (WTO, 2001). Moreover, the Doha Declaration begins:

We recognize the gravity of the public health problems afflicting many developing and least-developed countries, especially those resulting from HIV/AIDS, tuberculosis, malaria and other epidemics. We stress the need for the WTO TRIPS Agreement to be part of the wider national and international action to address these problems ... we reaffirm the right of WTO members to use, to the full, the provisions in the TRIPS Agreement, which provide flexibility for this purpose. (WTO, 2001)

For 't Hoen *et al.*, 'this landmark event represented the first significant push back to the relentless march to strengthen private intellectual property rights without regard for societal consequences in poor countries' (2011). But while this has been declared and reaffirmed at the WTO, the United States has pushed for even more stringent controls on compulsory licences and parallel imports, and, in many cases, has been able to establish stronger mechanisms in bilateral trade agreements (so-called 'TRIPS-plus regulations') (Kerry and Lee, 2007).[10]

The Brazilian and South African experiences teach us that political will, combined with economic and legal resources, can be used to increase access to expensive treatments in the global south. And while much remains to be done in this area, the experience of scaling up access to antiretroviral treatment is celebrated by many in global health as one of the most remarkable achievements in recent decades (UNAIDS, 2009). Yet, at the same time, there are dissenting views on this and, in particular, there is a school of thought that says it is a mistake to focus on scaling up treatment to antiretroviral therapy.

Scaling up treatment

The speed at which new medical technologies, including medications, are disseminated around the world is a critical issue in global health. It is at the root of a fundamental problem in our world – to what extent can scientific advancements be shared with the poorest, with those least able to pay? This problem has been at the centre of the global HIV/AIDS crisis since the development of antiretroviral therapy that transformed the HIV virus from a death sentence to something more akin to a manageable chronic condition.

The University of Copenhagen's Jens Kovsted has analyzed the global discourse on the scaling up of HIV/AIDS treatment, and found six central arguments raised *against* the scaling up of treatment in the global south. These arguments are listed below:

- Antiretroviral therapy is too expensive
- Health systems of the affected countries cannot support such a technically advanced treatment
- Focusing on antiretroviral therapy will divert resources from prevention
- It would exacerbate existing inequalities

■ It would lead to an increase in risk behavior
■ It is too complicated for poor settings; low compliance will lead to drug-resistant strains of HIV. (Kovsted, 2005)

Kovsted notes that when antiretroviral medicines were first introduced in the United States and the other OECD countries in 1996–97, 'most agencies and experts were agreed that scaling up to include any other than the wealthy and well-connected fraction of developing country populations would be quite impossible' (2005: 465). Due particularly to the cost of the medicine and the complexity of its administration, these agencies and experts deemed them to be beyond the reach of the global south. Since then – and it only has been fifteen years – a remarkable change has occurred in the global discourse on access to medicines, and all major international agencies, including the United Nations and the World Bank, now work with the goal of achieving universal access to antiretrovirals around the world. Indeed, the prevailing idea now is that ensuring access to HIV/AIDS medications is difficult and expensive but, nevertheless, a fundamental priority of global health.

Kovsted argues that in the fifteen years since the launch of antiretrovirals, only one of the six reasons first raised against the scaling up of treatment has been addressed. He finds that of the six reasons arguing against the scaling up of treatment, only the first – the cost of antiretroviral drugs – has been addressed as a result of dramatic decreases in the price of HIV/AIDs pharmaceuticals. The others remain unresolved.

Understanding the notion that antiretroviral medicines are too expensive for developing countries requires an analysis of the political economy of pharmaceuticals.[11] The price of medicine, after all, is not a science, but a reflection of market power (Farmer *et al.*, 2001; Zainol *et al.*, 2011). When first launched into the market, antiretroviral therapy cost between US$10,000 and US$15,000 per person per year, a cost that made it far too expensive for health care systems in the global south. Prices for antiretroviral medicines stayed high for the next five years. WHO data from 2001 indicate that only 2 per cent of people in advanced stages of HIV infection worldwide were receiving antiretroviral medicines in that year (WHO, 2002). During this same period, the brand-name pharmaceutical industry made record-breaking profits, far outpacing other companies in the Fortune 500 (Blech, 2006; Manners, 2006).

The global market for antiretroviral medicines changed dramatically in 2001, when Cipla (a generic manufacturer in India) entered the market, offering state-of-the-art 'triple combination therapy' for US$350 per person per year (Waning *et al.*, 2010). At the same time, civil society groups such as MSF and philanthropic organizations such as the Clinton Foundation supported new pressure from Brazil and South Africa for brand-name pharmaceutical companies to lower their costs. Between 2004 and 2008, the price for first-line antiretroviral drugs dropped by 30–68 per cent (AVERT, 2012) and, at the time of writing, Indian generic manufacturers supply the majority of antiretroviral medicines to countries in the global south (Waning *et al.*, 2010). Even so, this supply is threatened by TRIPS regulations, and any new medicines brought to market in the post-TRIPS environment are unlikely to be produced by generic manufacturers in India without significant legal challenges (Chatterjee, 2005; Havlir and Hammer, 2005).

Kovsted argues that, of the six arguments levelled in opposition to the scaling up of antiretroviral therapy in the global south, only the first argument (based on pricing of medicines) has been reasonably addressed. Let us now examine arguments 2–5, all of which Kovsted argues still reflect barriers to achieving universal access to HIV/AIDS drugs.

The second argument against the scaling up of antiretroviral therapy in the global south is based on the argument that health systems in the most affected countries cannot support such a technically advanced treatment. For example, Farmer *et al.* observe: 'much is made of the complexity of HIV management, which would defeat, according to conventional wisdom, the overburdened and undertrained health personnel in the countries most affected by HIV' (Farmer *et al.*, 2001: 407). And there certainly is a real danger of this occurring; health care systems around the world are overstretched, and incorporating a challenging new stream of services represents a formidable challenge, particularly in settings of 'epidemiological overlap', where health care services need to fight both communicable and non-communicable diseases.

The underlying challenge here is to strengthen health care systems and, in particular, primary health care systems. Such language is part of most initiatives that seek to scale up access to treatment (Kovsted, 2005), but many analysts warn that the opposite is occurring, and primary care systems in much of the global south are experiencing significant 'brain drain'. While globalization offers the potential for much good – for example, increasing the flow of medicines around the world – here, we are also concerned about its potential to inflict significant damage, with progressively more health care personal trained in the global south migrating to practice medicine in wealthier countries (see Crush, 2002).

While weakened health care systems are certainly a barrier to scaling up treatment, one can also argue that the HIV/AIDS crisis and the availability of efficacious treatment actually offer a tremendous opportunity to *strengthen* primary care around the world. Along these lines, Farmer *et al.* point out that while there are very real needs to strengthen health care infrastructure in the countries hardest hit by HIV, 'there is reason to believe that minor modifications could improve local capacity to care for those sick with advanced HIV disease' (Farmer *et al.*, 2001: 407). Indeed, that is what Famer and his colleagues at Partners in Health (PIH) have shown with remarkable power through their provision of HIV and tuberculosis care in the poorest parts of Haiti (Farmer, 1992; Farmer *et al.*, 2001). Their success is based on several factors, perhaps most notably their use of community health workers, or *accompagnateurs*. Integral to the PIH model, community health workers provide a range of services, including home visits to support directly-observed treatment regimens, nutritional support, and transportation stipends to patients. Farmer *et al.* have shown that local systems relying on community health workers can significantly improve adherence to treatment while, at the same time, supporting a community's capacity to respond to patient needs. Their work in Haiti has shown that community-based treatment of AIDS is highly effective in poor settings (Koenig *et al.*, 2004), work they have also replicated in Rwanda and other countries (Farmer *et al.*, 2001; Franke *et al.*, 2013). The experience of Brazil's National AIDS programme adds further optimism that HIV/AIDS medicines can be used with great effectiveness, even in the absence of the most advanced diagnostic tools.

The third argument against the scaling up of antiretroviral medicines in developing countries argues that a focus on these medicines will divert scarce resources from prevention. Kovsted argues that this is the key argument of 'economic pragmatists', who focus on finding the most cost-effective way to fight disease. Taken to an extreme, this position argues: 'Given that fiscal and human resources are scarce ... funds should be allocated to prevention. The fact that millions of infected people are left without antiretroviral treatment is perceived to be an unfortunate but unavoidable consequence of the efforts to avoid an even greater disaster in the future' (Kovsted, 2005: 467). Earlier in this book, I examined a similar notion with respect to the burden of chronic non-communicable diseases; that health services should delay focusing on these conditions until after communicable diseases are controlled. In both cases, the underlying logic is one of cost-effectiveness, the notion that health care decisions need to be guided by analysis of where scarce resources can have their greatest effect. And it is true that prevention is cheaper, more cost-effective, than treatment with expensive new drugs. Perhaps the greatest challenge that I see in global health is the urgent need to overcome this type of thinking that sees people as economic units; for, only when we go beyond simplistic/short-term cost–benefit thinking, can we get to a nuanced analysis of health care as a human right.

By 2005, the HIV/AIDS literature called for prevention *and* treatment, replacing talk of prevention *versus* treatment. And most recently, the discourse has shifted again, so that increasingly one hears of treatment *as* prevention. Stemming primarily from the work of a team of HIV researchers/scientists lead by Dr Julio Montaner, this approach emphasizes that the provision of antiretroviral therapy to infected people has beneficial effects in decreasing the rate at which they would transmit the virus to others (Harris and Montaner, 2011; Montaner, 2011). As is the case with MDA for lymphatic filariasis and other NTDs, the treatment *as* prevention paradigm in HIV/AIDS emphasizes that medicines have primary effects on the body of the sick person and very important secondary benefits for their communities. By treating an individual you decrease the likelihood that they will transmit the disease to others.

However, this is hampered by the quietly acknowledged double-standard that exists in the global discourse on scaling up access to antiretrovirals. A debate exists among specialists regarding when to start antiretroviral therapy in low- and middle-income countries – or perhaps this would be better phrased as 'among poor people in low- and middle-income countries', as there is little doubt that high-income groups in low- and middle-income countries will have access to the same standards of care as high-income groups in high-income countries. Bartlett and Shao (2009) note that, at present, treatment decisions in low- and middle-income countries rest on clinical assessment, and when available, immunological testing of the CD4 count. The better standard testing of viral-load is expensive and generally not available in poorer settings. The result is that 'by comparison with people in high-income countries, individuals in low- and middle-income countries might have very low baseline CD4 cell counts and more advanced disease by the time they start antiretroviral therapy' (Bartlett and Shao, 2009: 638–9).

And the implications of this can be severe: at the individual level, a later initiation of antiretroviral therapy has been shown to result in weaker immunological recovery, and 'more rapid progression to AIDS or death' (Bartlett and Shao, 2009: 639). At the community level, later initiation of therapy means that the preventive benefits of treatment are not realized as soon as they could be, meaning potentially avoidable transmission of HIV to uninfected people (Dabis et al., 2010). Notably, there are signs that this may be changing, though different thresholds continue to exist for different areas of the world. The latest WHO guidelines call for treatment to begin in 'resource poor' settings when a patient's CD4 cell count is at 350 cells/mm^3, whereas it used to recommend treatment initiation at 200 cells/mm^3. In contrast, recommendations in wealthy countries recommend earlier initiation of therapy, with a CD4 cell count of 500 cells/mm^3 ('t Hoen et al., 2011).

The unavailability of viral-load testing also hampers the clinical management of HIV. Consider that a patient on antiretroviral therapy will require continuous analysis of the effectiveness of their drug mix, and when so-called 'first-line' drugs begin to fail, a patient would be switched to 'second-line' (and, in high-income countries, eventually to 'third-line') drugs.[12] Knowing when to switch regimens is one of the most challenging aspects of HIV care, and physicians relying on cheaper CD4 counts rather than more expensive viral-load testing are at a disadvantage. Switching too soon means that months or years of potentially effective treatment is foregone. Switching too late is thought to reduce the effectiveness of the second-line drug regimen (Bartlett and Shao, 2009).

The fourth argument against scaling up treatment in the global south is based on the concern that doing so would exacerbate existing inequalities in those countries. The argument here is that expansion of treatment can be expected to be a top-down process, with treatment first being available in the high-resource urban areas of the developing world. Better-equipped and better-resourced hospitals in capital cities are the launching pad for expanding treatment into semi-urban and rural areas; the populations served by these specialty centres and clinics will not be representative of the population, neither will this strategy reflect the underlying epidemiology of HIV/AIDS along the social gradient. Rather, it will reflect population inequities in access to medical care. For Kovsted, 'initial discrimination is increasingly perceived as an unfortunate but unavoidable consequence of scaling up HAART [highly active antiretroviral therapy]' (2005: 473). In other words, the idea that expanding treatment will involve at least a short-term increase in inequalities remains accepted. Little more has been published in the global health literature on this, perhaps reflecting our collective inability to imagine how things could be otherwise.

The fifth argument against scaling up treatment raised by Kovsted is based on the moralistic idea that universalizing access to HIV/AIDS medicine will lead to an increase in risk behaviour. Similar arguments are raised in the harm reduction literature against safe-injection sites and needle-exchange programmes for injection drug users (Kerr *et al.*, 2005). In the HIV/AIDS literature, this concern has dovetailed with requirements from the United States that prevention programmes focus on abstinence. In contrast, Brazil has emphasized the mass distribution of condoms and aggressive advertising aiming to increase their use by young people. Brazil's programme has also focused on diminishing stigma associated with getting tested for HIV, which critics may also see as potentially increasing risk behaviour. Kovsted notes that there is no scientific basis for the belief that the availability of medicine for HIV/AIDS will lead to an increase in risk behaviour, but as an argument against the expensive scaling up of treatment, the notion is still part of the discourse.

Lastly, Kovsted identifies a school of thought opposed to the scaling up access to HIV/AIDS medicines that is based on the argument that the treatment is too complicated for poor settings, that the low compliance we might expect in these settings will lead to drug-resistant strains of HIV. Combined with a global health as 'threat' lens of analysis, one can see how the spectre of a drug-resistant strain of HIV may be a significant concern in populations where antiretroviral medicines have been used for the past fifteen years. But structural violence is at the root of this concern as well. Compliance with medical instructions is inextricably intertwined with patients' capacity not only to adhere to the prescribed medical regimen, but also their capacity and resources to provide for their living conditions. Farmer *et al.* poignantly argue: 'some have expressed alarm regarding the spread of drug-resistant virus if HAART is used where health infrastructure is weak. Just as it is possible to exaggerate the complexity of these regimens, so too is it possible to confound the main causes of acquired resistance' (Farmer *et al.*, 2001: 406–7). Failure to adhere to treatment is fundamentally associated with poverty and lack of resources – housing instability, lack of health insurance, and absence of addiction-treatment programmes for drug users. Adequately dealing with the problem of compliance requires dealing with these structural barriers, not the withholding of life-saving medicines from already marginalized peoples.

Conclusion

Ensuring access to live-saving medications is a critical challenge in global public health. And the failure to do so represents one of the most haunting fail-
ures of this field. In the case of HIV/AIDS, significant progress has been made,
although considered accounts warn of any premature celebration. Some analysts predict a 'treatment timebomb' ('t Hoen *et al.* 2011), as more and more
people are infected with HIV and those who are infected live for longer periods of time, as a result of treatment. Treatment costs are expected to rise with
development of new antiretroviral medications which will be launched with
more stringent patent protections, as a result of 'diminishing' options in
TRIPS-plus regulations.

Treating the sick is a critical aspect of reducing the burden of unnecessary
morbidity and premature mortality in the world. The other – perhaps even
more important aspect of reducing health inequities – calls for us to return to
the social/structural drivers of disease, with a focus on the social determinants
of health. It is here where two recent WHO Commissions have garnered a
great deal of attention, as well as criticism. In Chapter 7, I examine the WHO
Commission on Macroeconomics and Health as well as the more recent WHO
Commission on the Social Determinants of Health, considering both of their
conclusions within the context of the Latin American tradition of social medicine.

Reducing Health Inequities

Global health research and practice has been shaped by myriad actors – from university-based researchers to civil society organizations and philanthropic organizations to for-profit pharmaceutical companies and, of course, global institutions such as the International Monetary Fund, the World Bank, and the World Health Organization. And each of these groups undoubtedly contributes a unique vantage point, each with a varying level of commitment to reducing global health inequities, as well as different understandings of the determinants of disease around the world. At the level of *discourse*, global health has been shaped by each of these groups, but perhaps most of all, by two WHO Commissions: the 2001 Commission on Macroeconomics and Health (also known as the Sachs Report, after its lead author, Jeffrey Sachs) and the 2008 Commission on the Social Determinants of Health (CSDH).

These Commissions have done more than integrate the existing research on their issues and put forth recommendations. They have fundamentally altered what issues are emphasized in global health research and advocacy and, in the process, have shaped the kinds of research questions posed by investigators and the kinds of policy solutions debated by advocates. Together, these commissions 'frame' much of the global health inequity discourse. As I shall show, both of the reports have received important criticisms in the global health literature – the Sachs Report, in particular, for over-emphasizing the economic rationale for improving population health, and the CSDH for neglecting the truly structural roots of the social determinants of health.

In grappling with the outcomes the two WHO Commissions and contemporary efforts to improve global health and reduce inequities, I consider the Latin American tradition of social medicine and synthesize its core tenets with contemporary ideas on structural violence. Although largely ignored in the English-language literature, it is the tradition of social medicine that has done the most to conceptualize disease as a product of both biological and sociopolitical processes (Barreto, 2004; Guzmán, 2009). This tradition shares many similarities with the social determinants of health literature – yet, it expands the frame of the discussion and thereby opens up the 'solution space' in substantial ways.

The WHO Commission on Macroeconomics and Health

The WHO launched the Commission on Macroeconomics and Health (the Sachs Commission) in early 2000, with the goal of documenting the links between population health and global economic development. The Commission published its main report, *Macroeconomics and Health: Investing in Health for Economic Development*, in 2001. Its subtitle is a key reflection of its content and argument; the report placed primary emphasis on how improvements in population health can yield positive outcomes for economic development in low- and middle-income countries. According to the Commission's final report, 'Improving the health and longevity of the poor is an end in itself, a fundamental goal of economic development. But it is also a *means* to achieving the other development goals relating to poverty reduction' (WHO, 2001: 1; emphasis in original). The Sachs Commission – dominated by economists and finance industry experts, not epidemiologists or public health advocates – sought to create a 'business plan' to serve as a guide for global health activities. It concluded that a massive increase in international aid could very well wipe out the major diseases of poverty, but the report concentrated on HIV/AIDS, tuberculosis and malaria, largely ignoring NTDs and chronic non-communicable diseases. The Sachs Report estimated that investments of US$66 billion per year would produce a 'return' of more than US$360 billion per year by 2015–20, as 'investing in health' would lead to economically more productive populations (Smith, 2002).[1] The paradigm underlying the Sachs Commission is development and, in particular, development *within* the existing parameters of the macroeconomic global political system.

The Sachs Commission worked from the premise that poor health is a major determinant of poverty and economic underdevelopment. And while most scholars in global health emphasize that health and poverty are clearly connected in a cyclical way (with one influencing the other in a self-reinforcing loop), the major flow of the effect is from poverty to poor health, rather than the other way around, as posited by the Sachs Commission. In other words, they fundamentally changed the flow of cause and effect. This has serious implications for how we come to understand global health inequities and the solutions we may see as most effective. Along these lines, Howard Waitzkin observes:

> In asserting that disease is a major determinant of poverty, the authors of the report argue that investments to improve health form a key strategy towards economic development. They distance themselves from previous interpretations of poverty as a cause of disease... [And] shift emphasis from the social determinants of disease, such as class hierarchies, inequalities of income and wealth, and ethnic origin and racism. Although the authors refer to health as 'an end in itself', the focus on

economic productivity diminishes the importance of health as a fundamental human right. (2003: 523)

Waitzkin – along with many other critics of the Sachs Commission – decries
the use of DALYS and cost-effectiveness analysis, tools that many argue lead
to a de-humanized perspective on suffering, a perspective that reduces complex on-the-ground experiences with the cold calculus of business.

Most controversially, the Sachs Report recommended a wholesale retrenchment of universal welfare programmes in the global south. Instead, they called
for public financing to pay for a package of basic services for the poor, with
the private sector incentivized to supply additional services under market
mechanisms for the middle- and upper-classes. Waitzkin poignantly observes
that such a segmentation of health service provision would fundamentally
undermine national health programmes based on *solidarity*, 'where the system's quality depends on participation by both rich and poor' (2003: 523).
Moreover, the Sachs Report urged for public financing of privately provided
services, which they saw as providing a 'safety valve in case of failure of the
public system' (WHO, 2001: 7). Critics decried this as calling for the public
subsidization of for-profit providers, whereby public funds would be chan-
nelled to US-style health maintenance organizations, rather than to publicly-
administered health care systems. The Sachs Commission took a considerably
more progressive stand on TRIPS, urging that international trade agreements
'should be applied in a manner that gives priority to the health needs of the
poor' (WHO, 2001: 91) – but this position was lessened by the rest of the
Report's conclusions.

Other criticism of the Sachs Report focused on the underlying politics of
power in the Report's recommendations. For many analysts, the Report was
thoroughly steeped in outdated and discredited ideas based on development
and modernization theory. Debabar Banerji, for example, writes:

> Instead of giving primacy to the people in shaping their health services,
> ...[the Sachs Report] calls for 'donor's' imposition on the world's poor of
> prefabricated, selectively chosen, market- and technology-driven, exter-
> nally monitored, and dependence-producing programs. This is a compo-
> nent of a new version of colonialism and imperialism. (2002: 738)

Critics such as Banerji decried the Sachs Commission's underlying view of globalization, which they saw as belying a paternalistic tendency to impose views
from the global north on the global south. Instead of championing practical
solutions such as community health workers – which had already been shown
by Paul Farmer and others to offer significant improvement in treatment outcomes in even very poor settings – the Sachs Commission prized 'vertical programs' that target one disease at a time. Cuba, whose health care system is one
of the most successful in the world, is entirely ignored in the Sachs Report –
despite its long history of cooperation with other countries in the global south.

Along these lines, Alison Katz (2004) critiques the Sachs Commission for focusing almost exclusively on *medico-technological* solutions to problems that are best solved in the realm of public health, and for ignoring the *macro-economic* determinants of both poor health and poverty. Katz observes that the Commission on Macroeconomics and Health,

> despite its title, ignores all the major macroeconomic factors that deter-mine poverty and 'underdevelopment'. Quotation marks are used because in the logic of globalized capitalism, the poor countries have been developed precisely as intended, as cheap sources of primary mate-rials and labor for the rich countries ... With the exception of debt relief – which is dealt with in one sentence as something that should be 'deep-ened' – the report fails to mention a single element of significance to the international economic order ... These are the root causes of miserable living conditions in poor countries, and unless they are tackled, their people will struggle as best they can through bouts of frequent avoidable illness, sometimes ending in premature death. (2005: 176–7)

While described by Sachs as 'both compassionate and cost effective' (Sachs, 2001), the Report largely failed to place the health of poor people at the cen-tre of development discourse. Instead, it repeated and legitimized – through its branding as a WHO Commission – some of the basic assumptions of modern-ization theory. From this perspective, 'developing' countries need to be helped along the epidemiological transition through the donation of health care tech-nologies and structural adjustment programmes that push market mechanisms for the delivery of public goods. The fundamental causes of poverty in the global south – including long histories of colonialism and imperialism, military dictatorships, and current trade rules that heavily favour industrialized coun-tries – were ignored.

The WHO Commission on the Social Determinants of Health

The WHO followed the 2001 Commission on Macroeconomics and Health with a new venture, which began in 2005 and culminated in the publication of the 2008 report *Closing the Gap in a Generation*. Unlike the Sachs Report, the CSDH was headed by one of the most respected health researchers in the world today – Sir Michael Marmot, one of the lead authors of the influential Whitehall studies on the social gradient in health in Britain (see Marmot, 2004). Marmot and his colleagues framed their work very differently than did the Sachs Commission, explicitly focusing on health equity as its fundamental issue, ultimately concluding that 'reducing health inequalities is ... an ethical imperative. Social injustice is killing people on a grand scale' (WHO, 2008a: iix). The CSDH took an openly progressive political stance, emphasizing that 'it does not have to be this way and it is not right that it should be like this. Where systematic differences in health are judged to be avoidable by reasonable action they are, quite simply, unfair. Putting right these inequities – the huge and remediable differences in health between and within countries – is a matter of social justice' (WHO, 2008a: iix).[2] The CSDH openly questioned the benefits of globalization for the world's poor, observing that increasingly transnational risks are borne by low- and middle-income countries, while the financial benefits of new global trade agreements are unequally distributed in favour of high-income regions.

The CSDH has been hailed by academic reviewers – some have claimed that with its 'landmark' report, 'the two worlds of science and policy have collided in an exceptionally productive way'; that it 'creates a pathway by which to improve health for all citizens of the world by integrating the worlds in which policy makers live with those of workers in population health' (Berkman and Sivaramakrishnan, 2008: 557). The CSDH has also been described as 'an unprecedented global effort to understand the extent and nature of social inequities in health worldwide and what is needed to ameliorate them' (Bates *et al.*, 2009: 1002).

Overall, the report presents twelve objectives categorized into three broad principles:

1   Improve daily living conditions

- A more equitable start in life
- A flourishing living environment
- Fair employment and decent work
- Universal social protection
- Universal health care

2   Tackle the inequitable distribution of power, money and resources

- Coherent approach to health equity
- Fair financing
- Market responsibility
- Improving gender equity for health
- Fairness in voice and inclusion
- Good global governance

3   Measure and understand the problem and assess the impact of action

- Enhanced capacity for monitoring, research and intervention. (WHO, 2008a)

The report emphasized the need for the pragmatic improvement of day-to-day living conditions for the world's poor. Building on a large literature on the health effects of childhood deprivation, the CSDH took a 'lifecourse' perspective and called for a major emphasis on early child development and education. At the same time, it called for strengthened social policies and legislation for working age populations, emphasizing the need to 'improve the working conditions for all workers to reduce their exposure to material hazards, work-related stress, and health-damaging behaviours' (WHO, 2008a: 6). Moreover, the CSDH called for living wage legislation, and emphasized the need to 'establish and strengthen universal comprehensive social protection policies that support a level of income sufficient for healthy living for all' (WHO, 2008a: 7).

Global health inequities are at the heart of the report. At its strongest, the report is a denunciation of these inequities. The Commission describes the forty-year gap in life expectancy from the poorest to the richest as four decades that are 'denied' (WHO, 2008a: 166). At the same time, it documents *within* country inequities based on a variety of factors – economic, political, and gender-based. The Commission calls for a refocusing of much of the global discourse on health, away from development towards equity. In effect, the CSDH takes explicit aim at the Sachs Commission's foundation. The report states:

> Economic growth is without question important, particularly for poor countries, as it gives the opportunity to provide resources to invest in improvements of the lives of their population. But growth by itself, without appropriate social policies to ensure reasonable fairness in the way its benefits are distributed, brings little benefit to health equity. (WHO, 2008a: 1)

The CSDH report builds on a rapidly growing literature that critiques the notion that increasing economic productivity, measured as Gross Domestic Product per capita, is the fundamental metric by which we should assess public policy. The CSDH explicitly bring *distribution* into its analysis, thereby opening the discussion to terms such as 'social justice', 'equity', and 'fairness'. This is a remarkable change from the Sachs Commission's focus on charity, development and modernization through the expansion of markets.

The CSDH also breaks with the Sachs Commission's view on the centrality of health care services. The CSDH – in line with its fundamental grounding in the social determinants of health literature – radically expands the frame under which we might understand the causes of disease. While not discounting the importance of the health care sector, the CSDH emphasizes living conditions, social policies, and economic systems – what we can describe as *structural violence*. The CSDH does not discount the importance of *equitable access* to health care services: 'Traditionally, society has looked to the health sector to deal with its concerns about health and disease. Certainly, maldistribution of health care – not delivering care to those who most need it – is one of the social determinants of health.' (WHO, 2008a: 1). However, they do not place great emphasis on the development and expansion of health care services as the means by which to reduce health inequities in the world today. The CSDH's report states, for example:

> the high burden of illness responsible for appalling premature loss of life arises in large part because of the conditions in which people are born, grow, live, work, and age. In their turn, *poor and unequal living conditions are the consequence of poor social policies and programmes, unfair economic arrangements, and bad politics.* (WHO, 2008a: 1, emphasis added)

The CDSH recommended revising the MDGs. It 'proposes that the multilateral community revise existing global development frameworks to incorporate health equity and social determinants of health indicators more coherently' (WHO, 2008a: 171). If adopted – and it has not been at this point – such changes to the MDGs would significantly alter global health discourse and research priorities amongst the major funders. Probably no organization other than the WHO has the global authority to make these calls, and even critics of the report laud the fact that, thanks to the Commission, worldwide attention has turned to issues of global health inequities (Guzmán, 2009). At its core, the report questions the progress made in the new global era: 'While the risks associated with globalization – related to health, trade and finance, or human security – are increasingly transnational and disproportionately experienced in low- and middle-income countries, the benefits remain profoundly unequally distributed in favour of high-income regions' (WHO, 2008a: 166).

The CSDH's approach was a break with previous WHO-authored reports – yet, as I shall discuss, critics have charged that it did not do enough, and what it did do was done without the necessary historical perspective that would have identified the lineage of many of its key recommendations.

While clearly a departure from the Sachs Commission, the CSDH is not revolutionary in tone or in content. And critics argue that, as much as the CSDH vehemently opposes existing patterns of inequities, its recommendations arguably will have little impact on the lives of the world's poor. It is they who suffer from 'neglected diseases' and are increasingly seen as risk carriers – those who would bring Chagas with them to North America, or those who would spread multi-drug resistant tuberculosis, rather than as persons at risk of dying prematurely from readily treatable diseases. Debabar Banerji questions the 'apolitical and ahistorical' nature of the CSDH, noting that 'despite suffering from sustained and almost intolerable political and economic attacks from outside, the heroic efforts of the people and the government of Cuba to retain one of the best health care systems in the world ought to have served as a shining example to anybody discussing social determinants of health' (Banerji, 2006: 641). Yet, Cuba does not feature in the CSDH, and was altogether ignored by the Sachs Commission. Along these lines, Olivia Arellano *et al.* – while supporting the CSDH's work overall – argue that:

the report does not discuss the limitations on the reduction of social and health inequalities imposed by capitalism in general and by specific capitalist formations ... there is no discussion about the contraction posed by adopting a 'politically correct' concern over poverty, which proposes to reduce social and health differences, *while at the same time, ferociously defending the market economy.* (2008: 257; emphasis added)

Arellano *et al.* conclude that the CSDH only partly fulfils its promise; that it is to be commended for reversing the neoliberal perspective of the Sachs Commission that saw population health as primarily a route to economic growth and, instead, posited health equity as a fundamental goal, an ethical imperative, in and of itself. At the same time, Arellano *et al.* suggest that the CSDH ultimately falls short on its conceptualization of the root causes of disease – that although it speaks to the inequitable distribution of power, money and resources, it nevertheless fails to advance our understanding of the 'causes of the causes'. In their view, 'it is power disparities which produce health disparities' (Arellano *et al.*, 2008: 262). Due to its reliance on a public health/epidemiological perspective, the underlying power disparities are ignored. Arellano *et al.* argue that the Latin American tradition of social medicine offers a way forward.[3]

The Latin American tradition of social medicine

The Latin American tradition of social medicine has a long historical record. Its basic philosophy is radical, positing that a population's level of health cannot be understood – and thereby cannot be improved – without explicit engagement with its material conditions and its economic and political organization. Moreover, the tradition is centred on *social theory* – calling for 'critical and ideological analysis of what is usually presented as purely technical knowledge' (Tajer, 2003: 2023). It is known as both a body of literature and as a political movement, one that values the articulation between theory and social change.[4]

Social medicine differs from traditional public health in key ways. It rejects the tendency in some public health work to see populations as the sum of component individuals, and instead, argues that populations need to be understood in a far more holistic and historical way. Public health work focused on changing the behaviour of individuals, for example, takes far less precedence in the social medicine tradition. At the same time, the social medicine tradition takes health care institutions themselves as an object of study, rejecting their neutrality and seeing them as ideological and political agents (see, for example, Avilés' (2001) work featured in Chapter 3). Fundamentally, the social medicine tradition extends the socio-historical lens under which we view health problems – something almost entirely eschewed by a health promotion-focused public health. The social medicine tradition exists at the intersection of medicine, public health, and politically-engaged social science.

From the perspective of the tradition of Latin American social medicine, the CSDH's foundation in public health and epidemiology is overly-limiting. According to the Latin American Social Medicine Association's Rafael Guzmán:

> [these approaches] pay little attention to our current society as it is, focusing rather on the effects it produces within a model incorporating education, occupation, and income. The model itself is based on functionalist sociology, which sees the relationship between education, occupation, and income as deriving from socioeconomic stratification. According to this approach, one of the central measures of social justice or injustice is how equitably a society provides individuals with access to a good education. A quality education is supposed to ensure better jobs and consequently better incomes. These, in turn, permit better living conditions and thus better health. The only possible social transformations from this analytic perspective are changes within an inherently unequal society. Such changes remove only the most aggressive and lethal aspects of the social system (such as forced labor, child labor, occupational hazards, etc.). (Guzmán, 2009: 114–15)

Scholars from this tradition have criticized the CSDH's theoretical framework for not analyzing society as a whole and for not examining the logic of the current global capitalist order: accumulation of wealth, property, and social relations based on market rules. Instead, the CSDH focused on 'governance' of this very system; it does not seek to change it. It does not seek to abolish inequality but, rather, to limit its most pathogenic effects.

Guzmán argues that the CSDH made a strategic mistake in its conceptualization of inequity. He suggests that much of the report is actually focused on inequality, rather than inequity, with negative implications:

> If our analysis remains focused on inequality, it becomes distracted by the symptoms of the problem, rather than its determinants. Inequity reflects the essence of the problem; inequality is an empirical measure of inequity made apparent through statistical analysis ... Inequality is the observable and collective expression of inequity. *Inequalities are measured; inequities are judged.* (Guzmán, 2009: 116; emphasis added)

Critics of the report have argued that it does too little by way of judging. That is perhaps because there is a definite lack of consensus about the relative priority that ought to be placed on the idea of equity in health (Lee, 2010). Guzmán and other researchers from the social medicine tradition emphasize that, while they support the Commission in its call for social policies that reduce inequality in health, they see this as only one step in a larger process. They argue that we cannot limit the scope of the analysis to such policies. Instead, they call for a more radical approach – one that seeks to overcome the social inequities that produce health inequities in the first place; one that focuses our gaze on structural violence, and not merely its manifestation as disease outcomes.

Noticeably absent or underdeveloped in the report, according to these critics, is consideration of a number of important issues, including labour deregulation, the privatization of public services and social security, the exploitation of migrants, and discrimination according to skin colour, ethnicity, sexual orientation, or religion. Moreover, the social medicine tradition argues that the CSDH paid far too little attention to intellectual property rights and access to pharmaceuticals, subsidies to agricultural production by rich countries, and global warming and climate change.

It is these elements that are now at the core of Latin American social medicine (Waitzkin, 2011). Indeed, the Latin American tradition of social medicine stands in contrast to traditional biomedical approaches which isolate disease from its context. Olivia Arellano *et al.*, for example, note that biomedicine misinterprets 'social processes as biological, conceptualizing health phenomena in individualistic terms' (2008: 253). Instead, social medicine conceptualizes disease as the manifestation of structural violence.

Mauricio Barreto (2004) defines this tradition as encompassing a scientific discipline aiming to produce knowledge about the determinants of disease *and also* an act – epidemiological *praxis* – with a commitment to improving the health of populations. This framework is directly rooted in the work of Rudolph Virchow (1821–1902), a celebrated Prussian physician, pathologist, politician, and anthropologist (Brown and Fee, 2006; Rather, 1985; Virchow, 1958). Virchow's contributions to health research are wide-ranging and profound, but he is perhaps most famous for his conclusion that 'disease is not something personal and special, but only a manifestation of life under (pathological) conditions ... Medicine is a social science and politics is nothing else but medicine on a large scale' (1985 [1848]). Virchow's analysis was further developed by, amongst others, Chile's Salvador Allende. Allende's book *The Chilean Medico-Social Reality* (1939) presents an analysis heavily influenced by Virchow's ideas; the book conceptualizes a clear relationship between disease and social structure. Acknowledging the importance of Virchow's analysis and foreshadowing later developments in world systems theory, Allende emphasized the effects of economic underdevelopment and international dependency, as well as the effects of the country's foreign debt on the health of Chileans. Allende advocated for social, rather than purely medical, solutions for Chile's population health challenges: income redistribution, state regulation of food supplies, and a national housing programme, together with industrial reforms. Reflecting the ideals of social medicine, Allende did not see health care as an investment towards a more productive workforce but, rather, he saw health as an end itself (Waitzkin *et al.*, 2001).

The benefits of this approach are most clearly seen in Cuba's remarkable success in achieving high levels of population health (Spiegel and Yassi, 2004), with infant mortality rates and life expectancies that rival, and in many cases surpass, those of vastly richer countries. Cuba's focus on prevention is well-known, as is its appreciation of community versus individual health (Spiegel, 2006). Cuban medical diplomacy – which has sent tens of thousands of medical personnel across Latin American and Africa – has also been well-documented by researchers in the global south, and these accomplishments are celebrated by the tradition of social medicine. Yet, Cuba has not featured in the WHO Commissions, and the lessons that the country may offer the global south have been ignored.[5]

The principles of social medicine are also clearly at the heart of ongoing changes in the Venezuelan health care system. Under the *Barrio Adentro* programme, thousands of Cuban doctors have served in Venezuela, providing free, comprehensive care to the poorest segments of society (Muntaner *et al.*, 2006). *Barrio Adentro* has revolutionized Venezuela's health care system. It relies on community organization, a central principle of the programme, and the willingness of its physicians to live in the communities they serve – an act of solidarity seldom found in the global north. The programme is built on community-level 'Health Committees', a mechanism whereby Venezuelans participate in the day-to-day administration of their health care services. It is also a mechanism that enables *Barrio Adentro* medical personnel to enact a holistic and comprehensive model of health care services: when patients visit the clinic, not only are symptoms treated, but appropriate connections are made with other issues, including food security, sanitation, employment, and other social determinants of health. Yet, these 'horizontal' programmes, which nurture community involvement and support community empowerment, are not featured in the WHO-sponsored literature. To this day, the WHO-sponsored literature privileges technological and biomedical solutions and 'vertical' programmes that target one disease at a time, leaving underlying social conditions intact.

Conclusion

Globalization has opened new possibilities for collective solutions – whether through organizations such as MSF or Farmer's Partners in Health, or through 'south–south' collaboration in relation to the development, manufacture, and distribution of medicine. Understanding how these collective solutions could work is something with which sociologists need to be engaged. To do this, we need to bring structural violence to the centre of our theorizing, and we need to account for how large-scale social structures literally get 'under the skin'.

The Latin American tradition of social medicine has done more than any other body of scholarship to connect structural violence and its pathogenic manifestations. Yet, it has been largely ignored in the English-language literature on the social determinants of health. It has also been ignored by the WHO's Commissions – with the result being that neither the Sachs Report nor the CSDH give us a wholly adequate roadmap for understanding, and ultimately addressing, global health inequities in the world today.

Conclusion

We are told in most popular accounts of globalization that this is an era of great promise, where individuals can benefit from a newfound power to collaborate with one another, where barriers to communication are quickly being dismantled, and where an 'awareness of the world as a single place' is developing. For many scholars, globalization is producing a 'borderless world' – heralding a new age of collaboration and possibility for the development of human potential. Anthony Giddens, perhaps the most widely cited social theorist in this area, proclaims: 'In the new global electronic economy, fund managers, banks, corporations, as well as millions of individual investors, can transfer vast amounts of capital from one side of the world to another at the click of a mouse' (Giddens, 2000: 9). Similarly, Ulrich Beck has deemed globalization: 'A new kind of capitalism, a new kind of economy, a new kind of global order, a new kind of society and a new kind of personal life' (Beck, 1999: 2) – with new risks, but also with tremendous power. These positive portrayals of globalization are echoed in the popular press, which increasingly highlight the emerging economic power of countries such as Brazil and India (for example, see Friedman, 2005).

Yet, as Raewyn Connell points out, this is a very partial account of globalization, in which 'mainstream social theory sees and speaks from the global North' (2007: 50). Giddens, Beck, and other widely cited theorists of globalization seldom engage with the experiences and ideas of the global south. Connell points out: 'the fact that the majority [of the] world has deep prior experience of subjection to globalising powers is surely known to all the theorists. But this experience of subjection does not surface as a central issue in *any* of the theories of globalisation' (2007: 65). Connell argues – I think, with justification – that we have come to understand globalization by viewing it through a highly distorted lens, one that has marginalized the experiences of the majority of the world's people.

Building from Connell's argument, this book provides an alternative point of view, examining the new global era *not* from the perspective of communication technology or economic cooperation, but from something far more basic: the extent to which people of varying socioeconomic status can lead long and healthy lives. Centring our analysis on global health inequities means that we must question assumptions of modernization and 'development', and it leads us to question the often take-for-granted ideas regarding the benefits of globalization.

Running alongside the 'optimistic' accounts of globalization, we have another discourse: one that heralds a new age in medicine, with biomedical innovation grabbing public attention, and the latest discoveries in genetic medicine and pharmacology being lauded for their potential to treat an ever-increasing range of diseases. And this, too, turns out to be a highly selective portrayal. Certainly, biomedicine has achieved remarkable things, and I, too, celebrate them. Yet, when our analysis is focused on global health inequities, a different picture emerges. It is in this stage of globalization, after all, where more than 1 billion people remain exposed to neglected tropical diseases by virtue of living in poor and marginalized conditions, representing unnecessary morbidity, social exclusion and, in many cases, premature mortality. It is in this stage of globalization where tuberculosis – an infectious disease for which effective treatment was developed more than twenty-five years ago – still kills more than 1 million people every year. It is in this stage of globalization where more than 2 million children die every year from diarrhoeal diseases – deaths that could be avoided with improved living conditions and the most basic of primary health care service. At the same time, new barriers are being erected to stop the generic manufacturing of badly-needed HIV medicines by companies in the global south.

This level of health inequity – inequality that is 'avoidable, unnecessary, and unfair' – is greater than at any other point in history. These patterns of inequity are driven by social, political, and economic arrangements. They are shaped by uneven access to health care services but, primarily, by our living conditions – the social determinants of health. Following Paul Farmer, I would argue that these arrangements can be termed *structural violence* – as they are embedded in our politics and economics, and because, ultimately, they *cause* harm to people. Perhaps most importantly to me, recognizing structural violence as the fundamental cause of global health inequity means that we can do something about it – for these social, political, and economic arrangements are not static; nor are they immutable. They change over time, and they *can be improved* over time through concerted collective effort.

Recognizing structural violence does not mean that we will not be inspired by advances in biomedicine – but we will be increasingly worried about its distribution. And that is what is happening in the world today with antiretroviral treatment for HIV/AIDS. Recognizing structural violence means that we will also not be satisfied with seeing the solutions to global health problems as remediable only by biomedicine. We would welcome new treatments for NTDs – but at the same time, recognize that fully addressing the problem will require not only more treatment, but also improvements in living conditions.

Structural violence is not something that will wither away, as one might assume based on modernization theory. It is not enough to expect that health inequities will diminish over time – based on research data, we know that this is not the case. Empirical studies in countries of the global south have shattered the notion of a universal epidemiological transition, and instead, demonstrate that socioeconomic and political marginalization inevitably results in segmented 'epidemiological worlds', with the rich and poor experiencing radically different *capabilities* to lead long and healthy lives. And it is contemporary expressions of structural violence that continue to lead to premature mortality in the global south today, as seen in trade agreements that restrict generic production of antiretroviral medicines, protecting patents over patients.

Structural violence is, admittedly, a nebulous term. It can be used to describe a very wide range of situations – from gross violations of human rights to high levels of income inequality to complex international trade agreements that limit our capacity to distribute medicines to those most in need. For some, this represents a fundamental liability – for, if structural violence can manifest in so many different ways, it ceases to be a useful explanatory force, becoming instead a 'black box' (Janes and Corbett, 2009). Moreover, structural violence cannot be measured in the same way that economic activity can be measured; we have no metric for structural violence that mirrors the specificity of gross domestic product per capita (the most common measure of a country's economic development), or the Gini coefficient (a commonly used measure of inequality). As such, the positivist disciplines of the social sciences (including epidemiology and quantitative sociology) have been hard pressed to incorporate the concept into their theories. And the interpretivist disciplines, including anthropology and qualitative sociology, may likewise avoid the concept, as it challenges ethnographic research to move from its traditional focus on the local and presents a stronger *determinism* than is usually welcomed in those disciplines.

Despite these drawbacks, I believe that structural violence needs to take a central role in social science research on health. Using the concept of structural violence with nuance is possible, and offers us a way of understanding the very real constraints under which our 'lifestyle' choices are made. Doing so may yield breakthroughs in our understanding of global increases in, for example, diabetes and obesity. Empirical work shows that the prevalence of these conditions is rapidly increasing in the global south (Hawkes, 2006; Webber *et al.*, 2012). And there are signs that they are increasing particularly among the poor. But how are we to understand the 'generative mechanisms', the causes of this growing burden? Is it the result of choices exerted by individuals over their diet and level of physical exercise? Is it the result of local-level policies that inhibit green spaces in our cities, that neglect public transportation, and push people towards sedentary lifestyles? Or is it influenced by global forces – the food systems we live under, and the policies under which food is labelled and sold? Naturally, all these factors come into play – with our individual choices being constrained by the structure in which we live, and our individual/collective agency being capable of changing those structures, at least with some level of success over time. Incorporating structural violence into our work is not meant to negate individual-level factors; however, it is meant to add nuance to the causal theories we might develop, helping us to contextualize the agency of individuals.

Taking structural violence as the starting point in our theories of global health is entirely possible. David Coburn (2000, 2004), for example, has shown how we can expand the 'frame' of the income inequality hypothesis, moving beyond a traditional positivistic account of the pathogenic effects of inequality towards a more holistic analysis that models both the causes and effects of inequality. This is a critical difference – for, if we fail to incorporate the causes of inequality into our analyses, we miss out on the 'generative mechanisms' that lead to health inequities (Scambler, 2001). The deep structural roots remained obscured, and our knowledge is limited as a result. More importantly, our capacity to think of, propose, and implement structural solutions is inhibited – leading to the continuation of avoidable, unnecessary, and unjust patterns of disease in the world.

This, I would argue, is happening right now with our thinking about chronic non-communicable diseases, neglected tropical diseases, and access to medicines. The deep structural roots of these issues are hidden, often pushed aside by leading agencies in these fields. For example, most of the global health literature on obesity has focused on individual behaviour – diet and level of physical exercise – without examining economic and political forces that influence the cost and availability of nutritious food in the neighbourhood. Most of the literature on NTDs acknowledges that these conditions thrive in poverty, yet seldom questions the political economy of that poverty. Much of the global literature on antiretroviral therapy has examined the extent to which patients adhere to their doctor's prescribed regimen – ignoring that adherence to a prescription regimen is highly affected by the socioeconomic resources of the individual and their community, and that the production and distribution of medicine is tightly controlled by global trade rules written in favour of for-profit companies over the needs of the poor.

Much of our work on global health has been overly narrow in its focus. The Latin American tradition of social medicine offers an alternative perspective, urging us to connect structural violence and its pathogenic manifestations. In Chapter 7, we saw that the basic philosophy of social medicine is radical, in that it addresses root causes. Above all, this tradition argues that a population's level of health cannot be understood – and therefore cannot be improved – without explicit analysis of its material conditions, and its economic and political organization.

A focus on structural violence is badly needed in global health, and offers us a way of overcoming the limitations of the now-dominant features of this area of research: a tendency to view global health through the lens of *securitization* and an implicit reliance on the epidemiological transition model, with its outdated and discredited foundation in modernization theory.

As we saw in Chapter 1, from the perspective of securitization, global health matters because it is a *threat* to the populations in the rich industrialized countries. Research and policy guided by this perspective seeks to protect populations in the global north from 'Third World' diseases. For example, we saw in Chapter 5 that NTDs continue to exert a tremendous toll on the health of the poorest of the poor. Every year, they cause more deaths than the 2004 Christmas tsunami. Yet, NTDs rarely make the news – for their victims are cordoned off by poverty and political marginalization. The exception to this is when an NTD such as Chagas is 're-branded' to become a *global* threat – something that can break the bounds of geography and threaten the populations of the north (Hotez *et al.*, 2012).

An alternative perspective on global health is rooted in the idea of health equity. In this light, global health matters because it is a telling marker of injustice in the world. It is a sensitive indicator of the well-being of the world's population. Recognizing health as a human right, research and policy guided by this perspective seeks to improve the overall level of the world's population, but is aware that overall improvements are not enough. Indeed, work done under this perspective recognizes that overall improvements may be realized while the condition of the worst-off stagnates, or even deteriorates. Recognizing global health as an issue of equity leads us to say that this is not good enough.

There are promising developments in this area of work, developments that lead me to believe that the case for global health equity is strengthening. In sociology, anthropology, public health, epidemiology, and related fields, the literature on the social determinants of health has shown remarkable growth in the past thirty years – first, establishing the empirical foundations of the social gradient in health, to more nuanced theories pointing to the pathogenic effects of area-level inequality, the experience of discrimination, and the 'intersection' of race, class, and gender. This work is slowly beginning to 'scale up' – and though much remains to be done, there is the potential for the social determinants of health literature to develop into a truly global area of research.

We need to ground global health research in questions of equity. Such work would prioritize inequities regardless of geographic location, and irrespective of their potential to spread to the well-off. A global perspective in health research must also temper our tendency to look for biomedical solutions to problems originating in social and economic inequality. If we fail in doing so – if global health remains focused on securitization and biomedicalization – the root causes of health inequities will remain obscured, and the promise of a better world envisioned by many globalization scholars will remain unattainable for most people.

Notes

I Introduction

1. Grady Memorial Hospital continues to offer health care services, upholding its mission to care for the under-served. It is one of the largest 'safety net' hospitals in the United States (see Dewan and Sack, 2008).

2. As with many other countries in Latin America, Venezuela's health care system has long-espoused the principle of universalism and public financing. But, in practice, inequities in access to health care services (and in health outcomes) have been quite substantial, and the presence of private schemes for delivery and financing have resulted in multi-tiered systems – private systems for the wealthy and under-funded public systems for the poor. Major changes in health care occurred under the Chavez government, most notably with the *Barrio Adentro* programme/mission. Under this programme, thousands of Cuban doctors have set up clinics in impoverished areas of the country, often over the opposition of the Venezuelan Medical Association (Muntaner *et al.*, 2008; PAHO, 2006). They provide free, comprehensive health care to populations who otherwise would have few options.

3. These programmes, a feature of International Monetary Fund (IMF) loan agreements in the 1990s (Ooms and Hammonds, 2009), lead to the retrenchment of the public sector and strengthened the push to privatize health care systems around the world, often with dire consequences for poor people's access to preventive and curative care (Birn and Dmitrienko, 2005; Homedes *et al.*, 2005; Lloyd and Weissman, 2002). Perhaps the most damaging evidence of the effects of structural adjustment programmes has been offered by the Nobel prize-winning economist Joseph Stigltz (2002). Health researchers have also documented the association between participating in IMF economic reform programmes and a significant independent risk of worsening tuberculosis incidence, prevalence, and mortality (Stuckler *et al.*, 2008).

4. The term 'global south' has come to replace 'developing' world and 'Third World' countries in many academic disciplines (see Dados and Connell, 2012), with the latter terms being seen as closely tied to outdated modernization/development theories and Cold War politics, respectively.

5. This was seen most clearly in 2012, when the publication of an editorial titled 'Chagas Disease: "The New HIV/AIDS of the Americas"' (Hotez *et al.*, 2012) in the specialist journal *PLoS Neglected Tropical Diseases* caught the attention of the US media. See Chapter 5 for details.

6. There are very few exceptions to the social gradient in health. Among them is breast cancer (Aitken *et al.*, 2010; Link *et al.*, 1998), which in some studies has

shown to have a higher prevalence among women from higher socio-economic classes.

7. Health research increasingly uses the language of compositional versus contextual/ecological factors. Compositional factors describe characteristics of individuals – for example, whether someone smokes tobacco, or if they exercise, or if their body mass index is over 30. Contextual/ecological factors, in contrast, describe the characteristics of the *places* in which these individuals live, including the level of income inequality, the level of poverty, the availability of healthy food, and environmental quality.

8. This is contrary to the classical position of structural-functionalists such as Davis and Moore (1945), who argued for the 'functional necessity' of stratification and might argue that its effect on health is an integral part of society's 'reward' system.

9. The notion of structural violence has been closely associated with the work of Paul Farmer since the 1990s. Yet, as Farmer points out, the concept has a longer historical legacy, usually traced to Johan Galtung (1969).

10. This perspective is also at play in the work of Farmer, who writes: 'Clearly we live in a time of unprecedented wealth and technological advancement. But a growing and globalizing market economy has not, as promised, lifted all boats. Instead, increasing world wealth has been linked to a sharp rise in inequalities' (1999: 280).

11. David Inglis and Debra Gimlin likewise call for a flexible understanding of globalization: 'we cannot define "globalization" in any narrow sense, but rather we must try to understand that term in as open-minded and flexible a manner as possible, without it conversely coming to mean everything and nothing' (2009: 6).

12. Dependency and world-systems theories are taken up in some detail in Chapter 3. Both are critiques of modernization theory, pointing out the Eurocentric and pro-capitalist ideological bias of that position. Both traditions emphasize that development does not, and cannot, occur 'naturally'; that the existing international economic order *blocks* the development of economies in the global south. Dependency theory describes the *development of underdevelopment*, arguing that so-called 'Third World' countries are cornered into the role of basic raw commodity production – a position where market volatility is particularly pronounced and harmful to the long-term economic growth of these countries. World-systems theory, rooted in the work of Immanuel Wallerstein, has been particularly influential in progressive economic thinking, though the health implications of his work are just beginning to be acknowledged.

13. Sleeping sickness (also known as 'human African trypanosomiasis') is caused by infection with a parasite, *Trypanosoma brucei*. It is spread to humans by tsetse flies. The infection process through two stages: the first involves headaches and fever, and is often undiagnosed. The second phase is associated with sleep disruptions, paralysis, progressive mental deterioration and, ultimately, results in death if untreated. Visceral leishmaniasis is caused by more than twenty species of the protozoan parasite *Leishmania* and can be transmitted to humans by some thirty species of sandflies. Infection is characterized by fever, enlarged spleen and liver, weight loss and anemia. Symptoms progress in severity over weeks or months. Symptomatic patients can die within months, if the infection is not treated (WHO, 2010b).

14. Along these lines, Stiglitz argues: 'TRIPS attempted (successfully) to restrict

access to generic medicines, putting these drugs out of the financial reach of most in the developing countries. When the trade ministers signed the TRIPS agreement ... they were in effect signing the death warrants on thousands of people in sub-Saharan Africa and elsewhere in the developing countries' (2008: 1701).

15. The marginalization of the Latin American tradition of social medicine from public health discourse in the global north mirrors the process observed by Raewyn Connell to be occurring in social science in general. In *Southern Theory*, Connell argues: 'Most theoretical texts in the social sciences are written in the global North, and most proceed on the assumption that this does not matter ... With few exceptions, mainstream social theory sees and speaks from the global North' (2007: 50).

2   Understanding Global Health

1. Only by ignoring the prevalence of infectious diseases amongst the most marginalized of the world's populations can we come to see diseases as 'controlled' – a notion emphasized in much of the contemporary literature on neglected tropical diseases, as well as on tuberculosis.

2. All 192 member countries of the WHO signed the FCTC in 2003. It became international law in 2005, and has now been ratified by more than 160 countries. The treaty contains a variety of anti-tobacco provisions, including measures to reduce the demand for tobacco (incorporating taxes, bans on advertising and sponsorship, and regulations on tobacco packaging and smoke-free environments), as well as to reduce the supply of tobacco (banning sales to minors) (Warner and Mackay, 2006; Mamudu and Glantz, 2009).

3. The clearest indication of this belief is the oft-quoted statement attributed to the 1965–69 US Surgeon General Dr William H. Stewart, who is said to have proclaimed it 'time to close the book on infectious disease as a major threat, declare the war against pestilence won, and shift national resources to such chronic problems as cancer and heart disease' (see, for example, McKeown, 2009). Yet, researchers have never been able to trace the quote to a document or speech (Spellberg, 2008). Nevertheless, the sentiment that health experts in the 1960s and 1970s were overly optimistic about the demise of infectious disease is widely agreed on.

4. The Millennium Declaration emerged as the focal point of UN work on development in 2000. It reaffirms member countries' commitment to the fundamental values of the UN, including the belief in solidarity, which it described as follows: 'Global challenges must be managed in a way that distributes the costs and burdens fairly in accordance with basic principles of equity and social justice. Those who suffer or who benefit least deserve help from those who benefit most.' The operationalization of this principle is one of the most contentious issues in global health, as seen, for example, in debates over patent protection for essential medicines.

5. Schreker (2012), for example, points out that new development assistance in the guise of the MDGs may be *less than* the 'capital flight' from sub-Saharan Africa following the 2008 financial crisis.

6. Protectionist measures for the agricultural sector are notoriously high in the high-income countries of the global north (Anderson and Martin, 2005). These meas-

ures – including tariffs on products from the global south – are still permissible under WTO regulations. Combined with export subsidies granted to major agricultural industries in the United States and other global north countries, the effect is a highly unequal playing field. In principle, the World Trade Organization's 1995 Agreement on Agriculture advocated global reductions in trade barriers, farm subsidies and government intervention in agricultural markets. Yet, this has not been achieved, and the global north has continued to retain a wide range of subsidies, particularly to large agricultural industries. McMichael observes that this is 'at the expense of much larger Southern farm populations who are threatened daily with imports (i.e., 'dumping') of cheap farm commodities from the North' (2012: 138). For more detailed accounts, see Stiglitz and Charlton (2005) and Lee (2006).

7. Critics, however, note that the level of funds allotted to malaria are 'paltry' (Teklemaimanot and Snow, 2002) in relation to the needs of Africa. The Global Fund has also been criticized for espousing a 'vertical' approach to treatment and prevention by launching disease-specific programmes. In contrast, a 'horizontal' approach would seek to strengthen primary health care systems, generating capacity to treat a wider range of conditions (McCarthy, 2007).

8. Tuberculosis and HIV spread particularly well in settings of poverty and inequality. As such, their epidemiology reflects common 'drivers'. Moreover, there are known synergistic interactions between these diseases, with increased HIV viral load increasing the risk of one contracting active tuberculosis. Similar synergistic interactions are found with HIV, sexually transmitted diseases and malaria (Corbett *et al.*, 2002; Fleming and Wasserheit, 1999; Van geertruyden and D'Allesandro, 2007).

9. The notion of 'risk environment' is receiving a great deal of attention in public health (see Rhodes, 2002).

10. Link and Phelan argue that fundamental causes of disease involve resources that enable individuals avoid disease. This is in contrast to 'proximal' risk factors of disease, which occur very close to the disease process itself. Link and Phelan argue that 'even if one effectively modifies intervening mechanisms or eradicates some diseases, an association between a fundamental cause and disease will reemerge' (1995: 81). Their analysis is a profound reconceptualization of the association between socioeconomic status and disease; seeing socioeconomic status as a 'fundamental cause' means that it is not enough to target the intervening factors that link socioeconomic status and disease (e.g., tobacco consumption). Link and Phelan emphasize: 'if one genuinely wants to alter the effects of a fundamental cause, one must address the fundamental cause itself' (1995: 88). The implications of this perspective for global health inequities are critical, for it reinforces the notion that structural violence – what we might see as the *starting point* in a long chain of events that ultimately results in inequitable patterns of population health – must be central to our theories and actions.

11. An important reason why it has been difficult to integrate structural violence into global health research revolves around the dominant methodology and epistemology of epidemiology and public health in general. Much of the research in this area reflects a positivist epistemology and quantitative methodology, ways of working that are not amenable to incorporating concepts that lack strongly validated 'measures'. But importantly, global health research is not confined to positivist statistical analysis. Indeed, the most exciting recent advances in this area of

work are a result of analyses driven by critical realism – an epistemology that posits that knowledge is not limited to that which can be directly measured, but that it also contains that which exists underneath the surface of observable phenomena and that can only be ascertained through theoretical reasoning (Coburn, 2004). Whilst open to quantitative research strategies and statistical analysis (Porpora, 2001), critical realism places emphasis on 'generative mechanisms' that exist beneath the surface of the phenomena we can measure with positivist methods (see Scambler, 2001). It is through this tradition that structural violence appears to be most useful as a guiding/orientating concept.

12. Mirroring, perhaps, Farmer's observation that 'the suffering of the world's poor intrudes only rarely into the consciousness of the affluent, even when our affluence may be shown to have direct relation to their suffering' (2003: 31).

13. While chronic non-communicable diseases are not the leading causes of death in sub-Saharan Africa, these conditions nevertheless contribute to a tremendous burden of preventable morbidity and premature mortality. Current data show that women aged 15–49 die from chronic non-communicable diseases in sub-Saharan Africa at a rate that is four times higher than that experienced by women in the high-income countries of the world (Alwan et al., 2011).

14. There is some debate in this literature with respect to how inequality may be associated with different health outcomes, with studies of mortality generally showing stronger relationships than studies of morbidity.

15. Indeed, Farmer warns us of relying too much on national boundaries: 'it is important to sound a warning about the habit of conflating the notion of society with that of nation-state. We already live in a global society. Thus, calls of a right to equity must necessarily contend with steep grades of inequality across as well as within international borders. Nationally farmed analyses ... may obscure their fundamentally transnational nature' (Farmer, 2003: 20).

16. The four typologies used by Moore divide the world using different metrics and different theories. The first typology is based on a standard World Bank definition of high versus low income per capita, with high income being defined as Gross Domestic Product per capita of over US$5,000. The second typology used membership in the Organisation for Economic Co-operation and Development. Both are traditional measures often used in comparative studies. Moore's third and fourth typologies, in contrast, are designed to capture theoretical divisions suggested by development and world-systems theory. The third typology contrasts core versus non-core countries, a distinction based on the presence or absence 'of a tie between countries in the trade of capital-intensive commodities' (Moore, 2006: 627). Countries not integrated into the trade of capital-intensive commodities are non-core, and participate in the world economy more as exporters of raw/unprocessed basic commodities. The fourth typology is based on world-systems theory, contrasting periphery and non-periphery countries.

17. Most ecological analyses of the income inequality hypothesis have been static in the sense that they have analyzed data from one particular point in time. This is partly attributable to the relative paucity of historical data on income inequality (Leigh and Jencks, 2007), particularly at levels of geography lower than the nation-state. However, there is reason to believe that the health effect of income inequality may lag, and income inequality in year 1 may influence health in year 1 + n (Laporte and Ferguson, 2003; Leigh and Jencks, 2007; Lynch et al., 2005), with some authors suggesting that a lag of up to 15 years may be appropriate

(Blakely *et al.*, 2000). More detailed accounts of the income inequality hypothesis are offered by Kawachi *et al.* (1999) and (De Maio, 2010a).

18. The income inequality – health literature has been very rooted in its operationalization of income inequality with the Gini coefficient (De Maio, 2007). While it is a popular and widely-accepted method, the Gini coefficient – as with any measure that seeks to reduce a complex phenomenon into a summary number – inevitably raises limitations. The Gini coefficient is derived from the Lorenz curve of the plot of cumulative percentage of the population by socioeconomic status and cumulative percentage of total income; a Gini coefficient of 0 reflects a perfectly equal society in which all income is shared equally, and a Gini coefficient of 1 represents a perfectly unequal society wherein all income is earned by one individual. The Gini coefficient's main weakness as a measure of income distribution is that it is incapable of differentiating different kinds of inequalities; Lorenz curves may intersect (reflecting differing patterns of income distribution) but may, nevertheless, result in the same Gini coefficient value. Together with colleagues in Argentina, I have tested the robustness of the income inequality hypothesis to varying measures of income distribution, testing the Gini coefficient against an alternative measure, the Generalized Entropy Index (see De Maio *et al.*, 2012b).

3 The Epidemiological Transition

1. Debate does exist, however, about the McKeown hypothesis. Colgrove (2002), for example, argues the hypothesis is flawed, pointing to debates within the field of historical demography that have raised doubts regarding McKeown's methods and conclusions (see also Link and Phelan, 2002). Wilkinson notes that 'while it is possible to argue the relative historical contributions of better nutrition, sewers, clean water supplies, improved housing, and, eventually, immunization to the long decline in mortality rates in the developed world, there can be no doubt that the enabling and sustaining power of economic growth was behind them all' (1994: 61–2). Economic growth underlies the historical analyses of McKeown as well as those of McKinlay and McKinlay, and, as I show in this chapter, economic growth is the lynchpin of Omran's theory of epidemiological transition.

2. Omran developed his model based on the literature on the demographic transition, which began to be developed in the 1920s and was fully stated by 1945. These earlier models were primarily focused on changes in fertility, rather than mortality (Feinleib, 2008).

3. The cholera outbreak has been traced to a base for Nepalese UN peacekeepers stationed next to Haiti's Artibonite River. Investigators matched the strain of cholera found in Haiti with a strain prevalent in Nepal in 2010, and noted that the disease was probably introduced to the Artibonite River through the dumping of sewage (cholera is spread through infected faeces) (Rosen, 2013). More than 8,000 Haitians have died as a result of this outbreak. Until this outbreak, Haiti had been free of cholera for more than a century (Farmer, 2011; Katz, 2013). The UN has invoked its legal immunity against calls for compensation (Lall and Pilkington, 2013).

4. The social gradient refers to a step-wise pattern observed as linking socioeconomic status and health outcomes. For the vast majority of health conditions, each

step downward in the socioeconomic hierarchy is associated with an increased probability of poor health. This is also often referred to as a 'linear' or 'curvilinear' relationship, in contrast to a 'threshold effect'.

5. McMichael (2012) points out that while Rostow's model was hailed in 1960s *laissez-faire* circles, it actually posits that an active state is fundamental in the *development* of markets and in the movement towards the stage of mass consumption.

6. It also urges us to remain vigilant to unacknowledged marginalizing effects of our theories – for example, in the simple distinction between 'groups at risk' and 'risk groups'; the former indicating a group that we focus on to aid and support, while the latter designates a potential threat, a group from whom populations need protection.

7. Along these lines, Barreto (2004) suggests that the rejection of the classic formulation of the epidemiological transition model by Latin American epidemiologists foreshadowed the damaging effects of globalization and neoliberal politics in the region. Rejecting the model relied on seeing relations of dependency and exploitation; it relied on theorizing and acknowledging social and political forces that have generated by what is now called 'epidemiological overlap' – the continued risk of premature death from infectious diseases for the poor majority and the growing presence of so-called 'diseases of affluence' (among all social classes).

4 Chronic Non-Communicable Diseases

1. There are significant conceptual and methodological difficulties associated with comparing the burden of one illness or one set of illnesses against another. Mortality indicators do not necessarily reflect a condition's burden in terms of pain, suffering and disability.

2. Our understanding of the burden of chronic non-communicable diseases has changed in recent years. Not only are these diseases now acknowledged to be the major drivers of mortality in most areas of the world but, even in countries where each individual non-communicable disease is thought to be relatively uncommon, their *combined burden* is now seen as substantial. Harvard University's Gene Bukhman describes this as the 'long tail' of global health equity. While in countries such as Rwanda, the leading causes of death and disability are infectious diseases (including respiratory infections, diarrhoeal diseases, HIV/AIDS and malaria), graphing the contributions of individual diseases produces a long-tail populated by non-communicable disease that adds to a significant overall burden (Bukhman and Kidder, 2011).

3. A significant component of COPD in low-income countries is generated by the use of biomass (wood, animal dung and crop waste) stoves inside the home ((Rubinstein *et al.*, 2011; Zeng *et al.*, 2012). These stoves are known to generate high levels of indoor air pollution with health-damaging chemicals.

4. The WHO's projections are clearly based on the notion of epidemiological transition, with the burden associated with communicable diseases such as tuberculosis being expected to diminish over time. We have seen that this model may have generalized validity, but that it leaves the question of heterogeneity, of inequality, in the margins.

5. These data support the warning issued by the *Lancet*'s Richard Horton: 'without concerted and coordinated political action, the gains achieved in reducing the burden of infectious disease will be washed away as a new wave of preventable illness engulfs those least able to protect themselves' (2005: 1514).

6. Sociologically, this entails a denial of the *sick role*. A foundational concept in medical sociology, the sick role is a normative social role with accompanying rights and obligations that sick people follow to legitimate their condition. There are four components to the sick role:

   - the sick person is exempt from 'normal' social roles
   - the sick person is absolved of personal responsibility – she or he is not to blame for their condition
   - the sick person should try to get well
   - the sick person should seek technically competent help and cooperate with a physician. (Parsons, 1951)

   With these four components of the sick role, Parsons believed he had discovered how society works to sanction certain illness situations as a legitimate condition. If a person falls ill, they fall within the medical system and they can fulfil the sick role; if they do not, their behaviour begins to verge on deviancy and falls outside of the medical system.

7. Unfortunately, welfare regime scholarship has mostly focused on the advanced industrialized countries of Europe and North America (Arts and Gelissen, 2002; Esping-Andersen, 1990). Far less is known about 'regime effects' in the countries of the global south.

8. India is the world's second largest producer and consumer of tobacco products.

9. Catastrophic spending was defined as chronic-disease-related hospitalization resulting in expenses which exceed a household's ability to pay by more than 40 per cent (Engelgau *et al.*, 2012; Xu *et al.*, 2003).

10. Burden of disease is typically measured in disability-adjusted life years (DALYs), a measure defined as the number of years of life lost due to disease, taking into account not only premature mortality, but also discounting for life 'lost' due to morbidity and disability (Asada, 2007; Barker and Green, 1996).

11. One of the clearest examples of epidemiological overlap is given by Alicia Hidron *et al.* (2010), in their study of Chagas cardiomyopathy in Santa Cruz, Bolivia. Their analysis acknowledges the general transition that is under way in Latin America – from high rates of infectious disease and premature deaths to a pattern characterized by deaths later in life associated with obesity, hypertension and diabetes. And they recognize that Chagas disease control programmes have made important progress in blocking vector- and transfusion *T. cruzi* infection. Yet, they note millions of people carry *T. cruzi* infection and, for a significant percentage, these infections will manifest in heart complications, including congestive heart failure. The distinction between infectious and chronic diseases is therefore less clear-cut than a simplistic reading of Omran's model would suggest.

12. 'Years of life lost' is an estimate of the burden associated with a disease in a particular population. If a person has a life expectancy of 75 years, and they die at age 55 due to lung cancer, the potential years of life lost is 75 – 55 = 20. For a detailed analysis of this concept, see Gardner and Sanborn (1990), as well as the annual *World Health Report* published by the WHO. Rubinstein *et al.* (2010)

provide a nuanced example of the value of this measure, estimating the burden of cardiovascular disease in Argentina.

13. This is a critical challenge that must be overcome. The need for a re-framing of chronic disease as a question of social justice has also been noted by David Stuckler *et al.*, who observe: 'Advocacy on non-communicable diseases has been described by young people as "dull" and "uninspiring," lacking an emphasis on social justice or inequality and missing a sense of outrage and urgency against continued inaction' (2011).

14. The gradient was steepest when measured by educational attainment. For example, in 'unadjusted' models, adults with low educational attainment were most likely to be obese (OR = 2.79, 95% CI = 2.28–3.31), followed by adults with medium–low (OR = 2.38, 95% CI = 2.00–2.82) and medium–high (OR = 1.63, 95% CI = 1.39–1.92) educational attainment, compared with adults with some post-secondary schooling. Models that 'adjusted' for other individual characteristics as well as for province of residence also produced gradient patterns, but with generally lower odds ratios (De Maio *et al.*, 2009).

15. As is the case with many population surveys, our study was based on self-reported data. In the case of diabetes, the respondent was asked if a medical professional had informed them that they had diabetes or high blood sugar. As such, our data on diabetes are influenced by access to the health care system. This has critical implications – for the data point to the prevalence of the condition, as well as the availability of resources to diagnose that condition. Increases in diabetes may signal a decreased level of *underdiagnosis* in the population, rather than an increase in actual diabetes prevalence (see Linetzky *et al.*, 2013).

16. This was the second time the UN held a high-level meeting on a health issue. The first meeting was held in 2001, and focused on the HIV epidemic. It led to the creation of the Global Fund to Fight HIV/AIDS, Tuberculosis and Malaria. For many, that meeting marked the turning point in the global fight against HIV (Alwan *et al.*, 2011).

17. Graham MacGregor, Chairman of World Action on Salt and Health (WASH), issued a sharp critique: 'We are shocked to hear that major Western countries, which are already reducing salt intake in their own countries, are trying to block salt reduction in all countries around the world. The WHO set a target of 5 gram a day in 1983, which was further endorsed in 2003 and 2006. This target was therefore suggested by Norway in the Outcomes Document for the NCD High Level Meeting on non-communicable diseases (NCDs) taking place on the 19th September, but has now been removed by the EU, Australia, Japan, US and Canada, who are refusing to support the recommendation and requested its removal in the July 29th version of the Document. This is a major step backwards, particularly in view of the fact that Canada, Australia and the United States all have salt reduction targets of 4, 5 or 6 gram a day. Very similar targets have been set across the EU (e.g. UK 6 gram a day). Without targets no action will take place and lives will be lost. Why are these countries denying the rest of the world the benefits of a target that would ensure a reduction in salt intake over the next decade, saving millions of lives through preventing strokes, heart attacks and heart failure? Is this due to the influence of the global food industry? We ask these countries to urgently reconsider their position and support the NCD Alliance's call on member states to make this a priority, as salt reduction has been shown to be one of the most cost-effective ways of tackling the NCD crisis'

(MacGregor, 2011). A similar critique was published by the World Heart Federation (2011).

Stuckler *et al.*'s analysis reinforces this position: 'At a preparatory meeting in New York representatives of the United States, Europe, and key Western allies, blocked consensus on action on non-communicable diseases after lobbying from the alcohol, food, tobacco, and drug industries. Negotiations have now stalled. When asked why Michelle Obama's successful childhood obesity programmes in the US should not be modelled in developing countries, a US official responded that they might harm American exports' (2011).

5 Neglected Tropical Diseases

1. There are five so-called 'tool ready' NTDs: lymphatic filariasis, onchocerciasis, schistosomiasis, soil-transmitted helminthiasis (including hookworm), and trachoma. Drugs for all of these conditions exist and have been found to be safe, available at low cost or, in some cases, through extraordinary donations from pharmaceutical companies (Zhang *et al.*, 2010).
2. The work of Chris Beyrer *et al.* (2007) presents the strongest evidence of the link between armed conflict and NTDs. They analyze the patterning of lymphatic filariasis in Burma and Chagas disease in Colombia, showing the links between systematic violations of human rights and NTDs.
3. Much controversy has arisen from new concerns over the spectre of a 'globalized' Chagas disease that follows immigration routes (Jackson *et al.*, 2009; Perez de Ayala *et al.*, 2009; Schmunis, 2007). In many ways, this issue marks a departure from the rest of the NTD literature by emphasizing a permeable point in what we might call the 'epidemiological boundary' separating the global south and global north.
4. Allotey *et al.*'s articles on social sciences research and neglected tropical diseases are particularly important – they highlight, for example, that the lack of sociological engagement with this field means that social and ecological factors have largely been side-lined in this research, which instead focuses on biomedical interventions (2010; see also Pokhrel *et al.*, 2011). Their bibliographic analysis of the NTD research literature suggests that less than 4 per cent of the work in this area is described as social science – and argue that this is an overestimate, with much of what is being classified as social science research being, in reality, clinical work. They conclude: 'there is little investigator driven social science and a poor presence of interdisciplinary science. The research needs more sophisticated funders and priority setters who are not beguiled by uncritical biomedical promises' (Reidpath *et al.*, 2011).
5. Both OneWorld Health and the Sabin Vaccine Institute have benefited from funding from the Bill & Melinda Gates Foundation. Indeed, the importance of the Gates Foundation in shaping contemporary global health research is hard to overstate. Its effects are well-described by McCoy and McGoey (2011).
6. Along with introducing DALYS, the 1993 World Development Report is remembered by many in global health research for its neoliberal recommendations that low- and middle-income countries should levy user fees on health services.
7. Efforts are under way to develop pharmaceuticals for leishmaniasis that are safer, cheaper, and easier to use (van Griensven *et al.*, 2010; Wakabi, 2007), and some

success has been reported by the Drugs for Neglected Diseases Initiative (DNDi), a not-for-profit partnership lead by *Médecins sans Frontières* (MSF). Commercial research and development for neglected diseases, however, continues to pale in comparison with expenditures on so-called 'me too' blockbuster drugs for hypertension, depression, arthritis, and other large markets.

8. It is important to note, however, that only a fraction of recipients of blood infected with *T. cruzi* go on to become infected themselves (Schmunis, 1991). Evidence of the rate at which *T. cruzi* passes from an infected mother to her foetus varies widely (Barona-Vilar *et al.*, 2012; Carlier *et al.*, 2011).

9. Patterns of immigrant health have received considerable attention in the social science and medical literature since the mid-1990s, particularly in the United States (Abraido-Lanza *et al.*, 2005; Kaplan *et al.*, 2004; Read *et al.*, 2005), where researchers have focused on the 'paradox' of good health given relatively poor socioeconomic conditions among Hispanic immigrants. In Canada, research on the health of immigrants has engaged with contrasting notions of 'sick immigrants' and 'healthy immigrants' (Beiser, 2005); the former describing immigrants as carriers of disease and as burdens on health and social welfare systems, and the latter acknowledging that, because of a number of factors (including self-selection, as well as Canadian immigration policies), immigrants to Canada tend to be healthier than the native-born population at the time of their arrival in the country (Gushulak, 2007; Hyman, 2004). Whilst empirical research has rejected the validity of the sick immigrant paradigm, it nevertheless still shapes anti-immigration ideologies, often interacting with ideas that immigrants take jobs away from the native-born population (De Maio, 2010b, 2012).

10. In particular, the triatomine bug that serves as the vector for *T. cruzi* differs between the Southern Cone and Central America. In the Southern Cone, *T. infestans* is the dominant vector, and insecticide spraying in the home and surrounding buildings (e.g., chicken coops) has shown success. In Central America, the dominant vectors are *Triatoma dimidiata* and *Rhodnius prolixus*. *Triatoma dimidata* can live in palm trees, and no effective methods for spraying palm trees exist (Hotez, 2008a).

11. Transmission via intra-domiciliary vectors refers to the spread of *T. cruzi* by bugs colonizing the home and neighbouring buildings (outhouses, barns, and so on).

6 Treating the Sick

1. Much has been written about the ways in which globalization has influenced health care systems, and empirical research has documented the deleterious effects of fee-for-service models on health care utilization, and the so-called 'exportation' of US-style managed care to countries in the global south (Iriart *et al.*, 2001; Waitzkin and Iriart, 2001). The effect was a 're-trenchment' of the welfare state in many Latin American countries in the 1990s, wherein public health systems were dismantled and privatized. Some of the most striking analyses have critiqued the IMF and the World Bank for pushing the commodification of health care in the global south (Kolko, 1999; Lloyd and Weissman, 2002; Ooms and Hammonds, 2009; Stuckler *et al.*, 2008). In the 1990s, this took the form of opposition against the recommendations of the 1993 *World Development Report*, wherein the World Bank advocated for a dismantling of then-existing

social/health insurance programmes in many Latin American countries, on the basis that they constituted 'subsidies to relatively affluent groups' (World Bank, 1993: 160). The World Bank argued that the universality of social/insurance programmes is a *regressive* feature, as benefits accrue to the middle classes. Pressure from the World Bank and the IMF for countries to adopt these changes was immense, with loans dependent on countries agreeing to move towards private markets as a condition of receiving funds (Armada *et al.*, 2001; Grembowski *et al.*, 2002).

2. CD4 cells – also called 'helper cells' – are an integral component of the body's immune system; they send signals that activate the body's immune response to viruses and bacteria. They become depleted with untreated HIV infection.

3. The WHO updated its guidelines for treatment initiation, and this has affected the estimated population in need of treatment. Based on their 2006 guidelines, which called for treatment to be initiated when a person had a CD4 cell count of <200 cell/mm^3, 52 per cent would be estimated to be receiving treatment. However, based on their updated 2010 guidelines, which call for treatment to be initiated when a person has a CD4 cell count of <350 cell/mm^3, only 36 per cent of the estimated population in need of treatment is thought to be receiving it (WHO, 2010a).

4. Treatment *as* prevention describes a paradigm shift in HIV care, wherein the provision of antiretroviral therapy to infected people was found to have beneficial effects in decreasing the rate at which they would transmit the virus to others ((Dabis *et al.*, 2010; Harris and Montaner, 2011; Montaner, 2011). Antiretroviral therapy, in other words, can decrease viral load in the infected person, decreasing the probability of the virus passing to their partner.

5. The number of deaths due to AIDS reflects both past prevalence and the past availability of effective treatment.

6. Rein describes the 'development lag' by which developing countries were granted a ten-year transition period as one of the concessions generated by the WTO negotiations on TRIPS. Rein observes: 'TRIPS calls upon developed country Members to provide incentives to locally-based enterprises for the purpose of encouraging technology transfer to the least developed countries. *This particular mandate does not provide any specific requirements or objectives*' (2001: 390; emphasis added).

7. Stiglitz's observation on TRIPS' flexibilities is worth quoting at length: 'The head of the WTO has been upset at my public criticisms of TRIPS, especially in those lectures in which I explain how the WTO is causing people to die because without access to generic medicines, the poor in developing countries suffering from life threatening diseases simply cannot afford to pay the "brand name" prices. He wrote me to remind me that I was forgetting about the *flexibilities*. But he is forgetting about the inflexibilities in these flexibilities. They are designed to make it difficult ... [for developing countries to produce generic medicines]. If the WTO really were interested in making sure people had access to generic medicines, the set of procedures would look very different' (Stiglitz, 2008: 1717).

8. Brazil's strategy has involved working with sex workers as key allies in the fight against HIV/AIDS. In this respect, it shows a tremendous contrast with the approach espoused by the United States. The US President's Emergency Fund for Aids Relief (PEPFAR) – one of the largest and most ambitious global health programmes ever put in place – explicitly requires programme participants to

denounce prostitution. In 2005, the Brazilian government turned down US$40 million from the United States rather than comply with that stipulation. For recent analyses of PEPFAR, see Jappah (2013), Ditmore and Allman (2010) and Cockerham and Cockerham (2010).

9. Buoyed by success in legal courts, civil society groups gone on to bring legal action against the South African government itself to push it to expand access the HIV medicines ever further by including the drug nevirapine, an antiretroviral used with pregnant HIV-positive women to inhibit transmission of the virus to the foetus (Singh *et al.*, 2007).

10. TRIPS-plus stipulations extend and deepen the intellectual property rights enshrined in TRIPS. They have been included in bilateral free trade negotiations initiated by the United States. Critics have argued that further extensions of patent rights and market protection are associated with increases in the costs of medicine, delays in the introduction of generics, and a weakened domestic capacity to produce medicines, favouring for-profit pharmaceutical multinational companies (Akaleephan *et al.*, 2009; Cohen-Kohler *et al.*, 2008; Kessomboon *et al.*, 2010).

11. Adding to the financial burden of antiretroviral therapy is the acknowledgement that, while medication is the most substantial component of its cost, other elements of clinical management – particularly laboratory testing – entail significant costs as well (Bartlett and Shao, 2009).

12. Switching from first- to second- to third-line drugs for HIV entails significant increases in the complexity of both cost and treatment.

7   Reducing Health Inequities

1. The Sachs Report estimated the required investments necessary to combat major endemic infections. It has been criticized for relying extensively on a disease-by-disease 'vertical' approach, rather than an integrated primary health care 'horizontal' approach.

2. In a thoughtful reflexive account of the CSDH and the reception its report received, Michael Marmot and Ruth Bell observe: 'From the start, the WHO Commission on the Social Determinants of Health built its case for taking action on the social determinants of health, *unashamedly*, on principles of social justice. ... Taking this position has brought praise and blame: praise for the Commission's boldness in putting fairness on the global health agenda in the face of the global model of economic growth as an end in itself, and blame for the Commission's unworldliness in apparently not recognizing that economic arguments push the political agenda' (2010: 1). See also Marmot (2009).

3. Raewyn Connell's fascinating critique of the assumptions underlying much of sociological theory produced in the global north is relevant here. In particular, Connell demonstrates how many of the key theorists in sociology – and, in particular, Giddens' and Becks' works on globalization – rely on a claim to universality. In contrast, work from the global south has been marginalized, deemed to lack such universality. Connell describes this dismissal: 'Intellectuals in the periphery cannot universalize a locally generated perspective because its specificity is immediately obvious. It attracts a name such as "African philosophy" or "Latin American dependency theory", and the first question that gets asked is

"how far is this relevant to other situations?"' (Connell, 2007: 44). In describing this perspective as the *Latin American* Tradition of Social Medicine, I mean to emphasize its geopolitical origins without diminishing its relevance for other areas. Indeed, I believe that this tradition is implicit – and unacknowledged – in the best aspects of the CSDH.

4. The Latin American Social Medicine Association (ALAMES), founded in 1984, serves as the key organization for this tradition, and is present across the region (Tajer, 2003).

5. For a detailed examination of Cuba's approach to medical education, see Huish (2009). Spiegel (2006) offers an important challenge to break the 'taboo' of learning from Cuba's example.

Bibliography

Abad-Franch, F., Santos, W. S. and Schofield, C. J. (2010) 'Research needs for Chagas disease prevention', *Acta Tropica*, 115(1–2): 44–54.

Abegunde, D. O., Mathers, C. D., Adam, T., Ortegon, M. and Strong, K. (2007) 'The burden and costs of chronic diseases in low-income and middle-income countries', *Lancet*, 370(9603): 1929–38.

Abraido-Lanza, A. F., Chao, M. T. and Florez, K. R. (2005) 'Do healthy behaviors decline with greater acculturation? Implications for the Latino mortality paradox', *Social Science & Medicine*, 61(6): 1243–55.

Acheson, D. (1998) *Independent Inquiry into Inequalities in Health* (London: Stationery Office).

Addiss, D. G. (2010a) 'The 6th Meeting of the Global Alliance to Eliminate Lymphatic Filariasis: A half-time review of lymphatic filariasis elimination and its integration with the control of other neglected tropical diseases', *Parasites & Vectors*, 3(1): 100.

Addiss, D. G. (2010b) 'Global elimination of lymphatic filariasis: addressing the public health problem', *PLoS Neglected Tropical Diseases*, 4(6): e741.

Ahmad, K. (2001) 'Roche gives in to Brazil over AIDS drug', *The Lancet Infectious Diseases*, 1(3): 138.

Aitken, Z., Walker, K., Stegeman, B. H., Wark, P. A., Moss, S. M., McCormack, V. A. and Silva, I. dos Santos (2010) 'Mammographic density and markers of socioeconomic status: a cross-sectional study', *BMC Cancer*, 10: 35.

Akaleephan, C., Wibulpolprasert, S., Sakulbumrungsil, R., Luangruangrong, P., Jitraknathee, A., Aeksaengsri, A., Udomaksorn, S., Tangcharoensathien, V. and Tantivess, S. (2009) 'Extension of market exclusivity and its impact on the accessibility to essential medicines, and drug expense in Thailand: analysis of the effect of TRIPs – Plus proposal', *Health Policy*, 91(2): 174–82. .

Allende, S. (1939) *La Realidad Médio-Social Chilena* [*The Chilean Medico-Social Reality*] (Santiago: Ministro de Salubridad).

Allotey, P. and Gyapong, M. (2005) 'The gender agenda in the control of tropical diseases: A review of current evidence (No. TDR/STR/SEB/ST/05.1) (Geneva: World Health Organization).

Allotey, P., Reidpath, D. D. and Pokhrel, S. (2010) 'Social sciences research in neglected tropical diseases 1: the ongoing neglect in the neglected tropical diseases', *Health Research Policy and Systems*, 8: 32.

Alwan, A., Galea, G. and Stuckler, D. (2011) 'Development at risk: addressing non-communicable diseases at the United Nations high-level meeting', *Bulletin of the World Health Organization*, 89(8): 546.

Alwan, A. and MacLean, D. R. (2009) 'A review of non-communicable disease in low- and middle-income countries', *International Health*, 1(1): 3–9.

Anderson, K. and Martin, W. (2005) 'Agricultural trade reform and the Doha development agenda', *The World Economy*, 28(9): 1301–427.

Ansell, D. A. (2011) *County: Life, Death and Politics at Chicago's Public Hospital* (Chicago: Academy Chicago Publishers).

Arellano, O. L., Escudero, J. C. and Carmona, L. D. (2008) 'Social determinants of health: perspective of the ALAMES working group on social determinants', *Social Medicine*, 3(4): 253–64.

Armada, F., Muntaner, C. and Navarro, V. (2001) 'Health and social security reforms in Latin America: the convergence of the World Health Organization, the World Bank, and transnational corporations', *International Journal of Health Services*, 31(4): 729–68.

Arts, W. and Gelissen, J. (2002) 'Three worlds of welfare capitalism or more? A state-of-the-art report', *Journal of European Social Policy*, 12(2): 137–58.

Asada, Y. (2007) *Health Inequality: Morality and Measurement* (Toronto: University of Toronto Press).

Ataguba, J. E., Akazili, J. and McIntyre, D. (2011) 'Socioeconomic-related health inequality in South Africa: evidence from General Household Surveys', *International Journal for Equity in Health*, 10(1): 48.

Auger, N., Giraud, J. and Daniel, M. (2009) 'The joint influence of area income, income inequality, and immigrant density on adverse birth outcomes: a population-based study', *BMC Public Health*, 9: 237.

Ault, S. K. (2008) 'Intersectoral approaches to neglected diseases', *Annals of the New York Academy of Sciences*, 1136: 64–9.

AVERT (2012) 'AIDS, drug prices and generic drugs', Retrieved 27 August 2012, from http://www.avert.org/generic.htm

Avilés, L. A. (2001) 'Epidemiology as discourse: the politics of development institutions in the Epidemiological Profile of El Salvador', *Journal of Epidemiology & Community Health*, 55(3): 164–71.

Backlund, E., Rowe, G., Lynch, J., Wolfson, M. C., Kaplan, G. A. and Sorlie, P. D. (2007) 'Income inequality and mortality: a multilevel prospective study of 521 248 individuals in 50 US states', *International Journal of Epidemiology*, 36(3): 590–6.

Baker, M. C., Mathieu, E., Fleming, F. M., Deming, M., King, J. D., Garba, A., Koroma, J. B., Bockarie, M., Kabore A., Sankara, D. P. and Molyneux, D. H. (2010) 'Mapping, monitoring, and surveillance of neglected tropical diseases: towards a policy framework', *Lancet*, 375(9710): 231–8.

Banatvala, N. and Donaldson, L. (2007) 'Chronic diseases in developing countries', *Lancet*, 370(9605): 2076–8.

Banerji, D. (2002) 'Report of the WHO Commission on Macroeconomics and Health: a critique', *International Journal of Health Services*, 32(4): 733–54.

Banerji, D. (2006) 'Serious crisis in the practice of international health by the World Health Organization: the Commission on Social Determinants of Health', *International Journal of Health Services*, 36(4): 637–50.

Barker, C. and Green, A. (1996) 'Opening the debate on DALYs (disability-adjusted life years)', *Health Policy and Planning*, 11(2): 179–83.

Barona-Vilar, C., Gimenez-Marti, M. J., Fraile, T., Gonzalez-Steinbauer, C., Parada, C., Gil-Brusola, A., Bravo, D., Gomez, M. D., Navarro, D., Perez-Tamarit, A., Fernandez-Silveira, L., Fullana-Montoro, A. and Borras, R. (2012) 'Prevalence of Trypanosoma cruzi infection in pregnant Latin American women and congenital transmission rate in a non-endemic area: the experience of the Valencian Health Programme (Spain)', *Epidemiology and Infection*, 140(1): 1896–903.

Barr, D. A. (2008) *Health Disparities in the United States: Social Class, Race, Ethnicity, and Health* (Baltimore: Johns Hopkins University Press).

Barraza-Llorens, M., Bertozzi, S., Gonzalez-Pier, E. and Gutierrez, J. P. (2002) 'Addressing inequity in health and health care in Mexico', *Health Affairs*, 21(3): 47–56.

Barreto, M. L. (2004) 'The globalization of epidemiology: critical thoughts from Latin America', *International Journal of Epidemiology*, 33(5): 1132–7.

Barreto, M. L., De Almeida-Filho, N. and Breilh, J. (2001) 'Epidemiology is more than discourse: critical thoughts from Latin America', *Journal of Epidemiology & Community Health*, 55(3): 158–9.

Bartlett, J. A. and Shao, J. F. (2009) 'Successes, challenges, and limitations of current antiretroviral therapy in low-income and middle-income countries', *The Lancet Infectious Diseases*, 9(10): 637–49.

Bartley, M. (2004) *Health Inequality: An Introduction to Theories, Concepts and Methods* (Cambridge: Polity).

Bartley, M., Blane, D. and Davey Smith, G. (eds) (1998) *The Sociology of Health Inequalities* (Oxford: Blackwell Publishers).

Basile, L., Jansa, J. M., Carlier, Y., Salamanca, D. D., Angheben, A., Bartoloni, A., Seixas, J., Van Gool, T., Cañavate, C., Flores-Chavez, M., Jackson, Y., Chiodini, P. L. and Albajar-Viñas, P. (2011) 'Chagas disease in European countries: the challenge of a surveillance system', *Euro Surveillance*, 16(37).

Bastien, J. W. (1998) *The Kiss of Death: Chagas' Disease in the Americas* (Salt Lake City: University of Utah Press).

Bates, L. M., Hankivsky, O. and Springer, K. W. (2009) 'Gender and health inequities: a comment on the Final Report of the WHO Commission on the Social Determinants of Health', *Social Science & Medicine*, 69(7): 1002–4.

Bayer, A. M., Hunter, G. C., Gilman, R. H., Cornejo Del Carpio, J. G., Naquira, C., Bern, C. and Levy, M. Z. (2009) 'Chagas disease, migration and community settlement patterns in Arequipa, Peru', *PLoS Neglected Tropical Diseases*, 3(12): e567.

Beaglehole, R., Bonita, R., Alleyne, G. and Horton, R. (2011a) 'NCDs: celebrating success, moving forward', *Lancet*, 378(9799): 1283–4.

Beaglehole, R., Bonita, R., Alleyne, G., Horton, R., Li, L., Lincoln, P., J. C. Mbanya, M. McKee, R Moodie, S. Nishtar, P. Piot, K. Srinath Reddy and D. Stuckler (2011b) 'UN High-Level Meeting on Non-Communicable Diseases: addressing four questions', *Lancet*, 378(9789): 449–55.

Beaglehole, R., Ebrahim, S., Reddy, S., Voute, J. and Leeder, S. (2007) 'Prevention of chronic diseases: a call to action', *Lancet*, 370(9605): 2152–7.

Beaglehole, R. and Yach, D. (2003) 'Globalisation and the prevention and control of non-communicable disease: the neglected chronic diseases of adults', *Lancet*, 362(9387): 903–8.

Beck, U. (1999) *World Risk Society* (Cambridge: Polity Press).

Beiser, M. (2005) 'The health of immigrants and refugees in Canada', *Canadian Journal of Public Health*, 96, Suppl. 2: S30–44.

Berkman, A., Garcia, J., Munoz-Laboy, M., Paiva, V. and Parker, R. (2005) 'A critical analysis of the Brazilian response to HIV/AIDS: lessons learned for controlling and mitigating the epidemic in developing countries', *American Journal of Public Health*, 95(7): 1162–72.

Berkman, L. F. and Kawachi, I. (eds) (2000) *Social Epidemiology* (New York: Oxford University Press).

Berkman, L. F. and Sivaramakrishnan, K. (2008) 'WHO Commission on the social determinants of health: a bold new venture', *European Journal of Public Health*, 18(6): 547.

Bernburg, J. G. (2010) 'Relative deprivation theory does not imply a contextual effect of country-level inequality on poor health. A commentary on Jen, Jones, and Johnston (68:4, 2009)', *Social Science & Medicine*, 70(4): 493–95; discussion 498–500.

Bethony, J. M., Diemert, D. J., Oliveira, S. C. and Loukas, A. (2008) 'Can schistosomiasis really be consigned to history without a vaccine?', *Vaccine*, 26(27/28): 3373–6.

Beyrer, C., Villar, J. C., Suwanvanichkij, V., Singh, S., Baral, S. D. and Mills, E. J. (2007) 'Neglected diseases, civil conflicts, and the right to health', *Lancet*, 370(9587): 619–27.

Bezruchka, S. (2006) 'Epidemiological Approaches', in D. Raphael, T. Bryant and M. Rioux (eds), *Staying Alive: Critical Perspectives on Health, Illness, and Health Care* (Toronto: Canadian Scholars' Press): 13–40.

Biggs, B., King, L., Basu, S. and Stuckler, D. (2010) 'Is wealthier always healthier? The impact of national income level, inequality, and poverty on public health in Latin America', *Social Science & Medicine*, 71(2): 266–73.

Biolo, A., Ribeiro, A. L. and Clausell, N. (2010) 'Chagas cardiomyopathy – where do we stand after a hundred years?', *Progress in Cardiovascular Diseases*, 52(4): 300–16.

Birn, A. E. and Dmitrienko, K. (2005) 'The World Bank: global health or global harm?', *American Journal of Public Health*, 95(7): 1091–2; author reply 1092.

Bisley, N. (2007) *Rethinking Globalization* (Basingstoke: Palgrave Macmillan).

Blakely, T., Kennedy, B. P., Glass, R. and Kawachi, I. (2000) 'What is the lag time between income inequality and health status?', *Journal of Epidemiology and Community Health*, 54(4): 318–19.

Blech, J. (2006) *Inventing Disease and Pushing Pills: Pharmaceutical Companies and the Medicalisation of Normal Life* (New York: Routledge).

Bobak, M., Murphy, M., Rose, R. and Marmot, M. (2007) 'Societal characteristics and health in the former communist countries of Central and Eastern Europe and the former Soviet Union: a multilevel analysis', *Journal of Epidemiology & Community Health*, 61(11): 990–6.

Böckerman, P., Johansson, E., Helakorpi, S. and Uutela, A. (2009) 'Economic inequality and population health: looking beyond aggregate indicators', *Sociology of Health & Illness*, 31(3): 422–40.

Bond, P. (1999) 'Globalization, pharmaceutical pricing, and South African health policy: managing confrontation with U.S. firms and politicians', *International Journal of Health Services*, 29(4): 765–92.

Boutayeb, A. (2006) 'The double burden of communicable and non-communicable diseases in developing countries', *Transactions of the Royal Society of Tropical Medicine and Hygiene*, 100(3): 191–9.

Bowman, N. M., Kawai, V., Levy, M. Z., Cornejo del Carpio, J. G., Cabrera, L., Delgado, F., Malaga, F., Cordova Benzaquen, E., Pinedo, V. V., Steurer, F., Seitz, A. E., Gilman, R. H. and Bern, C. (2008) 'Chagas disease transmission in periurban communities of Arequipa, Peru', *Clinical Infectious Diseases*, 46(12): 1822–8.

Bradshaw, D., Groenewald, P., Laubscher, R., Nannan, N., Nojilana, B., Norman, R., Pieterse, D., Schneider, M., Bourne, D. E., Timaeus, I. M., Dorrington, R. and

Johnson, L. (2003) 'Initial burden of disease estimates for South Africa, 2000', *South African Journal of Medical Sciences*, 93(9): 682–8.

Breckenkamp, J., Mielck, A. and Razum, O. (2007) 'Health inequalities in Germany: do regional-level variables explain differentials in cardiovascular risk?', *BMC Public Health*, 7: 132.

Brenière, S. F., Bosseno, M. F., Noireau, F., Yacsik, N., Liegeard, P., Aznar, C. and Hontebeyrie, M. (2002) 'Integrate study of a Bolivian population infected by Trypanosoma cruzi, the agent of Chagas disease', *Memórias do Instituto Oswaldo Cruz*, 97(3): 289–95.

Briceño-León, R. (2009) 'La enfermedad de Chagas en las Americas: una perspectiva de ecosalud' [Chagas disease in the Americas: an ecohealth perspective], *Cadernos de Saúde Pública*, 25, Suppl. 1, S71–82.

Briceño-León, R. (1990) *La Casa Enferma: Sociología de la Enfermedad de Chagas* (Caracas: Fondo Editorial Acta Cientifica Venezolana).

Briggs, C. L. and Mantini-Briggs, C. (2003) *Stories in the Time of Cholera: Racial Profiling During a Medical Nightmare* (Berkeley: University of California Press).

Brown, T. (2011) '"Vulnerability is universal": considering the place of "security" and "vulnerability" within contemporary global health discourse', *Social Science & Medicine*, 72(3): 319–26.

Brown, T. M. and Fee, E. (2006) 'Rudolf Carl Virchow: medical scientist, social reformer, role model', *American Journal of Public Health*, 96(12): 2104–5.

Brunner, E. (1997) 'Stress and the biology of inequality', *British Medical Journal*, 314(7092): 1472–6.

Bukhman, G. and Kidder, A. (eds) (2011) *The PIH Guide to Chronic Care Integration for Endemic Non-Communicable Diseases* (Boston: Partners in Health).

Caldwell, J. C. (2001) 'Population health in transition', *Bulletin of the World Health Organization*, 79(2): 159–60.

Cardoso, F. H. (1972) 'Dependency and development in Latin America', *New Left Review*, 74: 83–95.

Carlier, Y., Torrico, F., Sosa-Estani, S., Russomando, G., Luquetti, A., Freilij, H. and P. A. Vinas (2011) 'Congenital Chagas disease: recommendations for diagnosis, treatment and control of newborns, siblings and pregnant women', *PLoS Neglected Tropical Diseases*, 5(10): e1250.

Cavalini, L. T. and de Leon, A. C. (2008) 'Morbidity and mortality in Brazilian municipalities: a multilevel study of the association between socioeconomic and healthcare indicators', *International Journal of Epidemiology*, 37(4): 775–83.

Cawthorne, P., Ford, N., Limpananont, J., Tienudom, N. and Purahong, W. (2007) 'WHO must defend patients' interests, not industry', *Lancet*, 369(9566): 974–5.

CDC (2011) 'Ten great public health achievements – worldwide, 2001–2010', *Morbidity and Mortality Weekly Report*, 60(24): 814–18.

Cedillos, R. A. (1988) 'The effectiveness of design and construction materials in Chagas' disease vector control', *Revista Argentina de Microbiología*, 20(1 Suppl.): 53–7.

Chatterjee, P. (2005) 'India's new patent laws may still hurt generic drug supplies', *Lancet*, 365(9468): 1378.

Chesnais, J. C. (1992) *The Demographic Transition: Stages, Patterns, and Economic Implications* (Oxford: Clarendon Press).

Chitsulo, L., Engels, D., Montresor, A. and Savioli, L. (2000) 'The global status of schistosomiasis and its control', *Acta Tropica*, 77(1): 41–51.

Coburn, D. (2000) 'Income inequality, social cohesion and the health status of populations: the role of neo-liberalism', *Social Science & Medicine*, 51(1): 135–46.

Coburn, D. (2001) 'Reasons to be sceptical of Marmot and Wilkinson', *British Medical Journal*, Electronic letter published on 30 July 2001: http://bmj.bmjjournals.com/cgi/eletters/2322/7296/1233#15812

Coburn, D. (2004) 'Beyond the income inequality hypothesis: class, neo-liberalism, and health inequalities', *Social Science & Medicine*, 58(1): 41–56.

Cockerham, G. B. and Cockerham, W. C. (2010) *Health and Globalization* (Cambridge: Polity Press).

Cohen-Kohler, J. C., Forman, L. and Lipkus, N. (2008) 'Addressing legal and political barriers to global pharmaceutical access: options for remedying the impact of the Agreement on Trade-Related Aspects of Intellectual Property Rights (TRIPS) and the imposition of TRIPS-plus standards', *Health Economics, Policy, and Law*, 3(Pt 3): 229–56.

Cohen, J. C. and Illingworth, P. (2003) 'The dilemma of intellectual property rights for pharmaceuticals', *Developing World Bioethics*, 3(1): 27–48.

Colgrove, J. (2002) 'The McKeown thesis: a historical controversy and its enduring influence', *American Journal of Public Health*, 92(5): 725–9.

Collins, J. W., Jr and David, R. J. (2009) 'Racial disparity in low birth weight and infant mortality', *Clinics in Perinatology*, 36(1): 63–73.

Connell, R. (2007) *Southern Theory: The Global Dynamics of Knowledge in Social Science* (Malden, MA: Polity).

Conteh, L., Engels, T. and Molyneux, D. H. (2010) 'Socioeconomic aspects of neglected tropical diseases', *Lancet*, 375(9710): 239–47.

Cook, I. G. and Dummer, T. J. (2004) 'Changing health in China: re-evaluating the epidemiological transition model', *Health Policy*, 67(3): 329–43.

Corbett, E. L., Steketee, R. W., ter Kuile, F. O., Latif, A. S., Kamali, A. and Hayes, R. J. (2002) 'HIV–1/AIDS and the control of other infectious diseases in Africa', *Lancet*, 359(9324): 2177–87.

Crager, S. E. and Price, M. (2009) 'Prizes and parasites: incentive models for addressing Chagas disease', *Journal of Law, Medicine & Ethics*, 37(2): 292–304.

Crush, J. (2002) 'The global raiders: nationalism, globalization and the South African brain drain', *Journal of International Affairs*, 56(1): 147–74.

CSDH (Commission on the Social Determinants of Health) (2008) *Closing the Gap in a Generation: Health Equity through Action on the Social Determinants of Health. Final Report of the Commission on Social Determinants of Health* (Geneva: World Health Organization).

Cwikel, J. (2006) *Social Epidemiology: Strategies for Public Health Activism* (New York: Columbia University Press).

Dabis, F., Newell, M. L. and Hirschel, B. (2010) 'HIV drugs for treatment, and for prevention', *Lancet*, 375(9731): 2056–7.

Dados, N. and Connell, R. (2012) 'The Global South', *Contexts*, 11(12): 12–13.

Danaei, G., Finucane, M. M., Lu, Y., Singh, G. M., Cowan, M. J., Paciorek, C. J., Lin, J. K., Farzadfar, F., Khang, Y. H., Stevens, G. A., Rao, M., Ali, M. K., Riley, L. M., Robinson, C. A. and Ezzati, M. (2011) 'National, regional, and global trends in fasting plasma glucose and diabetes prevalence since 1980: systematic analysis of health examination surveys and epidemiological studies with 370 country-years and 2.7 million participants', *Lancet*, 378(9785): 31–40.

Daniels, N., Kennedy, B. and Kawachi, I. (2000) *Is Inequality Bad for Our Health?* (Boston: Beacon Press).

Davey Smith, G. (2001) 'Reflections on the limitations to epidemiology', *Journal of Clinical Epidemiology*, 54(4): 325–31.

Davies, S. E. (2010) *Global Politics of Health* (Cambridge: Polity Press).

Davis, K. and Moore, W. E. (1945) 'Some principles of stratification', *American Sociological Review*, 10(2): 242–9.

Day, M. (2007) 'Threat to break patents saves Brazil $1bn in cost of HIV treatment, study shows', *British Medical Journal*, 335(7629): 1065.

De Maio, F. G. (2007) 'Income inequality measures', *Journal of Epidemiology and Community Health*, 61(10): 849–52.

De Maio, F. G. (2008) 'Ecological analysis of the health effects of income inequality in Argentina', *Public Health*, 122(5): 487–96.

De Maio, F. G. (2010a) *Health and Social Theory* (Basingstoke: Palgrave Macmillan).

De Maio, F. G. (2010b) 'Immigration as pathogenic: a systematic review of the health of immigrants to Canada', *International Journal for Equity in Health*, 9: 27.

De Maio, F. G. (2011) 'Understanding chronic non-communicable diseases in Latin America: towards an equity-based research agenda', *Globalization & Health*, 7(1): 36.

De Maio, F. G. (2012) 'Understanding the health transitions of immigrants to Canada: research priorities', *Journal of Health Care for the Poor and Underserved*, 23(3): 958–62.

De Maio, F. G., Corber, S. J. and Joffres, M. (2008) 'Towards a social analysis of risk factors for chronic diseases in Latin America', *LASA Forum*, 39(2): 10–13.

De Maio, F. G. and Kemp, E. (2010) 'The deterioration of health status among immigrants to Canada', *Global Public Health*, 5(5): 462–78.

De Maio, F. G., Linetzky, B. and Ferrante, D. (2012a) 'Changes in the social gradients for pap smears and mammograms in Argentina: evidence from the 2005 and 2009 National Risk Factor Surveys', *Public Health*, 126(10): 821–6.

De Maio, F. G., Linetzky, B., Ferrante, D. and Fleischer, N. L. (2012b) 'Extending the income inequality hypothesis: Ecological results from the 2005 and 2009 Argentine National Risk Factor Surveys', *Global Public Health*, 7(6): 635–47.

De Maio, F. G., Linetzky, B. and Virgolini, M. (2009) 'An average/deprivation/inequality (ADI) analysis of chronic disease outcomes and risk factors in Argentina', *Population Health Metrics*, 7(8).

De Vogli, R., Gimeno, D. and Mistry, R. (2009) 'The policies-inequality feedback and health: the case of globalisation', *Journal of Epidemiology and Community Health*, 63(9): 688–91.

De Vogli, R., Mistry, R., Gnesotto, R. and Cornia, G. A. (2005) 'Has the relation between income inequality and life expectancy disappeared? Evidence from Italy and top industrialised countries', *Journal of Epidemiology and Community Health*, 59(2): 158–62.

Deaton, A. (2002) 'The convoluted story of international studies of inequality and health', *International Journal of Epidemiology*, 31(3): 546–9.

Deaton, A. and Lubotsky, D. (2003) 'Mortality, inequality and race in American cities and states', *Social Science & Medicine*, 56(6): 1139–53.

Dewan, S. and Sack, K. (2008) 'A safety-net hospital falls into financial crisis', *New York Times*, 8 January, from http://www.nytimes.com/2008/01/08/us/08grady.html?pagewanted=all&_r=0.

Dias, J. C., Prata, A. and Correia, D. (2008) 'Problems and perspectives for Chagas disease control: in search of a realistic analysis', *Revista da Sociedade Brasileira de Medicina Tropical*, 41(2): 193–6.

Ditmore, M. and Allman, D. (2010) 'Implications of PEPFAR's anti-prostitution pledge for HIV prevention among organizations working with sex workers', *HIV/AIDS Policy & Law Review*, 15(1): 63–4.

Dorling, D., Mitchell, R. and Pearce, J. (2007) 'The global impact of income inequality on health by age: an observational study', *British Medical Journal*, 335(7625): 873.

Engelgau, M. M., Karan, A. and Mahal, A. (2012) 'The economic impact of non-communicable diseases on households in India', *Globalization & Health*, 8: 9.

Engels, D. and Savioli, L. (2006) 'Reconsidering the underestimated burden caused by neglected tropical diseases', *Trends in Parasitology*, 22(8): 363–6.

Esping-Andersen, G. (1990) *The Three Worlds of Welfare Capitalism* (Oxford: Polity Press).

Evans, T., Whitehead, M., Diderichsen, F., Bhuiya, A. and Wirth, M. (eds) (2001) *Challenging Inequities in Health: From Ethics to Action* (Oxford: Oxford University Press).

Farmer, P. (1992) *AIDS and Accusation: Haiti and the Geography of Blame* (Berkeley: University of California Press).

Farmer, P. (1996) 'Social inequalities and emerging infectious diseases', *Emerging Infectious Diseases*, 2(4): 259–69.

Farmer, P. (1999) *Infections and Inequalities: The Modern Plagues* (Berkeley: University of California Press).

Farmer, P. (2003) *Pathologies of Power: Health, Human Rights, and the New War on the Poor* (Berkeley: University of California Press).

Farmer, P. (2011) *Haiti After the Earthquake* (New York: PublicAffairs).

Farmer, P., Léandre, F., Mukherjee, J. S., Claude, M., Nevil, P., Smith-Fawzi, M. C., Koenig, S. P., Castro, A., Becerra, M. C., Sachs, J., Attaran, A. and Kim, J. Y. (2001) 'Community-based approaches to HIV treatment in resource-poor settings', *Lancet*, 358(9279): 404–9.

Farmer, P., Nizeye, B., Stulac, S. and Keshavjee, S. (2006) 'Structural violence and clinical medicine', *PLoS Medicine*, 3(10): e449.

Feachem, R. G. and Sabot, O. J. (2006) 'An examination of the Global Fund at 5 years', *Lancet*, 368(9534): 537–40.

Feagin, J. R. (2004) 'Social Justice and Sociology: Agendas for the Twenty-First Century', in W. K. Carroll (ed.), *Critical Strategies for Social Research* (Toronto: Canadian Scholars' Press Inc.): 29–43.

Feagin, J. R. and Vera, H. (2008) *Liberation Sociology* (2nd edn) (Boulder: Paradigm).

Feinleib, M. (2008) 'The epidemiologic transition model: accomplishments and challenges', *Annals of Epidemiology*, 18(11): 865–7.

Feliciangeli, M. D., Sanchez-Martin, M. J., Suarez, B., Marrero, R., Torrellas, A., Bravo, A., Medina, M., Martinez, C., Hernandez, M., Duque, N., Toyo, J. and Rangel, R. (2007) 'Risk factors for Trypanosoma cruzi human infection in Barinas State, Venezuela', *American Journal of Tropical Medicine and Hygiene*, 76(5): 915–21.

Ferrante, D., Linetzky, B., Virgolini, M., Schoj, V. and Apelberg, B. (2012) 'Reduction in hospital admissions for acute coronary syndrome after the successful implementation of 100% smoke-free legislation in Argentina: a comparison with partial smoking restrictions', *Tobacco Control*, 21(4): 402–6.

Finucane, M. M., Stevens, G. A., Cowan, M. J., Danaei, G., Lin, J. K., Paciorek, C. J., Singh, G. M., Gutierrez, H. R., Lu, Y., Bahalim, A. N., Farzadfar, F., Riley, L. M. and Ezzati, M. (2011) 'National, regional, and global trends in body-mass index since 1980: systematic analysis of health examination surveys and epidemiological studies with 960 country-years and 9.1 million participants', *Lancet*, 377(9765): 557–67.

Fleischer, N. L., Diez Roux, A. V. and Hubbard, A. E. (2012) 'Inequalities in body mass index and smoking behavior in 70 countries: evidence for a social transition in chronic disease risk', *American Journal of Epidemiology*, 175(3): 167–76.

Fleming, D. T. and Wasserheit, J. N. (1999) 'From epidemiological synergy to public health policy and practice: the contribution of other sexually transmitted diseases to sexual transmission of HIV infection', *Sexually Transmitted Infections*, 75(1): 3–17.

Ford, N., Wilson, D., Costa Chaves, G., Lotrowska, M. and Kijtiwatchakul, K. (2007) 'Sustaining access to antiretroviral therapy in the less-developed world: lessons from Brazil and Thailand', *AIDS*, 21, Suppl. 4: S21–29.

Frank, A. G. (1969) *Latin America: Underdevelopment or Revolution* (New York: Monthly Review Press).

Franke, M. F., Kaigamba, F., Socci, A. R., Hakizamungu, M., Patel, A., Bagiruwigize, E., Niyigena, P., Walker, K. D., Epino, H., Binagwaho, A., Mukherjee, J., Farmer, P. E. and Rich, M. L. (2013) 'Improved retention associated with community-based accompaniment for antiretroviral therapy delivery in rural Rwanda', *Clinical Infectious Diseases*, 56(9): 1319–26.

Frenk, J., Bobadilla, J. L., Sepúlveda, J. and Cervantes, M. L. (1989) 'Health transition in middle-income countries: new challenges for health care', *Health Policy and Planning*, 4(1): 29.

Frew, S. E., Liu, V. Y. and Singer, P. A. (2009) 'A business plan to help the "global South" in its fight against neglected diseases', *Health Affairs*, 28(6): 1760–73.

Friedman, T. (1990) *The Lexus and the Olive Tree* (London: Harper Collins).

Friedman, T. (2005) *The World is Flat: A Brief History of the Twenty-First Century* (New York: Farrar, Straus & Giroux).

Fuster, V., and Voûte, J. (2005) 'MDGs: chronic diseases are not on the agenda', *Lancet*, 366(9496): 1512–14.

Galtung, J. (1969) 'Violence, peace, and peace research', *Journal of Peace Research*, 6(3): 167–91.

Galvão, J. (2002) 'Access to antiretroviral drugs in Brazil', *Lancet*, 360(9348): 1862–5.

Garcia, J. and Parker, R. G. (2011) 'Resource mobilization for health advocacy: Afro-Brazilian religious organizations and HIV prevention and control', *Social Science & Medicine*, 72(12): 1930–8.

Gardner, J. W. and Sanborn, J. S. (1990) 'Years of potential life lost (YPLL) – what does it measure?', *Epidemiology*, 1(4): 322–9.

Gaylin, D. S. and Kates, J. (1997) 'Refocusing the lens: epidemiologic transition theory, mortality differentials, and the AIDS pandemic', *Social Science & Medicine*, 44(5), 609–621.

Giddens, A. (1990) *The Consequences of Modernity*. Cambridge: Polity.

Giddens, A. (2000) *Runaway World*. New York: Routledge.

Gold, J. (2002) 'Support required for antiretroviral uptake in developing countries', *Journal of HIV Therapy*, 7(3), 63–7.

Gómez, R. (2001) 'La transición en epidemiología y salud pública: ¿Explicacin o condena? [Epidemiological transition and public health: explanation or damnation?]', *Revista Facultad Nacional de Salud Pública*, 19, 57–74.

Grangeiro, A., da Silva, L. L. and Teixeira, P. R. (2009) 'Resposta à aids no Brasil: contribuições dos movimentos sociais e da reforma sanitária [Response to AIDS in Brazil: contributions of social movements and the sanitary reform]', *Revista Panamericana de Salud Pública*, 26(1): 87–94.

Greenberg, H., Raymond, S. U. and Leeder, S. R. (2011) 'The prevention of global chronic disease: academic public health's new frontier', *American Journal of Public Health*, 101(8): 1386–90.

Grembowski, D. E., Cook, K. S., Patrick, D. L. and Roussel, A. E. (2002) 'Managed care and the US health care system a social exchange perspective', *Social Science & Medicine*, 54: 1167–80.

Grove, D. I. (1990) *A History of Human Helminthology* (Oxford: C.A.B. International).

Gürtler, R. E., Kitron, U., Cecere, M. C., Segura, E. L. and Cohen, J. E. (2007) 'Sustainable vector control and management of Chagas disease in the Gran Chaco, Argentina', *Proceedings of the National Academy of Sciences of the United States of America*, 104(41): 16194–9.

Gushulak, B. (2007) 'Healthier on arrival? Further insight into the "healthy immigrant effect"', *Canadian Medical Association Journal*, 176(10): 1439–40.

Guzmán, R. G. (2009) 'Latin American social medicine and the report of the WHO Commission on Social Determinants of Health', *Social Medicine*, 4(2): 113–20.

Harling, G., Ehrlich, R. and Myer, L. (2008) 'The social epidemiology of tuberculosis in South Africa: a multilevel analysis', *Social Science & Medicine*, 66(2): 492–505.

Harris, M. and Montaner, J. S. (2011) 'Exploring the role of "treatment as prevention"', *Current HIV Research*, 9(6): 352–4.

Havlir, D. V. and Hammer, S. M. (2005) 'Patents versus patients? Antiretroviral therapy in India', *New England Journal of Medicine*, 353(8): 749–51.

Hawkes, C. (2006) 'Uneven dietary development: linking the policies and processes of globalization with the nutrition transition, obesity and diet-related chronic diseases', *Globalization & Health*, 2: 4.

Held, D., McGrew, A., Goldblatt, D. and Perraton, J. (1999) *Global Transformations: Politics, Economics and Culture* (Cambridge: Polity Press).

Heuveline, P., Guillot, M. and Gwatkin, D. R. (2002) 'The uneven tides of the health transition', *Social Science & Medicine*, 55(2): 313–22.

Hidron, A. I., Gilman, R. H., Justiniano, J., Blackstock, A. J., Lafuente, C., Selum, W., Calderon, M., Verastegui, M., Ferrufino, L., Valencia, E., Tornheim, J. A., O'Neal, S., Comer, R., Galdos-Cardenas, G. and Bern, C. *et al.* (2010a) 'Chagas cardiomyopathy in the context of the chronic disease transition', *PLoS Neglected Tropical Diseases*, 4(5): e688.

Hidron, A., Vogenthaler, N., Santos-Preciado, J. I., Rodriguez-Morales, A. J., Franco-Paredes, C. and Rassi, A., Jr. (2010b) 'Cardiac involvement with parasitic infections', *Clinical Microbiology Reviews*, 23(2): 324–49.

Holmes, S. M. (2012) 'The clinical gaze in the practice of migrant health: Mexican migrants in the United States', *Social Science & Medicine*, 74(6): 873–81.

Holveck, J. C., Ehrenberg, J. P., Ault, S. K., Rojas, R., Vasquez, J., Cerqueira, M. T., Ippolito-Shepherd, J., Genovese, M. A. and Periago, M. R. (2007) 'Prevention, control, and elimination of neglected diseases in the Americas: pathways to integrated, inter-programmatic, inter-sectoral action for health and development', *BMC Public Health*, 7: 6.

Homedes, N., Ugalde, A. and Forns, J. R. (2005) 'The World Bank, pharmaceutical policies, and health reforms in Latin America', *International Journal of Health Services*, 35(4): 691–717.

Horton, R. (2005) 'The neglected epidemic of chronic disease', *Lancet*, 366(9496): 1514.

Horton, R. (2007) 'Chronic diseases: the case for urgent global action', *Lancet*, 370(9603): 1881–2.

Hotez, P. J. (2007) 'Neglected diseases and poverty in "The Other America": the greatest health disparity in the United States?', *PLoS Neglected Tropical Diseases*, 1(3): e149.

Hotez, P. J. (2008a) *Forgotten People, Forgotten Diseases: The Neglected Tropical Diseases and their Impact on Global Health and Development* (Washington, DC: ASM Press).

Hotez, P. J. (2008b) 'The giant anteater in the room: Brazil's neglected tropical diseases problem', *PLoS Neglected Tropical Diseases*, 2(1): e177.

Hotez, P. J. (2008c) 'Stigma: the stealth weapon of the NTD', *PLoS Neglected Tropical Diseases*, 2(4): e230.

Hotez, P. J. (2009) 'Empowering women and improving female reproductive health through control of neglected tropical diseases', *PLoS Neglected Tropical Diseases*, 3(11): e559.

Hotez, P. J., Bethony, J. M., Oliveira, S. C., Brindley, P. J. and Loukas, A. (2008a) 'Multivalent anthelminthic vaccine to prevent hookworm and schistosomiasis', *Expert Review of Vaccines*, 7(6): 745–52.

Hotez, P. J., Bottazzi, M. E., Franco-Paredes, C., Ault, S. K. and Periago, M. R. (2008b) 'The neglected tropical diseases of Latin America and the Caribbean: a review of disease burden and distribution and a roadmap for control and elimination', *PLoS Neglected Tropical Diseases*, 2(9): e300.

Hotez, P. J., Dumonteil, E., Woc-Colburn, L., Serpa, J. A., Bezek, S., Edwards, M. S., Hallmark, C. J., Musselwhite, L. W., Flink, B. J. and M. E. Bottazzi (2012) 'Chagas disease: "the new HIV/AIDS of the Americas"', *PLoS Neglected Tropical Diseases*, 6(5): e1498.

Hotez, P. J. and Ferris, M. T. (2006) 'The antipoverty vaccines', *Vaccine*, 24(31/32): 5787–99.

Hotez, P. J. and Kamath, A. (2009) 'Neglected tropical diseases in sub-Saharan Africa: review of their prevalence, distribution, and disease burden', *PLoS Neglected Tropical Diseases*, 3(8): e412.

Hotez, P. J., Molyneux, D. H., Fenwick, A., Kumaresan, J., Sachs, S. E., Sachs, J. D. and Savioli, L. (2007) 'Control of neglected tropical diseases', *New England Journal of Medicine*, 357(10): 1018–27.

Hotez, P. J., Ottesen, E. A., Fenwick, A. and Molyneux, D. (2006) 'The Neglected Tropical Diseases: The Ancient Afflictions of Stigma and Poverty and the Prospects for their Control and Elimination', in A. J. Pollard and A. Finn (eds), *Hot Topics in Infection and Immunity in Children* (New York: Springer).

Hotez, P. J. and Pecoul, B. (2010) '"Manifesto" for advancing the control and elimination of neglected tropical diseases', *PLoS Neglected Tropical Diseases*, 4(5).

Huffman, S. A., Veen, J., Hennink, M. M. and McFarland, D. A. (2012) 'Exploitation, vulnerability to tuberculosis and access to treatment among Uzbek labor migrants in Kazakhstan', *Social Science & Medicine*, 74(6): 864–72.

Huish, R. (2009) 'How Cuba's Latin American School of Medicine challenges the ethics of physician migration', *Social Science & Medicine*, 69(3): 301–4.

Hyman, I. (2004) 'Setting the stage: reviewing current knowledge on the health of Canadian immigrants', *Canadian Journal of Public Health*, 95(3): 1–8.

Inglis, D. and Gimlin, D. (2009) 'Food Globalizations: Ironies and Ambivalences of Food, Cuisine and Globality', in D. Inglis and D. Gimlin (eds), *The Globalization of Food* (Oxford: Berg): 3–44.

Iriart, C., Merhy, E. E. and Waitzkin, H. (2001) 'Managed care in Latin America: the new common sense in health policy reform', *Social Science & Medicine*, 52: 1243–53.

Jackson, Y., Myers, C., Diana, A., Marti, H. P., Wolff, H., Chappuis, F., Loutan, L. and Gervaix, A. (2009) 'Congenital transmission of Chagas disease in Latin American immigrants in Switzerland', *Emerging Infectious Diseases*, 15(4): 601–3.

Janes, C. R. and Corbett, K. (2009) 'Anthropology and global health', *Annual Review of Anthropology*, 38: 167–83.

Jappah, J. V. (2013) 'The convergence of American and Nigerian religious conservatism in a biopolitical shaping of Nigeria's HIV/AIDS prevention programmes', *Global Public Health*, 8(3): 312–25.

Jauregui, A. (2012) 'Chagas disease, tropical insect-borne illness, may be "new HIV/AIDS of the Americas"', *Huffington Post*, 30 May.

Jen, M. H., Jones, K. and Johnston, R. (2009) 'Global variations in health: evaluating Wilkinson's income inequality hypothesis using the World Values Survey', *Social Science & Medicine*, 68(4): 643–53.

Jha, P., Jacob, B., Gajalakshmi, V., Gupta, P. C., Dhingra, N., Kumar, R., Sinha, D. N., Dikshit, R. P., Parida, D. K., Kamadod, R., Boreham, J. and Peto, R. (2008) 'A nationally representative case-control study of smoking and death in India', *New England Journal of Medicine*, 358(11): 1137–47.

Jones, A. (ed.) (2010) *Globalization: Key Thinkers* (Cambridge: Polity).

Jones, K. and Moon, G. (1992) 'Medical geography – global perspectives', *Progress in Human Geography*, 16(4): 563–72.

Joshi, S., Song, Y. M., Kim, T. H. and Cho, S. I. (2008) 'Socio-economic status and the risk of liver cancer mortality: a prospective study in Korean men', *Public Health*, 122(11): 1144–51.

Kaplan, M. S., Huguet, N., Newsom, J. T. and McFarland, B. H. (2004) 'The association between length of residence and obesity among Hispanic immigrants', *American Journal of Preventive Medicine*, 27(4): 323–6.

Katz, A. (2004) 'The Sachs report: Investing in Health for Economic Development – or increasing the size of the crumbs from the rich man's table? Part I', *International Journal of Health Services*, 34(4): 751–73.

Katz, A. (2005) 'The Sachs report: investing in health for economic development – or increasing the size of the crumbs from the rich man's table? Part II', *International Journal of Health Services*, 35(1): 171–88.

Katz, J. M. (2013) *The Big Truck that Went By: How the World Came to Save Haiti and Left Behind a Disaster* (Basingstoke: Palgrave Macmillan).

Kawachi, I., Kennedy, B. P. and Wilkinson, R. G. (1999) *The Society and Population Health Reader: Income Inequality and Health (Vol. 1)* (New York: New Press).

Kawachi, I., Subramanian, S. V. and Almeida-Filho, N. (2002) 'A glossary for health inequalities', *Journal of Epidemiology and Community Health*, 56(9): 647–52.

Kawachi, I. and Wamala, S. (eds) (2007) *Globalization and Health* (New York: Oxford University Press).

Kay, C. (1991) 'Reflections on the Latin American contribution to development theory', *Development and Change*, 22(1): 31–68.

Kearney, P. M., Whelton, M., Reynolds, K., Muntner, P., Whelton, P. K. and He, J. (2005) 'Global burden of hypertension: analysis of worldwide data', *Lancet*, 365(9455): 217–23.

Kerr, T., Tyndall, M., Li, K., Montaner, J. and Wood, E. (2005) 'Safer injection facility use and syringe sharing in injection drug users', *Lancet*, 366(9482): 316–18.

Kerry, V. B. and Lee, K. (2007) 'TRIPS, the Doha declaration and paragraph 6 decision: what are the remaining steps for protecting access to medicines?', *Globalization & Health*, 3: 3.

Kessomboon, N., Limpananont, J., Kulsomboon, V., Maleewong, U., Eksaengsri, A. and Paothong, P. (2010) 'Impact on access to medicines from TRIPS-Plus: a case study of Thai–US FTA', *Southeast Asian Journal of Tropical Medicine and Public Health*, 41(3): 667–77.

Kim, C. W., Lee, S. Y. and Moon, O. R. (2008) 'Inequalities in cancer incidence and mortality across income groups and policy implications in South Korea', *Public Health*, 122(3): 229–36.

Kim, J. Y., Millen, J. V., Irwin, A. and Gershman, J. (eds) (2000) *Dying for Growth: Global Inequality and the Health of the Poor* (Monroe: Common Courage Press).

King, C. H. and Dangerfield-Cha, M. (2008) 'The unacknowledged impact of chronic schistosomiasis', *Chronic Illness*, 4(1): 65–79.

King, H., Aubert, R. E. and Herman, W. H. (1998) 'Global burden of diabetes, 1995–2025: prevalence, numerical estimates, and projections', *Diabetes Care*, 21(9): 1414–31.

Kirk, S. F., Penney, T. L. and McHugh, T. L. (2010) 'Characterizing the obesogenic environment: the state of the evidence with directions for future research', *Obesity Reviews*, 11(2): 109–17.

Koch, E., Romero, T., Romero, C. X., Akel, C., Manriquez, L., Paredes, M., Roman, C., Taylor, A., Vargas, M. and Kirschbaum, A. (2010) 'Impact of education, income and chronic disease risk factors on mortality of adults: does "a pauper-rich paradox" exist in Latin American societies?', *Public Health*, 124(1): 39–48.

Koenig, S. P., Leandre, F. and Farmer, P. E. (2004) 'Scaling-up HIV treatment programmes in resource-limited settings: the rural Haiti experience', *AIDS*, 18, Suppl. 3: S21–25.

Kolko, G. (1999) 'Ravaging the poor: the International Monetary Fund indicted by its own data', *International Journal of Health Services*, 29(1): 51–7.

Koplan, J. P., Bond, T. C., Merson, M. H., Reddy, K. S., Rodriguez, M. H., Sewankambo, N. K. and Wasserheit, J. N. (2009) 'Towards a common definition of global health', *Lancet*, 373(9679): 1993–5.

Kovsted, J. (2005) 'Scaling up AIDS treatment in developing countries: a review of current and future arguments', *Development Policy Review*, 23(4): 465–82.

Krieger, N. (2005) 'Embodiment: a conceptual glossary for epidemiology', *Journal of Epidemiology and Community Health*, 59(5): 350–5.

Krieger, N. (2011) *Epidemiology and the People's Health: Theory and Context* (New York: Oxford University Press).

Krieger, N. and Davey Smith, G. (2004) '"Bodies count," and body counts: social epidemiology and embodying inequality', *Epidemiologic Reviews*, 26: 92–103.

Kruk, M. E. (2012) 'Globalisation and global health governance: implications for public health', *Global Public Health*, 7, Suppl. 1: S54–62.

Kuek, V., Phillips, K. and Kohler, J. C. (2011) 'Access to medicines and domestic compulsory licensing: learning from Canada and Thailand', *Global Public Health*, 6(2): 111–24.

Labonté, R., Schrecker, T., Packer, C. and Runnels, V. (eds) (2009) *Globalization and Health: Pathways, Evidence and Policy* (New York: Routledge).

Labonté, R. and Torgerson, R. (2005) 'Interrogating globalization, health and development: towards a comprehensive framework for research, policy and political action', *Critical Public Health*, 15(2): 157–79.

Lall, R. R. and Pilkington, E. (2013) 'UN will not compensate Haiti cholera victims, Ban Ki-moon tells president', *The Guardian*. 21 February. Retrieved from http://www.guardian.co.uk/world/2013/feb/21/un-haiti-cholera-victims-rejects-compensation.

Lammie, P. J., Lindo, J. F., Secor, W. E., Vasquez, J., Ault, S. K. and Eberhard, M. L. (2007) 'Eliminating lymphatic filariasis, onchocerciasis, and schistosomiasis from the Americas: breaking a historical legacy of slavery', *PLoS Neglected Tropical Diseases*, 1(2): e71.

Laporte, A. and Ferguson, B. S. (2003) 'Income inequality and mortality: time series evidence from Canada', *Health Policy*, 66(1): 107–17.

Larchanché, S. (2012) 'Intangible obstacles: health implications of stigmatization, structural violence, and fear among undocumented immigrants in France', *Social Science & Medicine*, 74(6): 858–63.

Le Loup, G., de Assis, A., Costa-Couto, M. H., Thoenig, J. C., Fleury, S., de Camargo, K., Jr. and Larouzé, B. (2009) 'A public policy approach to local models of HIV/AIDS control in Brazil', *American Journal of Public Health*, 99(6): 1108–15.

Lee, K. (2003) *Globalization and Health: An Introduction* (Basingstoke: Palgrave Macmillan).

Lee, K. (2010) 'How do we move forward on the social determinants of health: the global governance challenges', *Critical Public Health*, 20(1): 5–14.

Lee, Y. S. (2006) *Reclaiming Development in the World System* (Cambridge: Cambridge University Press).

Leigh, A. and Jencks, C. (2007) 'Inequality and mortality: long-run evidence from a panel of countries', *Journal of Health Economics*, 26(1): 1–24.

Lim, S. S., Gaziano, T. A., Gakidou, E., Reddy, K. S., Farzadfar, F., Lozano, R. (2007) 'Prevention of cardiovascular disease in high-risk individuals in low-income and middle-income countries: health effects and costs', *Lancet*, 370(9604): 2054–62.

Lincoln, P., Rundall, P., Jeffery, B., Kellett, G., Lobstein, T., Lhotska, L., Allen, K. and Gupta, A. (2011) 'Conflicts of interest and the UN high-level meeting on non-communicable diseases', *Lancet*, 378(9804): e6.

Lindoso, J. A. and Lindoso, A. A. (2009) 'Neglected tropical diseases in Brazil', *Revista do Instituto de Medicina Tropical de São Paulo*, 51(5): 247–53.

Linetzky, B., De Maio, F. G., Ferrante, D., Konfino, J. and Boissonet, C. (2013) 'Sex-stratified socio-economic gradients in physical inactivity, obesity, and diabetes: evidence of short-term changes in Argentina', *International Journal of Public Health*, 58(2): 277–84.

Link, B. G., Northridge, M. E., Phelan, J. C. and Ganz, M. L. (1998) 'Social epidemiology and the fundamental cause concept: on the structuring of effective cancer screens by socioeconomic status', *Milbank Quarterly*, 76(3): 304–75, 375–402.

Link, B. G. and Phelan, J. (1995) 'Social conditions as fundamental causes of disease', *Journal of Health and Social Behavior*, 35(Extra issue): 80–94.

Link, B. G. and Phelan, J. C. (2002) 'McKeown and the idea that social conditions are fundamental causes of disease', *American Journal of Public Health*, 92(5): 730–2.

Llovet, I., Dinardi, G. and De Maio, F. G. (2011) 'Mitigating social and health inequities: community participation and Chagas disease in rural Argentina', *Global Public Health*, 6(4): 371–84.

Lloyd, V. and Weissman, R. (2002) 'How International Monetary Fund and World Bank policies undermine labor power and rights', *International Journal of Health Services*, 32(3): 433–42.

Lobo, D. A., Velayudhan, R., Chatterjee, P., Kohli, H. and Hotez, P. J. (2011) 'The neglected tropical diseases of India and South Asia: review of their prevalence, distribution, and control or elimination', *PLoS Neglected Tropical Diseases*, 5(10): e1222.

Lorenc, T., Petticrew, M., Welch, V. and Tugwell, P. (2013) 'What types of interventions generate inequalities? Evidence from systematic review', *Journal of Epidemiology & Community Health*, 67(2): 190–3.

Lynch, J., Davey Smith, G., Harper, S., Hillermeier, M., Ross, N., Kaplan, G. A. and Wolfson, M. (2004) 'Is income inequality a determinant of population health? Part 1. A systematic review', *Milbank Quarterly*, 82(1): 5–99.

Lynch, J., Harper, S. and Davey Smith, G. (2003) 'Plugging leaks and repelling boarders – where to next for the SS income inequality?', *International Journal of Epidemiology*, 32(6): 1029–36.

Lynch, J., Harper, S., Kaplan, G. A. and Davey Smith, G. (2005) 'Associations between income inequality and mortality among US states: the importance of time period and source of income data', *American Journal of Public Health*, 95(8): 1424–30.

MacGregor, G. (2011) 'Salt reduction under threat at the UN High level meeting in New York', from http://www.ncdalliance.org/node/3502.

Magnusson, R. S. (2009) 'Rethinking global health challenges: towards a 'global compact' for reducing the burden of chronic disease', *Public Health*, 123(3): 265–74.

Malta, M., Magnanini, M. M., Mello, M. B., Pascom, A. R., Linhares, Y. and Bastos, F. I. (2010) 'HIV prevalence among female sex workers, drug users and men who have sex with men in Brazil: a systematic review and meta-analysis', *BMC Public Health*, 10: 317.

Mamudu, H. M. and Glantz, S. A. (2009) 'Civil society and the negotiation of the Framework Convention on Tobacco Control', *Global Public Health*, 4(2): 150–68.

Mamudu, H. M., Yang, J. S. and Novotny, T. E. (2011) 'UN resolution on the prevention and control of non-communicable diseases: an opportunity for global action', *Global Public Health*, 6(4): 347–53.

Manderson, L., Aagaard-Hansen, J., Allotey, P., Gyapong, M. and Sommerfeld, J. (2009) 'Social research on neglected diseases of poverty: continuing and emerging themes', *PLoS Neglected Tropical Diseases*, 3(2), e332.

Manners, S. (2006) *Super Pills: The Prescriptions Drugs We Love to Take*. Vancouver: Raincoast Books.

Mansyur, C., Amick, B. C., Harrist, R. B., & Franzini, L. (2008) Social capital, income inequality, and self-rated health in 45 countries. *Social Science & Medicine*, 66(1), 43–56.

Mantilla, B. (2011) Invisible plagues, invisible voices: a critical discourse analysis of neglected tropical diseases. *Social Medicine*, 6(3), 118–27.

Margellos, H., Silva, A., and Whitman, S. (2004) 'Comparison of health status indicators in chicago: are Black–White disparities worsening?', *American Journal of Public Health*, 94(1): 116–21.

Marmot, M. (2002) 'The influence of income on health: views of an epidemiologist. Does money really matter? Or is it a marker for something else?', *Health Affairs*, 21(2): 31–46.

Marmot, M. (2004) *Status Syndrome* (London: Bloomsbury).

Marmot, M. (2009) 'Closing the health gap in a generation: the work of the Commission on Social Determinants of Health and its recommendations', *Global Health Promotion*, Suppl. 1: 23–7.

Marmot, M. and Bell, R. (2010) 'Health Equity and Development: the Commission on Social Determinants of Health', *European Review*, 18(1): 1–7.

Marmot, M. and Wilkinson, R. G. (eds) (2006) *Social Determinants of Health* (2nd edn) (Oxford: Oxford University Press).

Martell, L. (2010) *The Sociology of Globalization* (Cambridge: Polity).

Martínez, C. S. and Leal, F. G. (2003) 'Epidemiological transition: Model or illusion? A look at the problem of health in Mexico', *Social Science & Medicine*, 57(3): 539–50.

Martorell, R. (2002) 'Obesity in the Developing World', in B. Caballero and B. M. Popkin (eds), *The Nutrition Transition: Diet and Disease in the Developing World* (London: Academic Press): 147–64.

Mathers, C. D., Ezzati, M. and Lopez, A. D. (2007) 'Measuring the burden of neglected tropical diseases: the global burden of disease framework', *PLoS Neglected Tropical Diseases*, 1(2): e114.

Mathers, C. D. and Loncar, D. (2006) 'Projections of global mortality and burden of disease from 2002 to 2030', *PLoS Medicine*, 3(11): e442.

Mayosi, B. M., Flisher, A. J., Lalloo, U. G., Sitas, F., Tollman, S. M. and Bradshaw, D. (2009) 'The burden of non-communicable diseases in South Africa', *Lancet*, 374(9693): 934–47.

McCarthy, M. (2007) 'The Global Fund: 5 years on', *Lancet*, 370(9584): 307–8.

McCord, C. and Freeman, H. P. (1990) 'Excess mortality in Harlem', *New England Journal of Medicine*, 322(3): 173–7.

McCoy, D. and McGoey, L. (2011) 'Global health and the Gates Foundation – in perspective', in S. Rushton and O. D. Williams (eds), *Partnerships and Foundations in Global Health Governance* (Basingstoke: Palgrave Macmillan).

McCracken, K. and Phillips, D. R. (2005) 'International Demographic Transitions', in G. J. Andrews and D. R. Phillips (eds), *Ageing and Place* (London: Routledge) 36–60.

McKeown, R. E. (2009) 'The epidemiologic transition: changing patterns of mortality and population dynamics', *American Journal of Lifestyle Medicine*, 3(1 Suppl.): 19S–26S.

McKeown, T. (1976) *The Modern Rise of Population* (London: Edward Arnold).

McKeown, T. (1979) *The Role of Medicine: Dream, Mirage, or Nemesis?* (2nd edn) (Princeton, NJ: Princeton University Press).

McKinlay, J. B. and McKinlay, S. M. (1977) 'The questionable contribution of medical measures to the decline of mortality in the United States in the twentieth century', *Milbank Memorial Fund Quarterly – Health and Society*, 55(3): 405–28.

McMichael, A. J. (1995) 'The health of persons, populations, and planets: epidemiology comes full circle', *Epidemiology*, 6(6): 633–6.

McMichael, P. (2012) *Development and Social Change: A Global Perspective* (5th edn) (Thousand Oaks, CA: Sage).

McNeil, D. G. (2012) 'Stubborn infection, spread by insects, is called "the new AIDS of the Americas"', *New York Times*, 28 May.

Mills, C. W. (1959) *The Sociological Imagination* (New York: Oxford University Press).

Montaner, J. S. (2011) 'Treatment as prevention – a double hat-trick', *Lancet*, 378(9787): 208–9.

Moore, S. (2006) 'Peripherality, income inequality, and life expectancy: revisiting the income inequality hypothesis', *International Journal of Epidemiology*, 35(3): 623–32.

Moore, S., Haines, V., Hawe, P. and Shiell, A. (2006) 'Lost in translation: a genealogy of the "social capital" concept in public health', *Journal of Epidemiology and Community Health*, 60(8): 729–34.

Morall, P. (2009) *Sociology and Health: An Introduction* (2nd edn) (New York: Routledge).

Morris, K. (2009) 'HIV drug patents in the spotlight', *Lancet Infectious Diseases*, 9(11): 660–1.

Moura, E. C., Malta, D. C., de Morais Neto, O. L. and Monteiro, C. A. (2009) 'Prevalence and social distribution of risk factors for chronic noncommunicable diseases in Brazil', *Revista Panamericana de Salud Pública*, 26(1): 17–22.

Moynihan, R. and Cassels, A. (2005) *Selling Sickness: How the World's Biggest Pharmaceutical Companies are Turning Us All Into Patients* (Vancouver: Greystone Books).

Muhumuza, S., Kitimbo, G., Oryema-Lalobo, M. and Nuwaha, F. (2009) 'Association between socio economic status and schistosomiasis infection in Jinja District, Uganda', *Tropical Medicine & International Health*, 14(6): 612–19.

Muntaner, C. (2003) 'Social epidemiology and class: a critique of Richard Wilkinson's income inequality and social capital hypothesis', *Rethinking Marxism*, 15(4): 551–4.

Muntaner, C., Armada, F., Chung, H., Mata, R., Williams-Brennan, L. and Benach, J. (2008) 'Venezuela's Barrio Adentro: participatory democracy, south–south cooperation and health care for all', *Social Medicine*, 3(4): 232–46.

Muntaner, C. and Lynch, J. (1999) 'Income inequality, social cohesion, and class relations: a critique of Wilkinson's neo-Durkheimian research program', *International Journal of Health Services*, 29(1): 59–81.

Muntaner, C., Lynch, J. and Davey Smith, G. (2001) 'Social capital, disorganized communities, and the third way: understanding the retreat from structural inequalities in epidemiology and public health', *International Journal of Health Services*, 31(2): 213–37.

Muntaner, C., Salazar, R. M., Benach, J. and Armada, F. (2006) 'Venezuela's Barrio Adentro: an alternative to neoliberalism in health care', *International Journal of Health Services*, 36(4): 803–11.

Murray, C. and Lopez, A. (eds) (1996) *The Global Burden of Disease* (Harvard: Harvard University Press).

Murray, L. R., Garcia, J., Munoz-Laboy, M. and Parker, R. G. (2011) 'Strange bedfellows: the Catholic Church and Brazilian National AIDS Program in the response to HIV/AIDS in Brazil', *Social Science & Medicine*, 72(6): 945–52.

Nabel, E. G., Stevens, S. and Smith, R. (2009) 'Combating chronic disease in developing countries', *Lancet*, 373(9680): 2004–6.

Navarro, V. (ed.) (2002) *The Political Economy of Social Inequalities: Consequences for Health and Quality of Life* (Amityville, NY: Baywood).

Nguyen, V. K. (2010) *The Republic of Therapy: Triage and Sovereignty in West Africa's time of AIDS* (Durham: Duke University Press).

Nunn, A. S., Fonseca, E. M., Bastos, F. I., Gruskin, S. and Salomon, J. A. (2007) 'Evolution of antiretroviral drug costs in Brazil in the context of free and universal access to AIDS treatment', *PLoS Medicine*, 4(11): 1804–17.

Offer, A., Pechey, R. and Ulijaszek, S. (2010) 'Obesity under affluence varies by welfare regimes: the effect of fast food, insecurity, and inequality', *Economics and Human Biology*, 8(3): 297–308.

Okie, S. (2006) 'Fighting HIV – lessons from Brazil', *New England Journal of Medicine*, 354(19): 1977–81.

Ollila, E. (2005) 'Global health priorities – priorities of the wealthy?', *Globalization & Health*, 1(1): 6.

Olshansky, S. J., Antonucci, T., Berkman, L., Binstock, R. H., Boersch-Supan, A., Cacioppo, J. T., Carnes, B. A., Carstensen, L. L., Fried, L. P., Goldman, D. P., Jackson, J., Kohli, M., Rother, J., Zheng, Y. and Rowe, J. (2012) 'Differences in life expectancy due to race and educational differences are widening, and many may not catch up', *Health Affairs*, 31(8): 1803–13.

Olshansky, S. J. and Ault, A. B. (1986) 'The fourth stage of the epidemiologic transition: the age of delayed degenerative diseases', *Milbank Memorial Fund Quarterly*, 64(3): 355–91.

Omran, A. R. (1971) 'The epidemiologic transition. A theory of the epidemiology of population change', *Milbank Memorial Fund Quarterly*, 49(4): 509–38.

Omran, A. R. (1983) 'The epidemiologic transition theory. A preliminary update', *Journal of Tropical Pediatrics*, 29(6): 305–16.

Omran, A. R. (1996) *The Epidemiologic Transition in the Americas* (Washington, DC: Pan American Health Organization).

Ooms, G. and Hammonds, R. (2009) 'Scaling up global social health protection: prerequisite reforms to the International Monetary Fund', *International Journal of Health Services*, 39(4): 795–801.

Ooms, G., Stuckler, D., Basu, S. and McKee, M. (2010) 'Financing the Millennium Development Goals for health and beyond: sustaining the "Big Push"', *Globalization & Health*, 6: 17.

Opie, L. H. and Mayosi, B. M. (2005) 'Cardiovascular disease in sub-Saharan Africa', *Circulation*, 112(23): 3536–40.

Orsi, J. M., Margellos-Anast, H. and Whitman, S. (2010) 'Black–White health disparities in the United States and Chicago: a 15-year progress analysis', *American Journal of Public Health*, 100(2): 349–56.

Osler, M., Christensen, U., Due, P., Lund, R., Andersen, I., Diderichsen, F. and Prescott, E. (2003) 'Income inequality and ischaemic heart disease in Danish men and women', *International Journal of Epidemiology*, 32(3): 375–80.

Osler, M., Prescott, E., Gronbaek, M., Christensen, U., Due, P. and Engholm, G. (2002) 'Income inequality, individual income, and mortality in Danish adults: analysis of pooled data from two cohort studies', *British Medical Journal*, 324(7328): 13.

Ottesen, E. A., Hooper, P. J., Bradley, M. and Biswas, G. (2008) 'The global programme to eliminate lymphatic filariasis: health impact after 8 years', *PLoS Neglected Tropical Diseases*, 2(10): e317.

PAHO (2006) *Mission Barrio Adentro: The Right to Health and Social Inclusion in Venezuela* (Caracas: PAHO).

Pande, R. P. and Yazbeck, A. S. (2003) 'What's in a country average? Wealth, gender, and regional inequalities in immunization in India', *Social Science & Medicine*, 57(11): 2075–88.

Parsons, T. (1951) *The Social System* (London: Routledge & Kegan Paul Ltd).

Pays, J. F. (2012) 'No, Chagas disease is not the new AIDS of the Americas!', *Bulletin de la Société de Pathologie Exotique*, 105(5): 337–48.

Pearce, N. (2004) 'The globalization of epidemiology: introductory remarks', *International Journal of Epidemiology*, 33(5): 1127–31.

Pei, X. and Rodriguez, E. (2006) 'Provincial income inequality and self-reported health status in China during 1991–7', *Journal of Epidemiology & Community Health*, 60(12): 1065–9.

Perel, P., Casas, J. P., Ortiz, Z. and Miranda, J. J. (2006) 'Noncommunicable diseases and injuries in Latin America and the Caribbean: time for action', *PLoS Medicine*, 3(9): e344.

Perez de Ayala, A., Perez-Molina, J. A., Norman, F. and Lopez-Velez, R. (2009) 'Chagasic cardiomyopathy in immigrants from Latin America to Spain', *Emerging Infectious Diseases*, 15(4): 607–8.

Petryna, A. (2009) *When Experiments Travel: Clinical Trials and the Global Search for Human Subjects* (Princeton: Princeton University Press).

Phillips, D. (1994) 'Does epidemiological transition have utility for health planners?', *Social Science & Medicine*, 38(10): vii–x.

Pickett, K. E., Kelly, S., Brunner, E., Lobstein, T. and Wilkinson, R. G. (2005) 'Wider income gaps, wider waistbands? An ecological study of obesity and income inequality', *Journal of Epidemiology and Community Health*, 59(8): 670–4.

Pickett, K. E. and Wilkinson, R. G. (2007) 'Child wellbeing and income inequality in rich societies: ecological cross sectional study', *British Medical Journal*, 335(7629): 1080.

Pirard, M., Iihoshi, N., Boelaert, M., Basanta, P., Lopez, F. and Van der Stuyft, P. (2005) 'The validity of serologic tests for Trypanosoma cruzi and the effectiveness of transfusional screening strategies in a hyperendemic region', *Transfusion*, 45(4): 554–61.

Pokhrel, S., Reidpath, D. and Allotey, P. (2011) 'Social sciences research in neglected tropical diseases 3: Investment in social science research in neglected diseases of poverty: a case study of Bill and Melinda Gates Foundation', *Health Research Policy and Systems*, 9(1): 2.

Poortinga, W. (2006) 'Social capital: an individual or collective resource for health?', *Social Science & Medicine*, 62(2): 292–302.

Porpora, D. V. (2001) 'Do realists run regressions?', in J. López and G. Potter (eds), *After Postmodernism: An Introduction to Critical Realism* (London: Athlone Press): 260–6.

Porter, R. (1997) *The Greatest Benefit to Mankind: A Medical History of Humanity from Antiquity to the Present* (London: HarperCollins).

Prata, A. (2001) 'Clinical and epidemiological aspects of Chagas disease', *Lancet Infectious Diseases*, 1(2): 92–100.

Price-Smith, A. T. (2009) *Contagion and Chaos: Disease, Ecology, and National Security in the Era of Globalization* (Cambridge, MA: MIT Press).

Prothero, R. M. and Davenport, J. M. (1986) 'The geography of health in South-East Mexico: a research study and agenda', *Social Science & Medicine*, 22(12): 1321–7.

Ramachandran, A., Ramachandran, S., Snehalatha, C., Augustine, C., Murugesan, N., Viswanathan, V., Kapur, A. and Williams, R. (2007) 'Increasing expenditure on health care incurred by diabetic subjects in a developing country: a study from India', *Diabetes Care*, 30(2): 252–6.

Raphael, D. (ed.) (2004) *Social Determinants of Health: Canadian Perspectives* (Toronto: Canadian Scholars' Press).

Raphael, D., Bryant, T. and Rioux, M. (eds) (2006) *Staying Alive: Critical Perspectives on Health, Illness, and Health Care* (Toronto: Canadian Scholars' Press).

Rather, L. J. (ed.) (1985) *Collected Essays on Public Health and Epidemiology: Rudolf Virchow (Vols 1 and 2)* (Canton, MA: Science History Publications).

Read, J. G., Amick, B. and Donato, K. M. (2005) 'Arab immigrants: a new case for ethnicity and health?', *Social Science & Medicine*, 61(1): 77–82.

Reardon, S. (2011) 'U.N. summit on noncommunicable diseases. Meeting brings attention but little action on chronic diseases', *Science*, 333(6049): 1561.

Reidpath, D. D., Allotey, P. and Pokhrel, S. (2011) 'Social sciences research in neglected tropical diseases 2: a bibliographic analysis', *Health Research Policy and Systems*, 9(1): 1.

Rein, J. (2001) 'International governance through trade agreements: patent protection for essential medicines', *Northwestern Journal of International Law & Business*, 21(2): 379–408.

Reithinger, R., Tarleton, R. L., Urbina, J. A., Kitron, U. and Gürtler, R. E. (2009) 'Eliminating Chagas disease: challenges and a roadmap', *British Medical Journal*, 338: b1283.

Rhodes, T. (2002) 'The "risk environment": a framework for understanding and reducing drug-related harm', *International Journal of Drug Policy*, 13(2): 85–94.

Ribeiro, I., Sevcsik, A. M., Alves, F., Diap, G., Don, R., Harhay, M. O., Chang, S. and Pecoul, B. (2009) 'New, improved treatments for Chagas disease: from the R&D pipeline to the patients', *PLoS Neglected Tropical Diseases*, 3(7): e484.

Rivera, J. A., Barquera, S., Campirano, F., Campos, I., Safdie, M. and Tovar, V. (2002) 'Epidemiological and nutritional transition in Mexico: rapid increase of non-communicable chronic diseases and obesity', *Public Health Nutrition*, 5(1A): 113–22.

Robertson, R. (1992) *Globalization* (London: Sage).

Rosen, A. (2013) 'How the UN caused Haiti's cholera crisis – and won't be held responsible', *The Atlantic*, 26 February.

Rosenbaum, L. and Lamas, D. (2011) 'Facing a "slow-motion disaster" – the UN meeting on noncommunicable diseases', *New England Journal of Medicine*, 365(25): 2345–8.

Ross, N. A., Wolfson, M. C., Dunn, J. R., Berthelot, J. M., Kaplan, G. A. and Lynch, J. W. (2000) 'Relation between income inequality and mortality in Canada and in the United States: cross sectional assessment using census data and vital statistics', *British Medical Journal*, 320(7239): 898–902.

Rostow, W. W. (1960) *The Stages of Economic Growth: A Non-Communist Manifesto* (Cambridge, UK: Cambridge University Press).

Rubinstein, A., Colantonio, L., Bardach, A., Caporale, J., Marti, S. G., Kopitowski, K., Alcaraz, A., Gibbons, L., Augustovski, F. and Pichon-Riviere, A. (2010) 'Estimation of the burden of cardiovascular disease attributable to modifiable risk factors and cost-effectiveness analysis of preventative interventions to reduce this burden in Argentina', *BMC Public Health*, 10(627).

Rubinstein, A. L., Irazola, V. E., Bazzano, L. A., Sobrino, E., Calandrelli, M., Lanas, F., Lee, A. G., Manfredi, J. A., Olivera, H., Ponzo, J. and Seron, P. He. J. (2011) 'Detection and follow-up of chronic obstructive pulmonary disease (COPD) and risk factors in the Southern Cone of Latin America: the pulmonary risk in South America (PRISA) study', *BMC Pulmonary Medicine*, 11: 34.

Sachs, J. (2001) *Letter from the Chair, Commission on Macroeconomics and Health* (Geneva: World Health Organization).

Salomon, J. A. and Murray, C. J. L. (2002) 'The epidemiologic transition revisited: compositional models for causes of death by age and sex', *Population and Development Review*, 28(2): 205–28.

Samson, C. (2003) *A Way of Life That Does Not Exist: Canada and the Extinguishment of the Innu* (London: Verso).

Scambler, G. (2001) 'Critical realism, sociology and health inequalities: social class as a generative mechanism and its media of enactment', *Journal of Critical Realism*, 4: 35–42.

Scheper-Hughes, N. (1992) *Death Without Weeping: The Violence of Everyday Life in Brazil* (Berkeley: University of California Press).

Schmunis, G. A. (1991) 'Trypanosoma cruzi, the etiologic agent of Chagas' disease: status in the blood supply in endemic and nonendemic countries', *Transfusion*, 31(6): 547–57.

Schmunis, G. A. (2007) 'Epidemiology of Chagas disease in non-endemic countries: the role of international migration', *Memórias do Instituto Oswaldo Cruz*, 102, Suppl. 1: 75–85.

Schoj, V., Alderete, M., Ruiz, E., Hasdeu, S., Linetzky, B. and Ferrante, D. (2010) 'The impact of a 100% smoke-free law on the health of hospitality workers from the city of Neuquen, Argentina', *Tobacco Control*, 19(2): 134–7.

Schrecker, T. (2012) 'Multiple crises and global health: new and necessary frontiers of health politics', *Global Public Health*, 7(6): 557–73.

Schulz, A. J. and Mullings, L. (eds) (2006) *Gender, Race, Class, & Health: Intersectional Approaches* (San Francisco: Jossey-Bass).

Seear, M. (2007) *An Introduction to International Health* (Toronto: Canadian Scholars' Press Inc.).

Sen, A. (1981) *Poverty and Famines: An Essay on Entitlement and Deprivation* (Oxford: Oxford University Press).

Sen, A. (1999) *Development as Freedom* (Oxford: Oxford University Press).

Senior, K. (2007) 'Chagas disease: moving towards global elimination', *Lancet Infectious Diseases*, 7(9): 572.

Shaw, J. E., Sicree, R. A. and Zimmet, P. Z. (2010) 'Global estimates of the prevalence of diabetes for 2010 and 2030', *Diabetes Research and Clinical Practice*, 87(1): 4–14.

Shibuya, K., Hashimoto, H. and Yano, E. (2002) 'Individual income, income distribution, and self rated health in Japan: cross sectional analysis of nationally representative sample', *British Medical Journal*, 324(7328): 16.

Shilling, C. (2002) Culture, the "sick role" and the consumption of health', *British Journal of Sociology*, 53(4): 621–38.

Singh, J. A., Govender, M. and Mills, E. J. (2007) 'Do human rights matter to health?', *Lancet*, 370(9586): 521–7.

Skolnik, R. L. (2008) *Essentials of Global Health* (Sudbury, MA: Jones & Bartlett).

Smith, R. (2002) 'A time for global health', *British Medical Journal*, 325(7355): 54–5.

Smith, R. D., Correa, C. and Oh, C. (2009) 'Trade, TRIPS, and pharmaceuticals', *Lancet*, 373(9664): 684–91.

Sobal, J. (2001) 'Commentary: globalization and the epidemiology of obesity', *International Journal of Epidemiology*, 30(5): 1136–7.

Sobal, J. and McIntosh, W. A. (2009) 'Globalization and obesity', in D. Inglis and D. Gimlin (eds), *The Globalization of Food* (Oxford: Berg): 255–72.

Spellberg, B. (2008) 'Dr. William H. Stewart: mistaken or maligned?', *Clinical Infectious Diseases*, 47(2): 294.

Spiegel, J. M. (2006) 'Commentary: daring to learn from a good example and break the "Cuba taboo"', *International Journal of Epidemiology*, 35(4): 825–6.

Spiegel, J. M., Dharamsi, S., Wasan, K. M., Yassi, A., Singer, B., Hotez, P. J., Hanson, C. and Bundy, D. A. P. (2010) 'Which new approaches to tackling neglected tropical diseases show promise?', *PLoS Medicine*, 7(5): e1000255.

Spiegel, J. M. and Yassi, A. (2004) 'Lessons from the margins of globalization: appreciating the Cuban health paradox', *Journal of Public Health Policy*, 25(1): 85–110.

Srinath Reddy, K., Shah, B., Varghese, C. and Ramadoss, A. (2005) 'Responding to the threat of chronic diseases in India', *Lancet*, 366(9498): 1744–9.

Starfield, B. and Birn, A. E. (2007) 'Income redistribution is not enough: income inequality, social welfare programs, and achieving equity in health', *Journal of Epidemiology & Community Health*, 61(12): 1038–41.

Statistics Canada. (2005) *Projections of the Aboriginal Populations, Canada, Provinces and Territories* (Ottawa: Statistics Canada).

Steinmann, P., Keiser, J., Bos, R., Tanner, M. and Utzinger, J. (2006) 'Schistosomiasis and water resources development: systematic review, meta-analysis, and estimates of people at risk', *Lancet Infectious Diseases*, 6(7): 411–25.

Stevens, D., Siegel, K. and Smith, R. (2007) 'Global interest in addressing non-communicable disease', *Lancet*, 370(9603): 1901–2.

Stiglitz, J. E. (2002) *Globalization and its Discontents* (London: Allen Lane).

Stiglitz, J. E. (2006) *Making Globalization Work* (New York: W.W. Norton).

Stiglitz, J. E. (2008) 'Economic foundations of intellectual property rights', *Duke Law Journal*, 57: 1693–724.

Stiglitz, J. E. and Charlton, A. (2005) *Fair Trade for All: How Trade Can Promote Development* (New York: Oxford University Press).

Strong, K., Mathers, C., Leeder, S. and Beaglehole, R. (2005) 'Preventing chronic diseases: how many lives can we save?', *Lancet*, 366(9496): 1578–82.

Stuckler, D., Basu, S. and McKee, M. (2011) 'Commentary: UN high level meeting on non-communicable diseases: an opportunity for whom?', *British Medical Journal*, 343: d5336.

Stuckler, D., King, L. P. and Basu, S. (2008) 'International Monetary Fund programs and tuberculosis outcomes in post-communist countries', *PLoS Medicine*, 5(7): 1079–89.

Subramanian, S. V., Delgado, I., Jadue, L., Vega, J. and Kawachi, I. (2003) 'Income inequality and health: multilevel analysis of Chilean communities', *Journal of Epidemiology and Community Health*, 57(11): 844–8.

Subramanian, S. V. and Kawachi, I. (2003) 'In defence of the income inequality hypothesis', *International Journal of Epidemiology*, 32: 1037–40.

Subramanian, S. V. and Kawachi, I. (2007) 'Commentary: Chasing the elusive null – the story of income inequality and health', *International Journal of Epidemiology*, 36(3): 596–9.

Subramanian, S. V., Kawachi, I. and Smith, G. D. (2007) 'Income inequality and the double burden of under- and overnutrition in India', *Journal of Epidemiology & Community Health*, 61(9): 802–9.

Swai, B., Poggensee, G., Mtweve, S. and Krantz, I. (2006) 'Female genital schistosomiasis as an evidence of a neglected cause for reproductive ill-health: a retrospective histopathological study from Tanzania', *BMC Infectious Diseases*, 6: 134.

Sykes, A. O. (2002) 'TRIPS, pharmaceuticals, developing countries, and the Doha "solution"', *Chicago Journal of International Law*, 3(1): 47–68.

't Hoen, E. (2000) 'Campaign for Access to Essential Medicines at the Health Issues Group DE TRADE', Statement from Médecins sans Frontiéres (Brussels: MSF).

't Hoen, E. (2002) 'TRIPS, pharmaceutical patents, and access to essential medicines: a long way from Seattle to Doha', *Chicago Journal of International Law*, 3(1): 27–46.

't Hoen, E., Berger, J., Calmy, A., and Moon, S. (2011) 'Driving a decade of change: HIV/AIDS, patents and access to medicines for all', *Journal of the International AIDS Society*, 14: 15.

Tajer, D. (2003) 'Latin American social medicine: roots, development during the 1990s, and current challenges', *American Journal of Public Health*, 93(12): 2023–7.

Tarleton, R. L. and Curran, J. W. (2012) 'Is Chagas disease really the "new HIV/AIDS of the Americas"?', *PLoS Neglected Tropical Diseases*, 6(10): e1861.

Teklehaimanot, A. and Snow, R. W. (2002) 'Will the Global Fund help roll back malaria in Africa?', *Lancet*, 360(9337): 888–9.

Townsend, P. and Davidson, N. (eds) (1982) *Inequalities in Health: The Black Report* (Harmondsworth: Penguin Books).

Trouiller, P., Olliaro, P., Torreele, E., Orbinski, J., Laing, R. and Ford, N. (2002) 'Drug development for neglected diseases: a deficient market and a public-health policy failure', *Lancet*, 359(9324): 2188–94.

Turner, B. (2003) 'Social capital, inequality and health: the Durkheimian revival', *Social Theory & Health*, 1(1): 4–20.

UNAIDS (2009) 'AIDS Epidemic Update: November 2009' (Geneva: UNAIDS/World Health Organization).

UNDP (2000) *Human Development Report* (New York: Oxford University Press).

UNDP (2008) 'About the MDGs: Basics'. Retrieved 2 October 2008 from http://www.undp.org/mdg/basics.shtml

UNDP (2012) 'International Human Development Indicators'. Retrieved 13 August 2012 from http://hdrstats.undp.org/en/tables

United Nations (2011a) *The Millennium Development Goals Report* (New York: United Nations).

United Nations (2011b) *Political Declaration on HIV/AIDS: Intensifying our Efforts to Eliminate HIV/AIDS* (New York: United Nations).

Van geertruyden, J. P. and D'Alessandro, U. (2007) 'Malaria and HIV: a silent alliance', *Trends in Parasitology*, 23(10): 465–7.

van Griensven, J., Balasegaram, M., Meheus, F., Alvar, J., Lynen, L. and Boelaert, M. (2010) 'Combination therapy for visceral leishmaniasis', *Lancet Infectious Diseases*, 10(3): 184–94.

Veenstra, G. (2002) 'Income inequality and health. Coastal communities in British Columbia, Canada', *Canadian Journal of Public Health*, 93(5): 374–9.

Vega, J., Hollstein, R. D., Delgado, I., Perez, J. C., Carrasco, S., Marshall, G. and Yach, D. (2001) 'Chile: Socioeconomic differentials and mortality in a middle-income nation', in T. Evans, M. Whitehead, F. Diderichsen, A. Bhuiya and M. Wirth (eds), *Challenging Inequalities in Health: From Ethics to Action* (Oxford: Oxford University Press): 123–37.

Vio, F. and Albala, C. (2000) 'Nutrition policy in the Chilean transition', *Public Health Nutrition*, 3(1): 49–55.

Virchow, R. (1958) *Disease, Life, and Man: Selected Essays* (L. J. Rather, trans.) (Stanford, CA: Stanford University Press).

Virchow, R. (1985 [1848]) *Collected Essays on Public Health and Epidemiology* (Cambridge: Science History Publications).

Waitzkin, H. (2003) 'Report of the WHO Commission on Macroeconomics and Health: a summary and critique', *Lancet*, 361(9356): 523–6.

Waitzkin, H. (2011) *Medicine and Public Health at the End of Empire* (London: Paradigm Publishers).

Waitzkin, H. and Iriart, C. (2001) 'How the United States exports managed care to developing countries', *International Journal of Health Services*, 31(3): 495–505.

Waitzkin, H., Iriart, C., Estrada, A. and Lamadrid, S. (2001) 'Social medicine then and now: lessons from Latin America', *American Journal of Public Health*, 91(10): 1592–601.

Wakabi, W. (2007) 'Hope for improved leishmaniasis treatment in Africa', *Lancet Infectious Diseases*, 7: 1.

Wang, Y. (2001) 'Cross-national comparison of childhood obesity: the epidemic and the relationship between obesity and socioeconomic status', *International Journal of Epidemiology*, 30(5): 1129–36.

Waning, B., Diedrichsen, E. and Moon, S. (2010) 'A lifeline to treatment: the role of Indian generic manufacturers in supplying antiretroviral medicines to developing countries', *Journal of the International AIDS Society*, 13: 35.

Warner, K. E. and Mackay, J. (2006) 'The global tobacco disease pandemic: nature, causes, and cures', *Global Public Health*, 1(1): 65–86.

Waters, W. F. (2006) 'Globalization and local response to epidemiological overlap in 21st century Ecuador', *Globalization and Health*, 2: 8.

Webber, L., Kilpi, F., Marsh, T., Rtveladze, K., Brown, M. and McPherson, K. (2012) 'High rates of obesity and non-communicable diseases predicted across Latin America', *PLoS One*, 7(8): e39589.

Weiss, M. G. (2008) 'Stigma and the social burden of neglected tropical diseases', *PLoS Neglected Tropical Diseases*, 2(5): e237.

Whitehead, M. (1992) 'The concepts and principles of equity and health', *International Journal of Health Services*, 22(3): 429–45.

WHO (2001) *Macroeconomics and Health: Investing in Health for Economic Development* (Geneva: World Health Organization).

WHO (2002) *Coverage of Selected Health Services for HIV/AIDS Prevention and Care in Less Developed Countries in 2001* (Geneva: World Health Organization).

WHO (2003) *Communicable Diseases 2002: Global Defense Against the Infectious Disease Threat* (Geneva: World Health Organization).

WHO (2005) *Preventing Chronic Diseases: A Vital Investment* (Geneva: World Health Organization).

WHO (2007a) *Global Plan to Combat Neglected Tropical Diseases, 2008–1025* (Geneva: World Health Organization).

WHO (2007b) *World Health Report 2007: A Safer Future – Global Public Health Security in the 21st Century* (Geneva: World Health Organization).

WHO (2008a) *Closing the Gap in a Generation: Health Equity through Action on the Social Determinants of Health* (Geneva: World Health Organization).

WHO (2008b) 'The global burden of disease: 2004 update' (Geneva: World Health Organization).

WHO (2008c) *Towards Universal Access: Scaling Up Priority HIV/AIDS Interventions in the Health Sector* (Geneva: World Health Organization).

WHO (200d) *World Health Report.* (Geneva: WHO).

WHO (2010a) *Towards Universal Access: Scaling Up Priority HIV/AIDS Interventions in the Health Sector* (Geneva: World Health Organization).

WHO (2010b) *Working to Overcome the Global Impact of Neglected Tropical Diseases: First WHO Report on Neglected Tropical Diseases* (Geneva: World Health Organization).

WHO (2012a) *Accelerating Work to Overcome the Global Impact of Neglected Tropical Diseases: A Roadmap for Implementation* (Geneva: World Health Organization).

WHO (2012b) *World Health Statistics 2012* (Geneva: World Health Organization).

Wilkinson, R. G. (1994) 'The epidemiological transition: from material scarcity to social disadvantage?', *Daedalus*, 123(4): 61–77.

Wilkinson, R. G. (1996) *Unhealthy Societies: The Afflictions of Inequality* (New York: Routledge).

Wilkinson, R. G. (2000) *Mind the Gap: Hierarchies, Health and Human Evolution* (London: Weidenfeld & Nicolson).

Wilkinson, R. G. (2005) *The Impact of Inequality: How to Make Sick Societies Healthier* (New York: New Press).

Wilkinson, R. G. and Pickett, K. E. (2006) 'Income inequality and population health: a review and explanation of the evidence', *Social Science & Medicine*, 62(7): 1768–84.

Wilkinson, R. G. and Pickett, K. E. (2007) 'The problems of relative deprivation: why some societies do better than others'. *Social Science & Medicine*, 65(9): 1965–78.

Wilkinson, R. G. and Pickett, K. E. (2008) 'Income inequality and socioeconomic gradients in mortality', *American Journal of Public Health*, 98(4): 699–704.

Wilkinson, R. G. and Pickett, K. E. (2009a) 'Income inequality and social dysfunction', *Annual Review of Sociology*, 35: 493–511.

Wilkinson, R. G. and Pickett, K. E. (2009b) *The Spirit Level: Why More Equal Societies Almost Always Do Better* (London: Allen Lane).

Williams, S. J. (2005) 'Parsons revisited: from the sick role to...?', *Health*, 9(2): 123–44.

Wipfli, H. and Huang, G. (2011) 'Power of the process: evaluating the impact of the Framework Convention on Tobacco Control negotiations', *Health Policy*, 100(2–3): 107–15.

Wolf, M. (2004) *Why Globalization Works* (Yale: Yale University Press).

World Bank. (1993) *World Development Report 1993* (Washington, DC: World Bank).

World Bank. (2012) 'Haiti'. Retrieved 27 July 2012 from http://data.worldbank.org/country/haiti/

World Heart Federation. (2011) 'UN Member States jeopardise international progress on non?communicable disease epidemic'. Retrieved from http://www.world-heart-federation.org/fileadmin/user_upload/documents/press-releases/2011/Press_release_Ban_Ki-moon_Letter18Aug11.pdf

WTO. (2001) 'Declaration on the TRIPS agreement and public health'. Retrieved 26 August 2012 from http://www.wto.org/english/thewto_e/minist_e/min01_e/mindecl_trips_e.htm

WTO. (2012) 'TRIPS: Agreement on Trade-Related Aspects of Intellectual Property Rights'. Retrieved 26 August 2012 from http://www.wto.org/english/tratop_e/trips_e/t_agm1_e.htm

Xu, K., Evans, D. B., Kawabata, K., Zeramdini, R., Klavus, J. and Murray, C. J. (2003) 'Household catastrophic health expenditure: a multicountry analysis', *Lancet*, 362(9378): 111–17.

Young, T. K., Reading, J., Elias, B. and O'Neil, J. D. (2000) 'Type 2 diabetes mellitus in Canada's first nations: status of an epidemic in progress', *Canadian Medical Association Journal*, 163(5): 561–6.

Zacher, M. W. and Keefe, T. J. (2008) *The Politics of Global Health Governance: United By Contagion* (Basingstoke: Palgrave Macmillan).

Zainol, Z. A., Amin, L., Jusoff, K., Zahid, A. and Akpoviri, F. (2011) 'Pharmaceutical patents and access to essential medicines in sub-Saharan Africa', *African Journal of Biotechnology*, 10(10): 12376–88.

Zeng, G., Sun, B. and Zhong, N. (2012) 'Non-smoling-related chronic onstructive pulmonary disease: A neglected enity?', *Respirology*, 17 (6): 908–12.

Zhang, Y., MacArthur, C., Mubil, L. and Baker, S. (2010) 'Control of neglected tropical disesases needs a long-term comitmenent;. *BMC Medicine*, 8:67.

Index